DECEPTION AND ABUSE AT THE FED

ROBERT D. AUERBACH

DECEPTION AND ABUSE AT THE FED

Henry B. Gonzalez Battles Alan Greenspan's Bank

University of Texas Press ◀▶ AUSTIN

*The publication of this book was made possible in part by
a University Cooperative Society Subvention Grant
awarded by the University of Texas at Austin.*

Requests for permission to reproduce material from this work should be sent to:
Permissions
University of Texas Press
P.O. Box 7819
Austin, TX 78713-7819
www.utexas.edu/utpress/about/bpermission.html

⊗ The paper used in this book meets the minimum requirements of
ANSI/NISO Z39.48-1992 (R1997) (Permanence of Paper).

LIBRARY OF CONGRESS CATALOGING-IN-PUBLICATION DATA

Auerbach, Robert D.
Deception and abuse at the Fed : Henry B. Gonzalez battles Alan Greenspan's Bank /
by Robert D. Auerbach.
    p.   cm.
Includes bibliographical references and index.
ISBN 978-0-292-71785-5 (cl. : alk. paper)
1. Board of Governors of the Federal Reserve System (U.S.) 2. Governmental
investigations—United States—Case studies. 3. Greenspan, Alan, 1926- 4. Gonzalez,
Henry B. (Henry Barbosa), 1916-2000. I. Title.
HG2563.A94 2008
332.1'10973—dc22
                                                                2007051720

CONTENTS

ACKNOWLEDGMENTS

Both the United States and the account presented in this book benefited from the legislators who carried out their oversight responsibilities for the U.S. central bank during their service on the House of Representatives Banking Committee. (The committee, formerly called the Banking, Finance and Urban Affairs Committee, is now known as the Financial Services Committee; as was the custom in the House, I will refer to it as House Banking or the Banking Committee.) They include the late House Banking Committee chairmen Henry S. Reuss (D-WI; chairman, 1975–1980) and Henry B. Gonzalez (D-TX; chairman, 1989–1994; ranking member to 1998) as well as other members who served on the Banking Committee, including Representatives Barney Frank (D-MA, ranking member in 2003, chairman in 2007), Maurice Hinchey (D-NY), Jessie Jackson, Jr. (D-IL), Joseph P. Kennedy II (D-MA), Carolyn Maloney (D-NY), Maxine Waters (D-CA), and Melvin L. Watt (D-NC). Former congressman James Leach (R-IA; chairman, 1995–2000) was always accessible and knowledgeable, and provided funds for the Gonzalez investigation, in which I participated, of the airplane fleet contracted by the Federal Reserve System (the Fed). I was privileged to work with these members during the eleven years I served as a staff economist on the committee. I also benefited from my service as a staff adviser on monetary policy and the Federal Reserve to Beryl Sprinkel, undersecretary of the treasury for monetary affairs, during the first year of Ronald Reagan's administration.

I am indebted to Nobel laureate Milton Friedman, my professor and dissertation chairman, who drew my attention to central banking and continued to provide me with suggestions and encouragement until his death in 2006. Insightful suggestions from several of his letters to me appear in the book. He said he was looking forward to reading the book and liked the section of it I sent him in 2006, on whether it is important (or not) for Fed officials to be able to explain their actions (Chapter 9). Milton phoned me several times when I was working on congressional investigations of the Fed. He called once to say that someone had asked for his help in stopping me. Milton wanted me to know that he strongly objected to this call and that I should continue my efforts. In another call, we talked about the exemption given to the Fed by some "conservative" think tank members who were critical of the untethered powers of other governmental bureaucracies. I have always remembered his terse comment about this inconsistency of the conservative think tankers: "They aren't perfect."

My thanks also go to Anna Schwartz, at the National Bureau of Economic Research, who coauthored with Friedman three classic books, one of which, *A Monetary History of the United States, 1867–1960*, encompasses the early history of the Federal Reserve. I was honored that she agreed to be a discussant of a paper I presented at a meeting of the Western Economic Association in 2000, detailing the deceitful manner in which the Fed concealed transcripts of its meetings for seventeen years and misled Congress. She thought such actions were outrageous. She testified before the House Banking Committee on October 19, 1993, about numerous leaks of inside information from the Fed. She was one of Congressman Gonzalez's favorite witnesses. Two other witnesses at that same hearing also provided valuable testimony: James Meigs, an expert money-and-banking economist, and Robert Craven, an experienced broker who revealed some of the effects that leaks of inside information from the Fed have on securities markets (see Chapter 6).

Three days after Anna Schwartz testified, when the Fed was discussing in a secret meeting what actions it would take with regard to the Gonzalez investigation and hearings, a governor of the Fed, apparently displaying his historical perspective, paid an unintended tribute to a wonderful scholar. He suggested to the Federal Open Market Committee that it not disclose the transcripts of any of its meetings from before 1981, since "the very deep history first of all is less interesting, except to the Anna Schwartzes of the world perhaps" (FOMC transcript, October 22, 1993, 7).

I am especially indebted to Jake Lewis, who provided substantial expert knowledge and assistance. He has vast experience, going all the way back to 1958, when, as a reporter in Texas, he covered Gonzalez's unsuccessful gubernatorial campaign. Jake served on the House Banking Committee staff for twenty-seven years (1965–1992). He was a superb adviser and the go-to expert for the staff during the tenure of four Banking Committee chairmen, beginning with Wright Patman. He worked in the public interest on innumerable investigations and hearings as a primary force behind the scenes. He is the author of "Monster Banks: The Political and Economic Costs of Banking and Financial Consolidation" (*Multinational Monitor,* January–February 2005).

I was very fortunate to work with many other excellent House Banking Committee staff members, including Kelsay Meek, who served with Congressman Gonzalez for many years. He was staff director of the committee until 1994, then minority staff director until Gonzalez left Congress, in 1998. Kelsay used his outstanding writing ability to assist in the preparation of many speeches and played a constructive leadership role in Banking Committee oversight and investigations. Other valuable staff members include the late Paul Nelson, who served as staff director under House Banking chairmen Wright Patman, Henry Reuss, and Fernand St. Germain; Stefanie Mullin, who was the innovative and hard-working press secretary for the committee; and Armando Falcon, who served as a committee lawyer under Gonzalez and performed spectacularly during his five-year tenure as director of the Office of Federal Housing Enterprise Oversight (1999–2005), uncovering severe problems in government-sponsored enterprises operating in the mortgage market. Dennis Kane, an expert investigator, played a major role in assisting Gonzalez with an inquiry into $5.5 billion in loans extended to Saddam Hussein's Iraq government through an Atlanta banking operation (Chapter 4). Michael Crider served on the committee staff and participated in an investigation of Fed transcripts.

During the 1970s, I worked on hearings and oversight actions related to the Federal Reserve System, efforts that in 1980 produced legislation regulating the Fed. During those years I worked closely with three economists: Louis Gasper, of the House Banking Committee's Republican staff; the late Robert Weintraub, of the committee's Democratic staff; and James K. Galbraith, also of the Democratic staff. Galbraith, with whom I shared a small staff office in the 1970s and who is now my colleague at the LBJ School of Public Affairs, has been a very valuable source for discussing economic issues. I benefited also from discussions with David Meiselman, who wrote a classic book on interest rates and coauthored a famous study with Milton Friedman.

I gratefully acknowledge the Fed employees who publicly assisted the

Gonzalez investigation of abusive and deceitful practices in the Fed's management of its airplane fleet. The country owes these courageous longtime Federal Reserve Bank of Boston employees great praise for their efforts to improve the nation's central bank by publicly reporting problems with the Fed's management of its airplane fleet, which played a critical role in the nation's payment system. They were employed at the Fed's central management office, the Interdistrict Transportation System (ITS), at the Boston Fed, which managed the approximately fifty airplanes that flew each weekday night transporting paper checks. Three of these employees testified on September 16, 1997, before the House Banking Committee's Subcommittee on Domestic and International Monetary Policy: Thomas W. McFarland, manager, transportation operations; Thomas Hunt, senior analyst; and Charles Fazio, transportation analyst. After the congressional investigation was made public, in 1996, the Fed responded—and tried to cover the trail of its corrupt bookkeeping—by closing the ITS office where these experienced, longtime employees worked and moving its operations to the Atlanta Fed Bank. These Fed employees who were congressional witnesses displayed great courage and patriotism.

Thanks are also due to Ralph Nader, who sponsored a conference on the Federal Reserve on January 7, 2001, at the National Press Club; Jake Lewis and I had planned the event, and C-SPAN televised it. Former Fed employees provided important information on how the Fed treated workers who filed suits for racial discrimination, and Jim McTague, the Washington editor of *Barron's*, talked about how the Fed under Alan Greenspan treated reporters who were critical of its operations. Nader was also a witness at the July 26, 1996, hearings before the Senate Banking Committee to confirm Greenspan for a third four-year term as Federal Reserve chairman. He placed in the record a congressional report that covered Congressman Gonzalez's investigation, which I assisted, into the Fed's airplane fleet. On August 13, 1997, John Martin reported on part of this congressional investigation from a Federal Reserve airport facility for *ABC World News Tonight*. Both Nader and Martin provided a valuable public service. I thank Bill O'Reilly for allowing me to describe the shredding of Fed records on his television program following the publication of my article "That Shreddin' Fed" in *Barron's* in 2001.

I thank William V. Bishel, acquisitions editor, and Leslie Tingle, managing editor, at the University of Texas Press, as well as Kip Keller, copy editor, all of whom provided valuable suggestions on the manuscript and substantial assistance in preparing the book for publication. Stephen W.

Littrell, professional librarian at the University of Texas libraries, assisted with documentation.

My wife, Linda, provided encouragement and informed assistance during my work on this book. She was great.

Initially, I wanted to thank former Fed chairman Alan Greenspan for a qualified compliment that appeared in the transcript of a 1993 FOMC meeting. Greenspan said that "the productivity of Mr. Auerbach [was] extraordinary. He must be Fed trained." Greenspan said that Gonzalez's recent letter to him was thoughtful, because "leaks and public statements about FOMC meetings are a very serious matter that call into question the credibility of the Federal Reserve to manage its own operations" (FOMC transcript, July 1993, 72). This compliment did not take into account either the excellent Banking Committee staff members whom Gonzalez had assembled and who also assisted with his letters and investigations, or the steadfast, principled leadership of Henry Gonzalez. My appreciation was diminished when Greenspan retracted his compliment later in the meeting, after Governor John LaWare complained that Gonzalez was accusing the Fed of deliberately leaking inside information: "I'm surprised you feel that this is a thoughtful letter . . . He seems to regard this as an accepted practice of this institution!" LaWare added that with respect to the immediate release of Fed policy, "even if I believed that was the right way to go—and I'm not sure I do—I wouldn't do it in light of this because this Congressman would declare victory and say 'Now I've got them.'" Greenspan replied, "I must humbly retract my statement with respect to the quality of the letter because I'm more inclined in your direction than not. To be exact, there are a few sentences in it that I think are reasonable" (77–78). With regard to the jocular description of my being "Fed trained," I would ascribe any such expertise to my two years' experience working inside the Fed bureaucracy.

My experience at the Kansas City Fed Bank was sometimes subjected to negative comments and false characterizations after I returned to the House Banking Committee staff in 1992. One news story reported: "'There apparently was a little bad blood' between Auerbach and the Fed at the time, said one source familiar with the Fed who spoke on condition of anonymity. . . . This was echoed by some other sources" (Cathy Christensen, "House Banking Aide Seen as Pointman in Gonzalez's Attacks on Fed," *Knight Ridder Financial News*, March 25, 1994). Of course, false accusations and worse go with the territory, as many dedicated congressional staff, reporters, and legislators are frequently reminded. Nevertheless, I was pleased to see that the reporter of this story checked with the Kansas City Fed Bank: "A Kansas City Fed spokesman said, 'He left here under good circumstances. He was regarded by those who worked with him as a productive member of the staff.'" I worked with some excellent people at the Fed, including Donald Kohn, who is now Fed vice chairman.

DECEPTION AND ABUSE AT THE FED

CHAPTER 1

HITTING A TANK
WITH A STICK

THE COMBATIVE HENRY B.

The amazing 1990s began with a recession, high unemployment, and victory in the first Gulf War. Soon, though, the economic good times rolled, as the promise of remarkable computer and Internet technologies was realized. The economy grew, unemployment dropped, the federal deficit changed to a rising surplus, and jubilant investors hung on to the stock-market balloon that rapidly inflated until the end of the decade. The spotlight focused on one man, who was cast as the country's economic "maestro." Alan Greenspan achieved saint-like status as he led the country's most powerful peacetime governmental bureaucracy: the nation's central bank, the Federal Reserve, the Fed.

Meanwhile, a relatively little-known man from Texas, Henry B. Gonzalez, who had risen to the chairmanship of the House Banking Committee, decided to carry out the responsibility assigned to that committee for overseeing the Fed. The Fed had frequently waved its "independent from politics" flag to ward off congressional intrusion. Now, under an enshrined leader, it appeared safe, except that Gonzalez seemed determined, and in 1992 had made public his suggestions for requiring accountability from Fed officials—who were shocked. The chairman of the "politically independent" Fed sought political help. Greenspan traveled to Little Rock, Arkansas, to talk to the president-elect, Bill Clinton. On December 14, 1992, at a then-secret meeting, Greenspan reported back to Fed officials about his conversation with Clinton, ten days earlier (selections from the transcript of the Fed meeting are in Chapter 10). The powerful Greenspan Fed was determined to stop Henry Gonzalez.

Despite the low odds of success, Gonzalez would not retreat from carrying out the responsibilities that the U.S. House of Representatives assigned to its Banking Committee for overseeing the nation's central bank. The Fed was so shrouded in mythology, and seemingly so guarded by its self-proclaimed need to act with absolute independence, that anyone aggressively poking it would be subject to trashing. Admiring politicians and a coterie of Fed watchers who earned their income by interpreting the Fed's garbled announcements would voice their disgust for anyone intruding on the Fed's advertised independence. Gonzalez compared his attempt to remedy severe problems at the Fed to hitting a Sherman tank with a stick. Those who knew Henry B., as he was called in his San Antonio district, knew that even later-model combat tanks would not have stopped him.

Gonzalez was certainly not driven by a need for power or fame. Jake Lewis, who served on the House Banking Committee staff under four chairmen and as a reporter had covered Gonzalez's unsuccessful campaign for governor of Texas, knew him well. In 1997, Lewis noted that thirty-six years in Congress had not changed Gonzalez: "'A lot of people come here [to Congress] and when they . . . rise to positions of power, you can't recognize them as the person that came here. But Henry today is, I think, exactly the same person that arrived in 1961.'"[1]

Gonzalez did not pay homage to rank or power, even his own after he became chairman of the House Banking Committee, which had more than fifty members, in 1989. When I arrived for a second period of service on the committee staff, I was proud to call him "Mr. Chairman." I had known him in the 1970s. He would occasionally join me in the cafeteria for lunch. He had not changed in 1992. He told me to drop the "Mr. Chairman" and call him "Henry." When I occasionally walked with him through the hallways of Congress, he would stop and talk to each of the employees, everyone from those cleaning the floors to Capitol Hill police officers. He knew not only many of their names, but also something about their families, and was interested in how they were getting along. When he walked to work along Pennsylvania Avenue, he would stop to speak to those begging and homeless, and there were many on the streets of the District of Columbia. Some of them offered him ideas that he seriously considered. This sincere interest in those far from positions of power carried over to his constituents. He would stay in his office until late at night, reading mail from constituents and writing notes to be included in the replies. One letter written to Gonzalez about banking issues was passed to me for a reply, and I wrote the customary constituent response, something like: "We thank you for your inquiry and we will look into it." Gonzalez drew an X through this weak dodge and wrote back to me in large letters: "No BS."

It would also be a weak dodge to say he was not on the best of terms with the Democratic leadership of the House. Gonzalez, a Democrat, had fought with the Democratic leadership to become chairman of a subcommittee, then to become the Banking Committee chairman, and finally, in a knock-down, drag-out battle, to retain his position as ranking member after he returned in 1998 from an absence due to illness. Shortly after I arrived, I accompanied Gonzalez to a chamber near the House floor. Speaker of the House Thomas Foley (D-WA) approached to speak with him, perhaps, I thought, about attending or holding a fund-raiser. After all, Gonzalez was chairman of the large Banking Committee. (In 2006 it had approximately seventy members and was called the Financial Services Committee.) Since legislation passing through this committee affected trillion-dollar financial conglomerates, the chairman could be a powerful fund-raiser. Before Speaker Foley could talk, Henry told him to "speak to the young man [who was not young] who works for me. He's an economist." Henry looked the other way, and Foley said hello to me and left.

Gonzalez was not afraid of losing. To illustrate this point, he told me that some years ago a friend who had campaigned for him, President Lyndon Baines Johnson, called him and complained. Henry, he asked, why were you the only one who voted against a bill I wanted? Gonzalez replied, "Mr. President, I'm glad to hear from you, but . . ." President Johnson interrupted with a laugh and said that there was no use trying to pressure Henry. He knew that Gonzalez was taking a principled stand.[2] The same principled stand prevailed in 1957, the year after Gonzalez's election to the Texas Senate. Senator Gonzalez holds the record for the longest filibuster in the history of that body, twenty-two hours straight, to defeat eight of ten proposed school segregation bills (another senator, Abraham Kazen, spoke for an additional fourteen hours as part of the same filibuster). Henry told me he kept going even when the lieutenant governor, who had a residence adjoining the Senate floor, appeared in the middle of the night and asked, in a profanity-laden question that made Henry laugh when he recalled the outburst, what it would take to shut him up. The filibuster was successful.[3]

As Banking chairman, Gonzalez shepherded passage of the bailout legislation that ended the decade-long savings and loan crisis, which lasted until the early 1990s. He had shown his skill as a committee chairman. Why not stop there? Why hit a stick against a tank driven by an enshrined national icon: Fed chairman Alan Greenspan?

A 1997 book review in the *Financial Times* stated that Greenspan is "widely called without a hint of hyperbole, the most powerful man in the world."[4] Why not follow the wise political practice of many others and join the chorus of admiration?

No governmental official—including occupants of the White House— had ever received more sustained applause than Alan Greenspan had enjoyed since being appointed chairman of the Federal Reserve. He adorned the covers of numerous newsmagazines and was the subject of an untold number of feature stories in major newspapers across the nation. He received an honorary knighthood from Queen Elizabeth II. An endless stream of superlatives described Greenspan as a wizard, a maestro, a genius. No praise was too extreme or too saccharine to be applied by the media or fawning members of both political parties in the Senate and the House. Almost all the press was favorable. Before the stock market bubble deflated in 2000, criticism was hard to find. Any negative comments that found their way into news stories were invariably balanced with fulsome praise. Most serious students of the Federal Reserve might have argued vigorously against the idea of early sainthood for Greenspan, but there was likely general agreement that the title "wizard" fit if one were trying to describe the amazing and long-running public relations success of Alan Greenspan, who was chairman of the Fed until January 2006, nearly nineteen years.

THE TANK'S SPECS

Greenspan drove a formidable tank, an approximately 23,000-person bureaucracy with immense powers. Among other things, the Fed approves or denies the purchase of competitor banks by trillion-dollar banking conglomerates, controls the nation's money supply, and manages targeted interest rates. And those are just part of its arsenal.

The Fed is led by nineteen unelected decision makers: the presidents of each of the twelve Federal Reserve district banks (Fed Banks) and the seven governors at its Washington, D.C., headquarters. The seven governors are nominated by the president and must be confirmed by the Senate. Each governor serves a fourteen-year term.[5] They can be fired only through congressional impeachment, which has never happened.[6] The

twelve Fed Bank presidents are internally appointed.[7] They are not subject to Senate confirmation, so their views, backgrounds, credentials, and
records do not have to pass public examination. The Fed headquarters, in
Washington, D.C., is run by the seven governors and is called the Board
of Governors, or just the board.[8] Twelve of these nineteen officials sit on
the Fed's most important policy-making committee, the Federal Open
Market Committee (FOMC).

Over this bureaucracy presides one of the seven governors, who is the
chairman of both central policy-making committees, the FOMC and the
Board of Governors. The chairman is nominated by the president and
confirmed by the Senate. He serves a four-year term as chairman and can
be reappointed and confirmed for additional terms.

Since 1951 the Fed and its chairmen have held increased power at
the expense of a greatly diminished U.S. Treasury Department. In 1951,
under the direction of President Harry Truman, the cooperation between
the U.S. Treasury and the Fed in controlling the nation's money supply
ended.[9] The Treasury gave up all power to issue money, retaining authority
over only the Bureau of Engraving and Printing, which it uses to fulfill
the Fed's orders for new currency and coins. Six Fed chairmen have served
under that agreement:

William McChesney Martin, Jr. (1951–1970)
Arthur F. Burns (1970–1978)
G. William Miller (1978–1979)
Paul Volcker (1979–1987)
Alan Greenspan (1987–2006)
Ben S. Bernanke (2006–present)

The Fed's unbridled lobbying powers can shoot down most of the problems it perceives coming from Congress. During my first term of service
on the House Banking Committee staff (1976–1981), I helped the Banking
Committee chairman, Henry Reuss, uncover how the Fed used the banks
it regulated to lobby against bills the Fed did not like. The lobbying campaign orchestrated by the Fed managed to cripple the ability of private-
sector and governmental auditors to examine significant parts of the Fed's
operations. That trophy for the Fed's lobbying success is still on the Fed's
shelf.

At the time, few members of Congress were willing to incur the wrath
of powerful bankers in order to argue for a complete independent audit
of the Fed's books. The need to appease financial interest groups trumped

any public interest on that issue. That did not detour Reuss. He told the House of Representatives that this lobbying organized by the Fed would be illegal if the Fed used appropriated funds to organize the private-sector bankers who did it.[10]

The Fed did lose some battles. Reuss was victorious in passing a congressional resolution that directed the Fed to regularly and publicly report to Congress on Fed policies, beginning in 1975.

The Greenspan Fed (1987–2006) was more proficient than its predecessors at lobbying. Its liaison staff could bring the famous chairman to a member's office. What a wonderful opportunity to have a one-on-one with the nation's sage, who could offer advice about the economy or his views on undesirable legislation, defined as any that would impair the Fed's independence, the all-purpose banner that could be waved to shield Fed officials from accountability. The Fed knew that even friendly legislation invites ornaments (amendments) from unfriendly members. At meetings with friendly members, issues such as corruption and lies uncovered by congressional investigations could be quietly trivialized and swept under the Fed's lumpy rug. Greenspan even visited president-elect Bill Clinton in Arkansas in 1992, reporting back that Clinton's body language and peripheral comments were consistent with independence for the Fed. (See Chapter 10 for the full story.)

Any sensitive subject could be handled during Greenspan's visits to congressional offices. For example, those questioning the Fed's contention that it was not covered by the Civil Rights Act of 1964 were assured that it fully subscribed to civil rights, even though it might be facing certain problems in that area.

The Fed could not silence or intimidate Gonzalez. Greenspan and his staff of lobbyists made the rounds in Congress without making any sales that mattered to Gonzalez. The congressman saw to it that the Banking Committee would maintain an arm's-length relationship with Greenspan and institute actual checks and balances. Gonzalez wanted action taken on issues that were important to the country. The heat generated by the Fed and its sympathizers never caused Gonzalez to stop an investigation. There was an attack against Gonzalez's ancestry. In February 1995, a national newspaper, *USA Today*, defended the Fed chairman by attacking Gonzalez with a blatant ethnic slur in its main editorial: "Fortunately, for most Americans, Greenspan and other members on the Fed board tuned out the noise. They rejected the Mexican approach to economics, easy money for fast growth, whatever the consequences. Instead they tweaked up interest rates. Seven times."[11] Greenspan's actual policy in 1994 was revealed more than five years later. He had informed Congress and the public in 1994 that he was taking a preemptive strike against inflation even though there was little inflation. Now there is a record of what he was secretly and continually telling Fed officials (see Chapter 11).

The vicious editorial in *USA Today* was not the only personal attack Gonzalez faced during his rise to the chairmanship of the Banking Committee. Despite these attacks, many legislators stood with him. When the Democrats lost the House of Representatives in 1994 and Henry went from being chairman of the Banking Committee to being ranking member, Congressman Joseph Kennedy (D-MA), a Banking Committee member and a strong Gonzalez supporter, asked Henry B. how he liked being in the minority. Henry laughed and said he had always been a minority. All of us at the meeting laughed; we knew being in the minority would not hurt Henry B.

Gonzalez could not be swayed by campaign donations. That kind of offer would receive a stiff rebuke. He did not hold fund-raisers for anyone. A group representing large banks once called me because it wanted to hold a dinner to honor the chairman of the Banking Committee; I put the caller on hold and checked with Gonzalez. Without hesitation he said to tell them he did not take free meals. Few other members were as careful to avoid this possible conflict of interest with the oversight functions assigned to the Banking Committee.

Given the sea of money surrounding political campaigns, Gonzalez's strict adherence to principle may certainly have seemed eccentric and out of place. But his stand had valuable payoffs for his public service. Overseeing the Fed bureaucracy, which has established barriers to transparency, is very difficult unless the many honest people inside the bureaucracy, who may know of severe problems, trust the integrity of the investigator. Many Fed employees knew about Gonzalez. In one period in 1994 he spoke in the House chamber night after night for weeks while Congress was in session. He was sometimes mocked for addressing the empty room at the end of the day's regular session. But from feedback we received, it was apparent that, thanks to C-SPAN, people were listening. People came to him because they trusted him. Fed officials quietly blasted him. Someone at the Fed told me that Gonzalez was called an old buzzard and I was called his henchman. Although I was certainly not the only person on the excellent committee staff, I was deeply honored to be associated with Henry.

BATTLE LINES

Much of this book is based on investigations of the nation's central bank, the Fed, in which I assisted Henry B. Gonzalez. Some material is also from my work with Henry Reuss, a previous chairman of the Banking Committee. Here are some of the severe problems described in the book:

- The shielding of powerful Fed officials from individual accountability to Congress and the public by falsely declaring—for seventeen years—that it had no transcripts of its meetings
- The shredding of official source records during the 1990s
- The leaking of inside information that could be exploited for billions of dollars
- A policy to manipulate the stock and bond markets in 1994 under cover of a preemptive strike against inflation
- Faulty bank-examination practices, as revealed by the $5.5 billion sent to Saddam Hussein from a small Atlanta branch of a foreign bank
- Stonewalling congressional investigations and misleading the *Washington Post* about the $6,300 in hundred-dollar bills found on the Watergate burglars
- Billion-dollar loans to foreign countries without congressional authorization
- Employee theft of more than the officially reported $500,000 in cash from the central bank's enormous vault facilities
- Corrupt accounting practices at the Fed's second-largest vault facility, which stored $80 billion in cash
- Denying that the Fed was covered under the Civil Rights Act of 1964 and firing women who sued for racial discrimination
- Retaliation by the Fed against critical reporters
- Falsified records and shady operations regarding the Fed's fleet of fifty-plus airplanes, including paying for a "phantom" backup airplane at Teterboro Airport

How to explain the lies, deceptions, and abuse at the Fed described in this book, given its excellent personnel? The Fed did many activities well with a staff and officials, including Chairman Greenspan, who were predominantly conscientious, capable people.[12] I am a former Fed employee, as Greenspan told the FOMC (cited in the acknowledgments). The coexistence of conscientious personnel with the lies and deceptions discussed in this book presents a central question. Why did Fed officials, aided by their staff, behave duplicitously? A major reason for this behavior, advanced long ago, relates to all governmental bureaucracies. The primary objective and rationale of the officials who run a governmental bureaucracy such as the Fed is to *preserve and enhance the power and prestige of the bureaucracy,* sometimes even if its policies are harmful to the public. One reason for this is that bureaucratic success is measured by power and prestige, not profits. If the Fed's success were measured by profits, it could appear efficient and very profitable, since the governmental presses print new money on its command. Instead, Fed officials' legacies and reputations are dependent on what happens to the bureaucracy.

I call this explanation the "preservation hypothesis."[13] It is borrowed from a famous sociologist, Max Weber (1864–1920), who emphasized the tendency of a governmental bureaucracy to preserve itself: "The individual bureaucrat is thus forged into the [bureaucracy's] mechanism. They have a common interest in seeing that the mechanism continues its functions and that the societally exercised authority carries on."[14] The preservation of power in combination with secrecy is directly applicable to the Fed: "The pure interest of the bureaucracy in power, however, is efficacious far beyond those areas where purely functional interests make for secrecy. The concept of the 'official secret' is the specific invention of bureaucracy, and nothing is so fanatically defended by the bureaucracy as this attitude, which cannot be substantially justified beyond these specifically qualified areas."[15]

From this perspective, how likely is the head of a powerful governmental bureaucracy such as the Fed, with all the acclaim and prestige that comes with such a position, to accept a policy that severely reduces its power and prestige by injuring its reputation?

Some of Greenspan's prior views, brought from the private sector, enhanced or conflicted with this preservation motive at the Fed. He experienced serious conflicts between his position as the nation's top regulator and his long devotion to and association with novelist and philosopher Ayn Rand's economic views, which strongly rejected regulation, intrusion, and ownership by the government. He could hide these antigovernment views behind equivocating language or constrain them in garblings, but he could not erase his record as king of the Fed bureaucracy.

In an austere room at the Fed headquarters, at 20th and Constitution in Washington, D.C., hang the large framed pictures of the past chairmen of the Fed. As cheery as a mausoleum, the room was designed to preserve in dignity the memories of the men who have been at the helm of this great ship. That room is next to the large meeting room for the Fed's two top policy-making committees. The picture gallery is both a symbol of the importance of the legacy that will follow from the decision making next door, and a shrine to the preservation of the bureaucracy. It also stresses the importance of the officials who will be remembered as kings of the proceedings.

For many reasons, the motives of Fed officials to preserve its power and prestige may well be in accord with the public interest. Determining just where this effort crosses the line and begins to harm the public interest can be an especially hazy, or even nonexistent, task for Fed bureaucrats, who have an incentive to form a united front against criticism and close accountability. They are joined by a large number of admirers and protectors, many of whom distrust other governmental bureaucracies that operate with insufficient congressional oversight, but grant a special exemption to the bureaucracy handling the nation's money supply.

The account presented in this book will, I hope, help eliminate that exemption. Free and informed public coverage aided by effective congressional oversight from legislators such as Henry B. Gonzalez is essential to diminish actions against the public interest by unelected governmental officials.

Gonzalez's efforts to turn the lights on at the Fed were not politically partisan. The bipartisan desire of legislators for transparency was evident in Greenspan's remarks at secret Fed meetings. During his testimony before the Banking Committee on October 13, 1993, Greenspan apparently thought that Republicans would protect him, but became alarmed when Republicans started asking penetrating questions. Former Banking Committee chairman Jim Leach (R-IA) had written a statement for the hearing record, describing how the Fed should be reformed: "The issues of greater transparency of FOMC decision making as well as greater budgetary openness can no longer be ducked."[16] At a secret meeting, Greenspan warned the FOMC: "Jim Leach, of course, was the one who concerned me the most because his view is that there will be some markup of some form on some legislation."[17]

Greenspan was also concerned with another Republican member of the Banking Committee. He called him "nonrational." He told the FOMC that Congressman Toby Roth (R-WI) was questioning him about the existence of Fed budget records.[18] Actually, Roth's primary concern, as he explained to Greenspan, was why large parts of the Fed should be off-limits to governmental auditors, as stipulated in a 1978 law. Roth also referred to legislative efforts by Congressman Lee Hamilton (D-IN, who in 2004 co-chaired the National Commission on Terrorist Attacks Upon the United

States, also known as the 9/11 Commission) to require the Fed to publish its budget in the official Budget of the United States Government and to include details Hamilton said were missing. When Roth asked why the Fed budget had not been published, Greenspan replied that it had a sixty-six-page budget. During a secret FOMC conference phone call, Greenspan attacked Roth:

> For example, there was Toby Roth out there, a Republican, who was saying that we don't publish our budget. I pick up a blue [document, a] budget of 66 pages and I look through it and I say: "This is the most detailed budget of expenses I have seen of a federal agency." Did Toby Roth say to me "Oh, I didn't know [about] that. May I take a look at it?" He went on as though I had not made a single remark. What we are confronted with here is a very peculiar degree of nonrationality. It's not irrational; it's nonrational. And I'm very much concerned that in the areas where it really matters to us we can become very vulnerable if we mishandle how we respond to this particular problem that we have with respect to these transcripts.[19]

Gonzalez was awarded the 1994 Profile in Courage Award at the Kennedy Library. He was recognized for launching congressional investigations into the corruption of the savings and loan industry and for probes into the sale of U.S. arms to Iraq before the Gulf War in 1991. Caroline Kennedy Schlossberg noted his "well-known insistence on ethical conduct, tireless pursuit of the truth, respect for the Constitution, and opposition to powerful special-interest groups." Gonzalez told the audience:

> In my time I have had the honor to be vilified for standing up against segregation. I have had the privilege of being a thorn in the side of unprincipled privilege, and the great joy of being demonized by entrenched special interests. I have had the special pride of seeing hard jobs completed: the great civil rights laws; the cleanup of corruption in the savings and loan industry; the enactment of Federal laws that help educate the poor, care for the sick, eradicate disease, and house the people. And I have endured the impatience and humiliation that comes along with sometimes falling short of the goal.[20]

Gonzalez was then leading the oversight investigations of the Fed.

CHAPTER 2

THE BURNS FED
Price Controls, Inflation, and the Watergate Cover-up
with a Distinguished Professor at the Helm

THE PROFESSOR FROM CENTRAL CASTING

Arthur Burns (1904–1987) dressed like a learned professor from central casting, complete with a tweed suit and pipe. The chairman of the world's most powerful central bank, along with his security detail, was said to arrive at embassies in Washington, D.C., for meetings or formal social gatherings in his unassuming car, fit for an ivory-tower professor, while other central bankers and finance ministers playing the role of diplomats arrived in limousines.

At House Banking hearings, an out-of-place professor might have been expected to humbly share his wisdom and its limitations and to be honored to hear from the people's representatives. In reality, Burns was a tough old bird who would not alter his position an inch. Magisterial, he rained condescension on questioners like a prickly professor having to answer irritating questions from unprepared undergraduates.

Unlike Greenspan, who would assume some of the same erudite style, Burns had been a professor, an acclaimed scholar with a long, distinguished academic career. He began his academic career at Rutgers University (1927–1930), where one of his students was future Noble laureate Milton Friedman. Burns spent thirty-five years (1934–1969) as a professor at Columbia University, where Alan Greenspan was one of his students.[1] Many of the terms still used to describe business cycles were developed by Burns and Wesley C. Mitchell, his collaborator and former teacher.[2] It is evidence of the great public esteem accorded Burns's advice that his counsel, like Greenspan's, was solicited by presidents from both political parties. Burns served as Fed chairman (1969–1978) during the Nixon and Ford administrations. He served in the presidential administrations of John Kennedy, a Democrat, and Republicans Dwight Eisenhower, Richard Nixon, and Ronald Reagan.

Many would agree that he had the right to assume a haughty style, even if some legislators found that it impaired communication. His style may have shielded him from questions about basic problems at the Fed.

Inside the Fed, Burns assumed a similarly commanding style that fostered strict censorship of its large staff of economists, a policy that, as *Business Week* reported in 1979, continued when his successor, G. William Miller, became Fed chairman: "'Burns ran a one-man show. As far as he was concerned, he was the monetary policy in the Federal Reserve System,' observes Denis S. Karnosky, who recently resigned as vice-president of research in St. Louis after more than 12 years at the Fed bank."[3] The article goes on to state that "the pressure for noncontroversy is being applied in varying degrees throughout the system and that the disarray surfacing in New York and Philadelphia [at the Fed Banks in those cities] is spreading." In the New York Fed Bank, "many economists charge that bank officials alter the conclusions of their research to conform to what those officials think will please the Washington Fed staff and Paul A. Volcker, president of the New York Fed. Says one New York economist: 'The tone of every article is written to order.'"[4] I relate my experience with censorship at the Kansas City Fed in Chapter 9.

LOBBYING AND DIVERSIONARY PERFORMANCES

The Fed went to elaborate efforts to influence new members on the Banking Committees as a way to circumvent the "unfriendly" chairmen. For example, Burns, frustrated by House Banking chairman Wright Patman (committee chairman, 1963–1975), held many breakfasts with the numerous new members. Patman used to joke that Burns's breakfasts were affecting the price of egg futures.[5]

The lobbying campaign ran into a snag engineered by a committee staff member. Burns was incensed that an economist on the staff of House Banking advised members, especially Chairman Henry Reuss (who succeeded Patman), to legislate a requirement that the Fed periodically report to Congress. The culprit was the late Robert E. Weintraub, who gave up a tenured position as professor of economics at the University of California, Santa Barbara to join the staff. He had been a marine in the South Pacific during World War II and was a University of Chicago PhD who campaigned for slow money growth. Bob persuaded members of the need to mandate Fed reports at public hearings. He also spoke with members of the Senate Banking Committee who had been contacted by Burns. Burns lobbied hard to stop this intrusion on the Fed's "independence," but in 1975 a House resolution initiated the Fed's semiannual hearings at the Banking Committees.[6]

Burns, vigorously waving the Fed's mythical flag of independence, was very upset at being the first Fed chairman to be formally invited, by force of a congressional resolution that would later be incorporated into a law, to regularly testify to Congress about what the Fed was doing. Weintraub liked to describe one particular reaction to his work. After coming around a corner at a White House reception, he found himself alone with Burns, who, according to Weintraub, dropped the (expletive deleted) bomb on him and left.

Burns's required appearances before the House Banking Committee always attracted overflow crowds and wide TV coverage. At long last there was a slight lifting of the curtain of secrecy. Burns was expected to be revealed as the exalted wizard behind the curtain, deigning to explain some of the knobs and controls of his policy apparatus. The dog and pony shows fell far short of this expectation.

Burns sometimes gave answers as if he were instructing the legislators, lecturing in his nasal monotone. Such belittlement discouraged critical questions from members who did not want to be part of a student-teacher performance on national TV. Each of the approximately fifty House Banking Committee members was allotted five minutes to question the Fed chairman. Burns's answer might consume the full allotment, preventing a follow-up question. Generally, the exchanges contained little or no content relating to Fed policies and operations. Burns told Senate Banking chairman William Proxmire: "I would like to see interest rates where they are, or even come down, but they may have to go up." Proxmire responded "as an overflow crowd in the hearing room erupted in laughter: 'I keep nailing that custard pie to the wall.'"[7]

In the 1970s, technical details about Fed policy did not make the evening news on the major networks; a report on the Fed hearings was sometimes reduced to pictures of a cash-register drawer opening to signify that the central bank had something to do with money.[8] Veteran NBC reporter Irving R. Levine would say, "This is Irving R. Levine," in his distinctive voice. Shown against the backdrop of the empty chamber where the House Banking Committee held its hearings, he read his report from large cards held by an assistant. In the days before cable, his success depended in large part on his short report being selected for the evening news. If the renowned Fed chairman contradicted someone else in the government, that was the kind of confrontational tidbit that could draw attention in a short sound bite. These selected "news" items shed little, if any, light on problems at the Fed.

AN INCONSISTENT "CONSERVATIVE"

A biographer wrote that when President Eisenhower nominated Burns as chairman of the Council of Economic Advisers, "Republicans worried over the appointment despite Burns' economic conservatism. He had remained a Democrat throughout his academic years. His tweed suit and professorial manner reminded party stalwarts of the New Dealers they had worked so hard to oust."[9]

Burns's record, including information on transcripts of the Fed's then-secret meetings, cannot be readily tagged with a convenient label such as "economic conservatism." Burns stood firm against giving away interest-rate control when pushed to do so by House Banking chairmen Wright Patman and Henry Reuss or when subjected to tough questioning from members who wanted lower interest rates. Interest-rate management was central to the Fed's policy. Fed chairmen since 1951 had stood firm on this front; otherwise, short-term interest-rate policy would be subject to congressional pressures.[10] Conservatives and many others believed this was a necessary stance for central banks to take in order to prevent rapid inflation. Yet it was clearly inconsistent for Burns to publicly appear to protect the Fed from these attacks while thrusting what conservatives saw as another dagger into the heart of free markets: wage, price, and dividend controls.[11]

FOMC transcripts from 1972 indicate that Burns advocated wage and price controls and even controls on dividends.[12] House Banking chairman Patman, a leading liberal Democrat from Texas, also advocated wage and price controls. In an effort to reduce inflation, Richard M. Nixon (president, 1969–1974) introduced wage and price controls in 1971. At FOMC meetings in 1971 and 1972, Burns told Fed officials that he strongly supported these controls and had been in favor of them before Nixon suggested that they be used.[13] The Nixon administration's wage and price controls self-destructed in 1973 because of rising inflation.[14] Four years later, Burns told the Senate Banking Committee that the country needed an "incomes policy," and he called on the federal government to cut in half the pay increase for governmental employees.[15]

While Burns was advocating fighting inflation with price controls and an income policy, he also was using the Fed's assigned ammunition to stimulate the economy. Tape recordings from President Nixon's office reveal a sustained effort by administration officials to pressure Burns to stimulate the economy with low interest rates by gunning the money supply right up to the November 1972 election.[16] Although administration officials were not always satisfied, and Burns may have acted solely on his own best judgment, the record is clear. The Burns Fed accelerated the growth of the money supply before the election and slammed on the brakes after the election.[17] Two Fed governors warned the distinguished chairman against fueling a more rapid inflation.[18] Price increases from a rise in the price of oil affected inflation in the early 1970s.[19] The continued rise in prices was nurtured by the Fed's fast money growth, earning the Burns Fed a low grade for its policies.[20]

By 1980, short-term interest rates targeted by the Fed were near 20 percent and inflation surged to 13.5 percent.[21] Burns had blamed inflation during his tenure on the Vietnam War, "oversized" wage increases in the steel industry, "oversized" wage increases by unions, and Congress (which raised the minimum wage and increased Social Security taxes).

Burns disliked the monetarist explanation put forward by Milton Friedman, who viewed fast money growth as the prime reason for sustained inflation. Burns came under wider political fire late in his term when he sought to raise interest rates to slow down money growth, which had ballooned far above the Fed's targets.[22] Using an analogy I heard him employ several times, Friedman compared instigating fast money growth while applying price controls to trying to hold down a cover on a boiling teapot.

THE KIDNAPPING EXCUSE FOR SECRECY

The culture of secrecy at the Fed could be both vivid and comical. House Banking chairman Patman once asked Burns for the salaries of Fed officials below the rank of the top officials, whose salaries were already made public.[23] Patman wanted the names and salaries of everyone in the Fed making more than $20,000 a year. Responding to Patman on June 25, 1974, Burns requested that Fed officials' salaries be kept secret, lest they be kidnapped and robbed: "In recent years, as you know, there have been numerous unfortunate incidents, such as kidnappings and robberies, perpetrated on individuals in the United States."[24]

Finally, Burns reluctantly allowed that his reply would "encompass approximately 1,000 employees," asking "that the names of the employees we will be supplying be maintained solely for your personal use and not made available to others." This subterfuge to prevent having to reveal public-sector expenses seemed so obviously drawn from whimsy that it served only to highlight the Fed's arrogance. More fundamentally, that arrogance and secrecy were means to preserve power, as described in Chapter 1.

A MASSIVE CONFLICT OF INTEREST

How could the secretive Fed bureaucracy survive in a democracy? In part because the Fed was regulating the very people charged with regulating it, a massive conflict of interest that still undermines Fed operations. House Banking chairman Patman's response to this problem is directly relevant to the type of corporate scandals uncovered after 2000 and the attention given to reducing conflicts of interest in corporate boards of directors. Patman directed that a study be made of the directors of the Fed Banks. Patman died in 1976, just before the final copy of this study—*Federal Reserve Directors: A Study of Corporate and Banking Influence*—was sent to the printer.[25] A new cover letter was prepared for the next House Banking chairman, Henry Reuss.

The study contained more than a hundred pages of diagrams of Fed Bank directors' corporate and banking connections. It examined the affiliations of the 9 directors in each of the 12 Fed Banks (108 directors), and the 161 directors at the branches of these banks, for a total of 269 directors. It showed that 73 of the 108 Fed Bank directors "are either now, or have been, officers, directors, or employees of financial institutions."[26] They were shown as being part of "interlocking directorships" that included the top one thousand industrial concerns and one hundred multibank holding companies. Reuss wrote in the introduction: "The survey of the 269 directors of the district bank and branch boards indicates only minimal representation for small business and only a scattering of input from the academic community. . . . *It is clearly evident that the Federal Reserve System is dominated by a very small universe of private corporations"* (emphasis added).[27]

EXTRACTING THE MINUTES

After the report was issued, Reuss was convinced that the minutes of the meetings of Fed Bank directors should not be secret. He asked Burns for the minutes of the directors' meetings. The request was met with the same defiant cordiality and feigned surprise that greets many requests for Fed records, a response similar to that received when requesting documents from some foreign governments.

The battle for the records pitted Burns against the new House Banking chairman. Although Reuss was a scholarly lawyer who loved academic discussions of different views of policy issues, he also had a magisterial style that could be quite confrontational. Burns's arrogance was no threat to him. This may explain why Burns shed his public persona as a tough old bird when meeting privately with Reuss. Reuss found a self-effacing professor pleading with him most pitifully to do something good for the country—and the central bank—by not asking for Fed records. Upon hearing of this tactic after the first meeting, the House Banking staff feared Reuss's magisterial style would be reduced to congenial accommodation. In staff-drawn cartoons of forthcoming meetings, the two chairmen sat at opposite ends of a very long table to prevent Reuss from giving away the store. Although he found it difficult to deny this humble Fed chairman, Reuss, an intelligent, well-educated legislator with high principles, would not relent from demanding the secret records.

On September 15, 1976, Burns responded to Reuss by affirming that he too wanted more diversity on the boards of directors, but assured Reuss that since the boards did not have much authority, he and Reuss should not waste each other's precious time reading minutes: "Neither of us will reach our common goal, however, by examining pages and pages of minutes of Directors meetings. . . . In any event, your and our objectives are the same, broader representation on the these Boards, and *we must not let debate cloud our thinking on this issue*" (emphasis added).[28]

Reuss replied eight days later: "So there will be no misunderstanding, I request that your office assemble the minutes . . . and deliver these documents to the Clerk of the Banking, Currency and Housing Committee . . . by 5 p.m. on October 15."[29] Burns did not meet the deadline. By November 12, Reuss had agreed to reduce the workload of copying five years' worth of minutes to the years 1972, 1974, and 1975. Burns finally agreed, adding, in a handwritten note, "P.S. Your press release after our talk was *very helpful* I appreciate it. A."[30]

Behind the scenes, the feelings at the Fed regarding greater transparency were not so cordial, as revealed in the FOMC transcripts that Burns left (upon his death, in 1987) to the Gerald R. Ford Presidential Library on the University of Michigan campus. The archivists of the National Archives and Records Administration only lightly edited the transcripts. St. Louis Fed president Lawrence K. Roos is reported as saying:

> I would also think that if this involves a lot of work, which it will, needless work, that someone on Mr. Reuss' Committee, a friendly individual should know what we're being called upon to do. *Because I think this can be used against Reuss if we react intelligently and as I see it in the St. Louis case, it's appalling how skimpy or meaningless our minutes are, I'm sure we did this with great wisdom knowing that a man named Reuss would ask for them. The minutes are really terribly shallow. Tell nothing.* (emphasis added)[31]

Finally, on December 20, 1976, after six months of letters and negotiations, the minutes were shipped; a handwritten note on Burns's cover letter to Reuss read, "Merry Christmas and Happy New Year to you and your family, Arthur." Reuss did not agree to one of the stipulations in Burns's lengthy letter. This "essential assumption" was that there be no public disclosure. The Fed chairman raised all manner of potentially dire consequences as reasons to keep the public from knowing what the central-bank district directors were doing. Burns even used the pretense that the Fed Banks were more like private corporations than part of a governmental bureaucracy responsible to the public: "They [the minutes] reflect, as would the minutes of any corporate board meetings, the directors' bona fide efforts to fulfill their fiduciary obligations through the candid exchange of views and through review of significant corporate issues."[32]

After reading the material, the staff (including the author) telephoned Reuss, who was in Milwaukee, his home district. Reuss asked the staff to assist in writing a speech that he would deliver on the House floor and to make the material available to the press.[33] He delivered a floor speech entitled "What the Secret Minutes of the Federal Reserve Banks Meetings Disclose." Reuss's investigation of the minutes led to the passage of the Federal Reserve Reform Act of 1977, which brought Fed Bank directors within the scope of federal conflict-of-interest laws.

MURDER AT THE RICHMOND FED
AND VACUUMED MINUTES

One important deficiency of the boards of directors' minutes was their failure to include details. They generally followed the above-cited practice from an official in the Fed bureaucracy: "Tell nothing." Reuss called attention to vacuumed minutes that reported the murder of a guard by another guard at a Fed bank: "VII. Deletions and Failure To Provide Important Details In The Directors' Minutes . . . (For example) After a murder and three related shootings inside the Richmond Federal Reserve Bank, there must have been quite a discussion at the next board of directors' meeting. However, the minutes of March 9, 1972, at Richmond report simply: 'Mr. Heflin reported on the incident last Tuesday, when one of the Bank's guards shot and wounded four other members of our Security force, one fatally. He said that the other three had been released by the hospital.'"[34]

The murder of a Fed guard and related events are a national-security problem involving the safety of the immense amount of currency and coins the Fed receives from the Bureau of Engraving and Printing. The Fed also examines and stores currency and coins for the entire banking system. Surely a threat to any part of this system would rate more than a two-sentence summary.

Despite this vigorous vacuuming, there was enough material in the hundreds of pages of minutes to reveal, after many weeks of combing, very disturbing facts that led to the discovery of the Fed's part in the Watergate cover-up.

BURNS, THE BURGLARS, AND THE *POST*

Burns, a top Nixon administration official, appeared to have escaped the 1972 Watergate scandal with his honor and prestige intact. Burns's directive to keep the "System" from getting involved blocked congressional investigations into the source of the $6,300 found on the Watergate burglars. It was also used as the basis for issuing false or misleading information to the *Washington Post*, according to the documents shown here.

Five burglars, acting on instructions from the Nixon administration, broke into the Democratic National Committee offices in the Watergate Office Building, part of a large hotel-apartment-office complex overlooking the Potomac. They were arrested at approximately 2:30 A.M. on June 17, 1972.[35] Six thousand three hundred dollars in new hundred-dollar bills, numbered in sequence, was found on the burglars. The Philadelphia Fed Bank notified the Board of Governors about some of this money on June 20, three days after the Watergate break-in. The following day, Burns sent a directive to all the Fed Banks. The existence of the directive and Burns's reported desire to keep the Fed from getting involved were revealed in the minutes of a Philadelphia Fed Bank meeting on June 22, 1972 (Fig. 2-1). In the minutes, a Fed official reports: "Mr . . . said that Chairman Burns doesn't want the System to get involved and issued a directive to all Reserve Banks on June 21, which said in effect that the System was co-operating with law enforcement agencies but should not disclose any information to others."

Two days after the Watergate break-in, Senator William Proxmire, chairman of the Financial Affairs Subcommittee, specifically requested that Burns report to Congress about the $6,300 rumored to have been paid to the Watergate burglars.[36] Burns replied in a letter dated the same day: "We at the Board have no knowledge of the Federal Reserve Bank which issued those particular notes or the commercial bank to which they were transferred."[37]

What did the Board of Governors staff know forty minutes later? According to the Fed's annotated "Chronology Listing of the Events of the Watergate Matter as they Relate to the Federal Reserve System," forty minutes after the Burns's reply to Proxmire was sent, the Fed contacted the FBI (Fig. 2-2). The Fed was told "of two Federal Reserve offices that had issued currency notes in the Watergate matter." One day later, June 20, 1972, the Fed's "Chronology" records: "Federal Reserve Board staff [was] informed that . . . ten notes had been shipped by the Reserve Bank to Girard Trust Company in Philadelphia on April 3, 1972." Later the same day the staff at the Miami Fed facility "advised the Board they had given the FBI the following information—seven $100 notes listed by the FBI had been paid by Miami to Republic National Bank of Miami on April 19, 1972."[38]

Several notations in the "Chronology" indicate that the FBI had asked the Fed not to disclose this information to anyone. Henry B. Gonzalez observed twenty-one years later that officials of the FBI may well have been part of the cover-up: "The Acting Director of the FBI, who may have been given the information, testified that he burned some Watergate files."[39] Gonzalez was referring to L. Patrick Gray (1916–2005). Gray was

Discount Rate

Mr. ⌐   reported that he noted a general satisfaction with the
current trend of monetary policy at the Federal Open Market Committee meeting
on June 20. Problems were anticipated later in the year, however, as a
stimulative fiscal policy places more burden on monetary policy.

Mr. ⌐   said that market relationships and the overall stance of
monetary policy indicated that the discount rate should not be changed and he
so recommended.

Thereupon, the directors resolved unanimously,

That the existing rates on discounts
and advances be continued.

Other Matters

Mr. ⌐   reported that $6,300 in one hundred dollar bills had been
found on the persons arrested for breaking into the Democratic National
Committee headquarters in Washington. The FBI came to this Bank and said that
ten new 3-C notes numbered in sequence were among those found. This Bank
informed the FBI that they were part of a shipment sent to the Girard Bank on
April 3. Mr. ⌐   also said that the Washington Post had called to verify
a rumor that these bills were stolen from this Bank. The Post was informed
of the CV&D thefts but told they involved old bills that were ready for
destruction.

Mr.   said that Chairman Burns doesn't want the System to get
involved and issued a directive to all Reserve banks on June 21, which said
in effect that the System was cooperating with law enforcement agencies but
should not disclose any information to others.

Mr. ⌐   reported that the Board of Governors had formally issued the
revised regulations D and J which will be sent to banks tomorrow. He said

FIGURE 2-1. A page from the minutes of a board of directors meeting at the
Federal Reserve Bank of Philadelphia, June 22, 1972. The minutes show that the
Philadelphia Fed Bank misled the *Washington Post* about the source of some of
the money used to pay the Watergate burglars. The minutes were made public by
House Banking chairman Henry Reuss.

acting FBI director for less than a year (1972–1973). On June 26, 2005, three days before his death from pancreatic cancer, Gray was interviewed on ABC's *This Week* by George Stephanopoulos. Gray said he was called to the White House while he was the acting director of the FBI and given documents that had been found in the safe of a Watergate conspirator who was later convicted. Gray said White House counsel John Dean assured him that the documents were not Watergate related and instructed him in the presence of another high White House official, John Ehrlich-

---

Chronology Listing of the Events of the Watergate Matter
as they Relate to The Federal Reserve System

1. June 19 (9:45 a.m.) John Rippey, Assistant to the Board, received
    a call from Howard Shuman, Administrative Assistant to Senator Proxmire,
    requesting information on currency involved in the Watergate matter.

2. June 19 - During course of day Mr. Shuman called three more times for
    progress reports.

3. June 19 (2:15 p.m.) Letter of same date from Senator Proxmire received
    at the Board, requesting information on currency involved in Watergate
    matter.

4. June 19 (4:20 p.m.) Chairman Burns' letter of reply to Senator Proxmire
    was sent to the Hill. Chairman's letter indicated we had, at that time,
    no knowledge of the Federal Reserve bank which issued the particular
    notes or of the commercial bank to which they were transferred.

5. June 19 (5:00 p.m.) Mr. McIntosh contacted the FBI at Chairman's
    suggestion and was given the names of two Federal Reserve offices
    that had issued the currency notes in the Watergate matter.

7. June 20 (11:55 a.m.) Mr. Shuman called for a progress report and Mr.
    Rippey confirmed that we were in contact with the FBI.

8. June 20 (12:00 noon) Federal Reserve Board staff informed that the
    Philadelphia Reserve Bank had provided FBI information regarding the
    currency on June 19. (Information indicated that ten notes had been
    shipped by the Reserve Bank to Girard Trust Company in Philadelphia
    on April 3, 1972.

9. June 20 (2:20 p.m.) Federal Reserve Board staff (T. J. O'Connell, General
    Counsel) contacted U. S. Attorney for District of Columbia, Hal Titus,
    regarding the Shuman request for information. At this time the U. S.
    Attorney informed the Board that he was opposed to any disclosure of
    investigative evidence for the reason that such prior disclosure might
    well impede the investigation then underway.

10. June 20 (late afternoon) Miami facility staff advised the Board they
    had given the FBI the following information - seven $100 notes listed
    by the FBI had been paid by Miami to Republic National Bank of Miami
    on April 19, 1972.

11. June 20 (late afternoon) Senator Proxmire released press statement
    criticizing the Federal Reserve System for "their refusal to cooperate".

Photocopy from Gerald R. Ford Library

FIGURE 2-2. "Chronology Listing of the Events of the Watergate Matter as They Relate to the Federal Reserve System." A record of stonewalling worthy of an executive-branch agency in the Nixon administration. Source: Arthur Burns Collection, Gerald R. Ford Presidential Library.

12. June 20 (3:45 p.m.) Mr. Rippey read following statement to Mr. Shuman:
     "We have been in touch with the FBI and the U.S. Attorney's Office
     which is conducting the investigation. We are advised that disclosure
     of any information that might be in existence at the Federal Reserve
     Banks could be prejudicial to the conduct of the investigation and
     any subsequent prosecution, and consequently should not be released to
     anyone other than the investigative authorities."

13. June 20 (4:00 p.m.) Same statement read to the staff of House Legal and
     Monetary Affiars Subcommittee.

14. June 21 - Federal Reserve Board issued press release dated June 21
     stating the FRS was cooperating fully with law enforcement agencies
     in ascertaining the facts. The statement indicated that the U. S.
     Attorney had advised the System against disclosure of information
     at that time.

15. June 22 - Letter of this date received at the Board from Congressman
     Patman requesting information on the currency involved in the Watergate
     matter.

16. June 28 - Governor Robertson replied to Congressman Patman's letter of
     June 22, reiterating our cooperation with the officials in the
     investigation.

FIGURE 2-2. Continued

man, to make sure that they never saw the light of day. Gray said that at a later date he retrieved these documents, which he had placed in a FBI safe, took them to his Connecticut home, and burned them in the fireplace.

Five days after the break-in, June 22, 1972, at a board of directors meeting of officials at the Philadelphia Fed Bank, it was recorded in the minutes that false or misleading information about the $6,300 had been provided to a reporter from the *Washington Post* (see Fig. 2-1, under "Other Matters"). Bob Woodward told me he thought he was the *Washington Post* reporter who had made the phone inquiry. The reporter "had called to verify a rumor that these bills were stolen from this Bank," according to the Philadelphia Fed minutes. The Philadelphia Fed Bank had informed the Board on June 20 that the notes were "shipped from the Reserve Bank to Girard Trust Company in Philadelphia on April 3, 1972" (Fig. 2-2, item 8). The *Washington Post* was informed that thefts had occurred, but was "told they involved old bills that were ready for destruction" (Fig. 2-1). Three people had been named in a complaint filed before U. S. Magistrate Richard A. Powers with "the abstraction on or about June 29, 1971, of $900,000 in U.S. Federal reserve notes of $100 denominations from the Federal Reserve Bank of Philadelphia where they were employed as clerks in the Currency Verification and Destruction Unit."[40] The *Washington Post* and the chairmen of the congressional banking committees were not given information about the trail of the funds back through the Girard bank so that the source or sources could be determined.

Despite efforts by Senator Proxmire and House Banking chairman Patman, Burns steadfastly refused to supply information given to the Fed about the $6,300 found on the Watergate burglars. Burns wrote that the Fed was cooperating with the U.S. Attorney, adding:

> None of us here at the Board feel that any good purpose would be served by going back a third time to the U.S. Attorney.
> Your charge that the Board "is covering up for someone high in the Executive Branch" is deeply resented. This charge is totally without foundation. (see Fig. 2-3)

Proxmire responded: "In fact, *the situation is even worse than I thought.* I now find that the U.S. Attorney did not ask in any formal way that you withhold the information from me and that in addition neither you nor he made any independent judgment that the information I sought could impair the investigation or harm the right of a defendant" (see Fig. 2-4; emphasis added).

Nearly two decades later, Gonzalez referred to Burns's denial of information in his opening statement to Fed chairman Alan Greenspan and sixteen other Fed officials who were congressional witnesses:

> The Acting Director of the FBI, who may have been given the information, testified that he burned some Watergate files. The Nixon administration asked him to limit the FBI's investigation of the burglars' financing on the grounds that further inquiry would "uncover CIA assets and sources." Gosh, that sounds familiar. [Gonzalez was referring to the same type of warnings he received in the 1990s in an effort to stop his investigation of $5.5 billion in loans sent to Iraq's Saddam Hussein.] What was the Federal

July 28, 1972

The Honorable William Proxmire
Chairman
Joint Economic Committee
Washington, D. C.

Dear Mr. Chairman:

Our general counsel, Mr. O'Connell, has reported to me that at
the conclusion of a conference with your staff yesterday afternoon,
he was asked to consult once again with the U.S. Attorney for the
District of Columbia regarding the Watergate affair.

Twice before he has consulted with the U.S. Attorney on this question, most recently on Wednesday of this week. Twice before I
have consulted not only with the Board's legal advisers but also
with the other Members of the Board, including Vice Chairman
Robertson, who is, as you know, a lawyer with considerable
experience in law enforcement.

Our legal advisers have recommended that the Board honor the
judgment of the U.S. Attorney. The Board unanimously has decided
to do so, after reviewing the question yesterday morning. We feel
that the responsible course is to extend to the enforcement authorities the cooperation they say is necessary for the successful investigation and prosecution of this case. None of us here at the Board
feel that any good purpose would be served by going back a third
time to the U.S. Attorney.

Your charge that the Board "is covering up for someone high in
the Executive Branch" is deeply resented. This charge is totally
without foundation.

So that the record will be complete, I respectfully request that this
letter be inserted at an appropriate place in the record of the hearing.

Sincerely yours,

(signed) Arthur F. Burns

FIGURE 2-3. Letter from Fed chairman Arthur Burns to Senator William
Proxmire, July 28, 1972. Proxmire had charged the Board of Governors with
"covering up for someone high in the Executive Branch" who may have been
involved in Watergate. Burns informs him here that the accusation was "deeply
resented." Source: Arthur Burns Collection, Gerald R. Ford Presidential Library.

United States Senate

WASHINGTON, D.C. 20510

#933

August 1, 1972

Governor Arthur F. Burns
Chairman
Federal Reserve System
Washington, D.C. 20551

Dear Governor Burns:

At your request, your letter of July 28th relating to the Watergate affair will be inserted into the Record in full.

Once again, let me repeat that I regret very much the refusal of the Board to cooperate in the request which Congressman Patman and I have jointly made that the Board disclose information which we feel we have a right to secure.

In fact, the situation is even worse than I thought. I now find that the U.S. Attorney did not ask in any formal way that you withhold the information from me and that in addition neither you nor he made any independent judgment that the information I sought could impair the investigation or harm the right of a defendant.

Much of the information I sought is now public. As I thought, it clearly ties in the President's Re-election Committee with the bugging incident. I regret that the Federal Reserve System which had access to much of this information, refused it to me while passing it along to the Justice Department which has a clear conflict of interest in this case.

Sincerely,

William Proxmire, U.S.S.

FIGURE 2-4. Letter from Senator Proxmire to Fed chairman Burns, August 1, 1972. Responding to Burns's letter, Proxmire fires back—"The situation is even worse than I thought"—and goes on to imply that Burns lied about what the U.S. attorney had told him regarding the release of Watergate-related information. Source: Arthur Burns Collection, Gerald R. Ford Presidential Library.

Reserve's role in this coverup? Did the Federal Reserve deliberately obstruct the Congress and the public?[41]

The Watergate scandal resulted in the criminal convictions of more than fifty people and in guilty pleas from nineteen corporations. Many administration officials had approved, taken part in, or later tried to cover up activities of the White House Special Investigation Unit, known as the "Plumbers" because they were supposed to fix leaks of information, which included the five Watergate burglars. The administration orchestrated and later tried to cover up other illegal activities, which were brought to light along with the Watergate revelations. These activities included "dirty tricks" against Democratic Party candidates running for election. The Plumbers had tried to enter the Democratic National Committee offices a number of times before they were caught.[42] Eventually the scandal led to Nixon's resignation, on August 9, 1974; he remains the only president who has resigned.

The Burns Fed not only kept the Fed from getting entangled in the Watergate cover-up, which the Fed's actions had assisted, but also allowed false statements about bills the Fed knew were issued by the Philadelphia Fed Bank to stand uncorrected. By blocking information from Congress and issuing false information during a perilous governmental crisis, the Fed imposed huge costs on a public already lacking the information to hold Fed officials accountable. Had the deception been discovered, the Fed chairmen following Burns might have been forced to rapidly implement transparency measures in order to restore the Fed's credibility. That would have reduced or eliminated many of the lies, deceptions, and corrupt practices that are described in this book.

BURNS FAILS THE AUDITION; HIS REPLACEMENT IS
DELAYED BY AN IRANIAN BRIBE SCANDAL

When Jimmy Carter was elected president (Democrat, 1977–1981), the Burns Fed was in the process of raising its short-term interest-rate targets in an effort to control the rapid money growth it had engineered.[43] The plans for more interest-rate increases drew criticism from House Banking chairmen Reuss and Proxmire. Although "Proxmire conceded that the recent rise in interest rates had been necessary," there was fear that further increases would cause serious harm. Reuss said that if Burns actually carried out this policy of raising interest rates, "the economy would be thrown in another recession."[44] Carter's chairman of the Council of Economic Advisers, Charles L. Schultze, warned that the interest-rate increases could weaken the economy. Hobart Rowen reported bitter feelings between Proxmire and Burns that were "thinly disguised" when Proxmire told Burns at a November 9, 1977, hearing: "We may be saying Auld Lang Syne, and in a way I hope we are, but we'll certainly miss you."[45]

Burns was not reappointed. It was unusual, even sad, to see the distinguished Burns all alone in the hallway of the Rayburn Office Building, at the House of Representatives, where only a few weeks before his every appearance on Capitol Hill was accompanied by a cadre of staff and guards. Burns finished his governmental career as ambassador to Germany (1981–1986). He died in 1987 at the age of eighty-three.

Carter nominated G. William Miller to be Fed chairman in 1978. Vice President Walter Mondale had conducted a secret search for a new chairman so as not to embarrass Burns. Miller's confirmation was delayed because of a widely publicized scandal at the company he headed, Textron. The Senate was investigating charges that executives of Bell Helicopter, a division of Textron, had made "concealed foreign payments" to officers of the Iranian army in order to sell them helicopters. The potential illegality involved the Securities and Exchange Commission requirement to report questionable payments. Miller testified he did not know that General Mohammed Khatemi, commander of the Iranian Air Force, owned a sales agency that received a $2.9 million commission on the sale of 500 Bell helicopters to Iran in 1973. Miller was then confirmed. The Justice Department then convened a grand jury to investigate charges that some Textron officials had obstructed the 1978 confirmation hearings. This action generated further adverse publicity. Neither episode appeared to impede Miller's job performance.[46]

Miller served only a short time, 1978 to 1979, before becoming secretary of the treasury. Although he was not well versed in monetary policy, he was instrumental in developing legislation in 1980 that required all private-sector banks to adhere to nationwide Fed-imposed reserve requirements—required cash reserves for checking deposits. The legislation also allowed all domestic depository institutions to purchase Fed services such as check clearing and Fed loans to banks. The Fed chairmen were now at the helm of an even more powerful bureaucracy, but one saddled with a big problem: inflation, which in the first quarter of 1980 reached an annual rate of more than 17 percent.

AFTER STOPPING RAPID INFLATION, VOLCKER IS UNDERMINED AND REPLACED

Paul Volcker, the new Fed chairman, was described as "a serious-minded, balding cigar-smoking man who, at 6 feet 7 inches, towers over most of those around him," "a Democrat who served as under secretary of the treasury for monetary affairs during the Nixon administration," and someone "regarded as skilled and highly competent by liberals and conservatives."[47]

Volcker took a large reduction in salary when he was promoted from president of the New York Fed Bank to Fed chairman. His annual salary, which had been $110,000 as president of the New York Fed Bank, was reduced to $57,500 as Fed chairman. This ridiculous pay scale was a product of the muddled organization of the Fed: Fed Banks could pretend to be private companies when it was convenient for them to do so. This pretense allowed them to reject the lower pay scales in the federal government. Twenty-four years later, in 2003, the same pay-scale embarrassment continued: the New York Fed Bank president was paid $310,000 a year, and Fed chairman Alan Greenspan was paid $171,900.

Volcker, who served two four-year terms as Fed chairman, steered a Fed policy that substantially reduced inflation before Alan Greenspan became Fed chairman, in 1987.[48] Prices for consumer goods and services that had risen more than 13 percent in 1980 dramatically fell in Volcker's second term. Prices rose slightly more than 1 percent in 1996.

Volcker hit the ground running. He held a news conference with an astounding message on stopping inflation, word of which "filtered through receptions Saturday night and into breakfast sessions Sunday morning" at the annual American Bankers Association (the largest banking trade association) convention in New Orleans; "the bankers expressed strong support."[49]

The Fed would now concentrate on controlling the money supply rather than interest rates, a view that pleased the group of economists called monetarists. "Miracles never cease," said Beryl Sprinkel, a monetarist who served in the Reagan administration in a position previously held by Volcker, undersecretary of the treasury for monetary affairs. Sprinkel later became the chairman of the Council of Economic Advisers.[50]

The Volcker Fed's remedy of slowing money growth was the major cause of a double-dip recession that saw a peak unemployment rate of 10.8 percent in 1982. This was the highest unemployment rate since the Great

Depression.[51] Volcker's slower money-growth policies did not please some people in the Reagan administration.

The Reagan administration's method of removing Volcker was an example of political manipulation of the "independent" Fed. Volcker had been outvoted on February 24, 1986, by Reagan appointees to the Board of Governors. The majority rejected an increase in the interest rates on loans that the Fed made to banks. Volcker reportedly said good-bye and abruptly left the meeting to prepare his resignation. The rebellious Fed governors, called "the gang of four," later backed down, but the unwelcome mat for the man whom James Baker (White House chief of staff and close adviser to the president) called the "known Democrat," as if the Fed chairman were a subversive, was never removed.[52]

Volcker offered his resignation at the end of his second term; he was pointedly not asked to remain. According to Bob Woodward: "Howard Baker [White House chief of staff after James Baker] called Jim Baker to report that Volcker didn't want to stay. Jim Baker was delighted. 'We got the son of a bitch,' he told a New York friend."[53] President Reagan, in a customary short pink-slip announcement, said he accepted Volcker's decision "with great reluctance and regret."[54] He nominated Alan Greenspan, who two months earlier had been informally notified that this would happen.

CHAPTER 3

THE MASTER OF GARBLEMENTS

THE ROAD TO HIGH OFFICE

Far from being an enshrined oracle who issued garbled messages that were dissected for meaning around the world, Alan Greenspan began his career as an aspiring musician. After graduating from George Washington High School in New York City in 1943, he enrolled in the Juilliard School that summer to study the clarinet. Greenspan, who qualified for a scholarship, became a competent clarinetist and saxophone player. He was hired by the Henry Jerome swing band in 1944. Henry Jerome had attended the same high school as Greenspan, a decade earlier. Greenspan played in the band and handled its bookkeeping. He also enrolled at New York University in 1944.[1]

Leonard Garment, who managed the band, would play a pivotal role in bringing Greenspan into the central government of the United States thirty years later. Garment became a lawyer and joined Richard Nixon's law firm. He later recommended that President Nixon appoint Greenspan chairman of the Council of Economic Advisers.

Greenspan realized that he was a competent musician, but not on a level with other musicians in the band. As a biographer noted: "Alan could either continue in music as a competent clarinetist and saxophonist who did a great job of preparing the group's tax returns, or else he could move on to something he could really excel at."[2] If Greenspan had continued his musical career, he would not have achieved his prominence as the conscientious, capable leader of the world's most powerful central bank.

Greenspan had a peculiar skill at making important contacts. He was affable, intelligent, somewhat aloof, and in possession of a sense of humor. His quiet, apparently reflective economic advice, later combined with his enshrined reputation, gave the impression of learned, thoughtful insights. He made important contacts throughout his career, both at his consulting firm and in the government. On the Washington scene, Greenspan showed up at cocktail parties, Gridiron Club dinners, private luncheons at major watering holes, etc., where he could make important contacts who would help him get good press.[3]

Greenspan's skill in presenting imprecise, sometimes near-meaningless, conflicting, yet learned-sounding views won him over-the-top adulation for his insights and abilities. In *Maestro*, his biography of Greenspan, Bob Woodward writes that Greenspan was described as a "math wiz" who "was always calculating probabilities."[4] The bar falls below "math wiz" when Woodward relates that Greenspan did not want to learn the modern statistics used by economists. The defense for the "maestro"'s lack of knowledge, according to Woodward: Greenspan knew that economists could end up addicted to such statistics. Woodward adds that Greenspan "would have been sucked in himself, but such study was not available when he was a student at New York University and Columbia in the 1940s and 1950s."[5] This leaves open the question described below of how Greenspan earned his PhD from New York University, in 1977.

After he earned his master's degree in 1950 from New York University's School of Commerce, Greenspan continued his graduate studies at Columbia, where Arthur Burns was one of his professors. Greenspan's views were importantly influenced by Burns: "Alan became more than just another one of Arthur Burns's students; they became lifelong friends despite the gap of a generation in their ages. . . . As a young Ph.D. candidate in 1950, Alan idolized the older man and sought to emulate him in every way, even once briefly taking up the pipe, which Burns smoked incessantly."[6]

Greenspan left Columbia without completing the PhD program. He became a partner in a consulting firm with William Townsend in 1953. The firm, originally founded in 1929, was now named Townsend-Greenspan and Company. When Townsend died, in 1958, Greenspan became the principal owner. The firm initially "consisted of five people—the two principals, two researchers, and a secretary, all crowded into a shabby office at 52 Wall Street."[7] As its business grew, the firm's staff increased to approximately twelve people by the mid-1960s, and it moved several times to more auspicious offices in New York.

In 1952, Greenspan joined a small circle of followers that gathered around Ayn Rand. He attended Saturday-night meetings in her Manhattan apartment. The group read drafts of sections of her forthcoming novel, *Atlas Shrugged*. She advocated a philosophy that opposed the modern welfare state and espoused self-interest as a guide for the optimal organization of society. Greenspan was not only a devoted follower of Rand, but also a frequent and active contributor to her antiregulation and antigovernment views. He was an ardent advocate for laissez-faire capitalism, a view holding that nearly all governmental activities and regulation are impediments to free markets and individual achievement. He advocated a return to the gold standard, which would eliminate the government's discretionary control of the money supply—a little surprising for someone who was to become the nation's most important regulator of the heavily regulated banking industry in a bureaucracy that had discretionary control over the nation's money supply.

Despite his strong beliefs against the wage and price controls that President Nixon had implemented, Greenspan accepted an appointment as chairman of the president's Council of Economic Advisers in 1974, while Burns was serving as chairman of the Fed. Nixon resigned before Greenspan's Senate confirmation. President Gerald R. Ford continued to support his confirmation against the strong objections of Senator William Proxmire, who became chairman of the Senate Banking Committee the following year. Proxmire questioned Greenspan's appointment on the grounds that Greenspan was opposed to consumer-protection laws, antitrust laws, and governmental regulation of business. Proxmire said that Greenspan "has the almost incredible posture for an economic realist in these days of opposing the progressive income tax."[8]

One biographer tried to summarize some of Greenspan's various views as of 2002, when Greenspan was leading the Fed: "King Alan was an unconventional economist by any measure. Part gold bug, part Austrian school free-market economist, part monetarist, with perhaps a dash of Keynesianism added for good measure, Alan had created his own school of economic theory that was fully understood only by himself."[9]

The conclusion that the views held by "King Alan" were "understood only by himself" goes too far. More accurately, he was a nimble bureaucrat who was able to serve under and win praise from Democratic and Republican presidents. He was able to sound convincing both as an Ayn Rand follower, arguing for unregulated free markets, and as the nation's most powerful regulator, defending nationalization of the Fed's check-clearing system (see Chapter 7). Rand's philosophy of adamantly rejecting governmental regulation did not appear to be merely a passing dalliance when Greenspan was young and impressionable. Greenspan invited Rand to his swearing in as President's Ford's chairman of the Council of Economic Advisors. Their relationship continued until her death, in 1982.

"TO BE BLUNT ABOUT IT, THE PRESIDENT HAS LOST CONFIDENCE IN HIS ADVISORS' ABILITY TO PREDICT THE FUTURE"

The Senate confirmed Greenspan. He began serving in 1974, the year after the U.S. entered a recession. The Ford administration and its chief economic adviser, Greenspan, focused on fighting inflation. This policy concentration brought into question the economic acumen of those who advised Ford.

The recession that began in 1973 lasted sixteen months.[10] The "official" unemployment rate (which underestimated unemployment) reached 9 percent, higher than the rate during any of the prior five recessions since World War II. Inflation also rose rapidly as a huge spike occurred in the prices of gasoline, fuel oil, and other energy goods.[11] This rise in price was largely an external "tax" collected by foreign oil producers: oil prices tripled from 1973 to 1974, and then rose 30 percent over the next four years.[12]

Three months after leaving his job as Ford's press secretary, Jerald F. Terhorst criticized the advice given by Ford's economists for fighting inflation while the country suffered a severe recession: "Ford relied heavily on the forecasts of his consultants, including Economic Council Chairman Alan Greenspan," adding, "To be blunt about it, the President has lost confidence in his advisors' ability to predict the future."[13]

The anti-inflation policy took a ludicrous turn when the Ford administration sought to fight it with lapel buttons and conferences. Ford organized "Whip Inflation Now" (WIN) meetings across the country and at the White House, replete with WIN lapel buttons. Admonitions about buying less-expensive goods to slow inflation were not helpful, especially for those facing unemployment or already out on the street. It was not an entirely logical suggestion, since a sustained rise in the average price of less-expensive goods and services is also inflationary.

The WIN conference at the White House and the lapel-button campaign during this severe recession were signs of detachment from reality.

This contribution to President Ford's loss to Jimmy Carter in 1976 may not have been given sufficient emphasis. Ford's pardoning of Nixon for alleged Watergate crimes, more easily understood and more politically damaging, receives more coverage.[14]

GREENSPAN'S SECRET PHD DISSERTATION

Greenspan returned to his consulting firm at the end of the Ford administration. He also returned to New York University, where he was awarded a PhD in 1977, the same year he left his position in the government. He submitted some papers in place of the usual PhD dissertation.[15] Normally, a PhD dissertation in a field such as economics must be in a form sophisticated enough to be usable in research, must make a contribution to the existing body of knowledge, and must be original, unpublished work. When approved, the PhD candidate is normally required to supply a bound copy of the dissertation, which remains in the university's library and is available for future researchers to consult.

It was surprising to find Greenspan's dissertation a secret. In his book about Greenspan, Justin Martin describes "a mild controversy" about the papers submitted: "The content totaled 176 pages and Greenspan gave it the prosaic title: 'Papers on Economic Theory and Policy.' Although the content was undoubtedly solid, this was not exactly groundbreaking academic level material, nor did the collection match the size and scope of the usual dissertation. For years after, Greenspan's Ph.D. would remain steeped in a mild controversy. *Critics questioned whether his work was sufficiently meritorious. And Greenspan didn't help matters by requesting that NYU withhold from public view the collection of articles that comprised his Ph.D. work*" (emphasis added).[16]

As of 2004, the New York University library would not allow Greenspan's dissertation papers to be seen by the public.[17] On January 9, 2004, I made a telephone request to see them, and was informed on January 10 that the Greenspan dissertation papers are in a safe in the library and are not allowed to be made public. My further inquiries, to the president of New York University, John Sexton, elicited two replies from the provost, David McLaughlin, that were worthy of bureaucrats at the Fed. The last reply is shown in Figure 3-1. He indicates that NYU officials could not find it in the specified library. Also, he says that in the 1970s it was the policy to not place dissertations in the library. Evidently, he wanted me to believe

New York University
A private university in the public service

David W. McLaughlin
Provost

Elmer Holmes Bobst Library
70 Washington Square South, Room 1221
New York, NY 10012-1091
Telephone: (212) 998-3077
Facsimile: (212) 995-3190
Email: david.mclaughlin@nyu.edu

Robert D. Auerbach
Professor of Public Affairs
Lyndon B. Johnson School of Public Affairs
The University of Texas at Austin
Drawer "Y"
Austin, Texas 78713-8925

August 12, 2005

Dear Professor Auerbach:

In further response to your letter dated July 13, 2005, I can tell you that it was the practice of the business school, during the 1970s, not to deposit dissertations with the library. Thus, a copy of Greenspan's dissertation is not in the Bobst Library.

We suggest that you contact Greenspan directly in order to obtain a copy of his dissertation.

Thank you,

Sincerely,

David W McLaughlin

David McLaughlin
Provost

cc: John Sexton
        President

FIGURE 3-1. Letter from New York University provost David W. McLaughlin to the author, August 12, 2005. A feeble defense of the absence of Greenspan's dissertation from the NYU library.

that NYU business PhDs just took their dissertations home and put them in a drawer in case anyone inquired.[18]

One possible argument for this secrecy is that Greenspan's dissertation contains proprietary information that can never be made public. This argument resembles the one made by the Fed to block exposure, and even to deny the existence, of the transcripts of its meetings that it had hidden for seventeen years (see Chapter 6).

SHIFTING THE TAX BURDEN TO LOWER INCOMES

As an adviser to Ronald Reagan and a private-sector consultant, Greenspan generally supported the large tax cuts pushed by the Reagan administration in 1981, although he gave priority to lowering inflation.[19] The tax cuts lowered the top tax rates on increases in income from 70 to 50 percent and reduced other tax rates on increases in income by 23 percent.[20] These tax-rate deductions went into effect over the next three years. Many people agreed that the previous rates had been too high, even confiscatory, and had impaired investment and economic growth. The tax reduction was followed by a large and growing, actual and projected, budget deficit.[21]

As early as 1981, doom-and-gloom projections, including one forecasting an imminent collapse, were issued regarding the funds available for Social Security pensions. Greenspan was appointed by Reagan to be chairman of a bipartisan commission to save Social Security (National Commission on Social Security Reform, 1981–1983).[22] Greenspan received praise for achieving a compromise solution in a crisis atmosphere. As the measure passed the Senate, it was reported that the changes would "assure the solvency of the Social Security for the next 75 years."[23]

A primary part of the Greenspan Commission's solution was an increase in the payroll tax rate over a phase-in period. The combined employee-employer payroll taxes (Social Security plus Medicare taxes) were raised 15 percent to 15.3 percent of wages for 1990 (still in effect in 2007). The tax fell only on lower incomes, $35,800 or less in 1984 ($97,500 in 2007).

The final plan has resulted in more funds being collected than are paid out every year thus far, imposing a larger than necessary tax increase on lower incomes. The tax helped finance other governmental spending, such as the wars in Afghanistan and Iraq. The payroll-tax increases combined with the Reagan tax cut have substantially shifted the tax burden to those with lower incomes.[24]

Twenty-two years after the commission claimed it had "saved" Social

Security for seventy-five years, Greenspan advocated an additional tax redistribution plan to save Social Security. Greenspan answered a question about the effects of taxes on the distribution of income in what was called his last appearance before the House Banking Committee, on July 21, 2005. Asked if tax cuts should provide more relief to the middle class, he said that as Fed chairman he looked only at the production effects of tax reduction (stimulating economic activity) and not at the effect on different income groups. Then he sermonized on his purity regarding this issue by saying the matter of who benefits from tax cuts must be decided by Congress; he would stay clear of that consideration. He ended with an aside that tarnished his purity a bit: he had always favored not taxing dividends. That sounds very much as though he has always advocated measures that affect income distribution, a necessary result of nearly all tax changes.[25]

CHARLES KEATING AND THE MOST EXPENSIVE FINANCIAL-INSTITUTION FAILURE IN U.S. HISTORY

Greenspan continued his consulting business. He was retained in 1984 by Charles H. Keating, Jr., the head of Lincoln Savings and Loan in California. Lincoln's collapse in 1989 was the most expensive financial-institution failure in U.S. history, costing more than $3 billion. Lincoln was a corrupt enterprise that stripped away many thousands of older people's savings. Instead of placing their funds in insured savings accounts, as many depositors expected, Lincoln used the funds to buy uninsured bonds from a real estate company, American Continental Corporation (ACC), which Keating operated. He had used ACC to buy Lincoln. He bought ACC with the proceeds of "junk bonds" (high-interest-paying bonds with lower credit ratings) sold by Michael Milken. Both Milken and Keating would serve time in prison. Criminal charges against Keating were later dismissed.

Lurid stories of how Lincoln misled these customers, costing them their life savings when Lincoln collapsed, were finally brought out in a San Francisco field hearing by House Banking chairman Gonzalez in January 1989.

Keating's attempt to keep Lincoln from failing included hiring a number of economists and a very prominent consultant who had been chairman of the Council of Economic Advisers. Alan Greenspan lobbied for Lincoln to obtain an exemption from the 10 percent limit on what were called "direct investments." The primary assets of savings and loans were home mortgages. If the 10 percent limit was lifted, more of the depositors' funds could be put in other investments.

Many of the savings and loans were insolvent and terminal. The income from the lower-interest mortgages they had sold in the 1970s failed to cover the cost of attracting new money in the higher-interest 1980s. The federal government refused to close the insolvent savings and loans. It would have had to use government-guaranteed deposit insurance to pay depositors. The government even passed legislation allowing phony assets to be put on the books at fake prices to make it look as if the firms were solvent.[26] Meanwhile, unsavory practices dominated much of the industry. Many of those who controlled the terminal and near-terminal S&Ls placed high-risk bets on speculative investments, and some made phony investments for personal gain. Eventually there were many criminal convictions.

Keating sent his distinguished, influential consultant, Alan Greenspan, to Congress to lobby senators for an exemption to the 10 percent limit. The expense statement from Townsend-Greenspan and Company, shown in Figure 3-2, details Greenspan's bill for his trip to Washington, D.C., on December 17, 1984, including his retainer of $25,000. Greenspan was scheduled to meet Keating's principal lobbyist, James Grogan, who would accompany him. Their schedule included meetings with the chairman of Senate Banking, Edwin Jacob "Jake" Garn (R-UT); Danny Wall, the committee's chief of staff, who would take over as director of the governmental regulatory board for S&Ls; and Senators John Glenn (D-OH) and Alan Cranston (D-CA). These last two senators would become part of the Keating Five, a group of senators who met with regulators to induce them to lay off of Keating.[27] Keating was generous with campaign contributions and in-kind payments.

Greenspan was also paid to write a letter on Keating's behalf. In 1985, he wrote to the governmental regulator, painting a picture of Lincoln management as "seasoned and expert" and as having "restored the association [i.e., Lincoln] to a vibrant and healthy state, with a strong net worth position, largely through the expert selection of sound and profitable direct investments." The bouquet of flowery praise included a final orchid: "Finally, I believe that denial of the permission Lincoln seeks would work a serious and unfair hardship on an association that has, through its skill and expertise, transformed itself into a *financially strong institution that presents no foreseeable risk*" (emphasis added).[28]

In *Maestro,* Woodward reports that Greenspan was "alternatively embarrassed, forthright and defensive" when Senator John McCain (R-AZ,

1131

TG

Townsend-Greenspan & Co., Inc.

180 Wall Street New York, N.Y. 10005 212-943-6916

December 20, 1984

PAUL, WEISS, RIFKIND, WHARTON & GARRISON
345 Park Avenue
New York, NY 10154

Attn: Mr. Arthur L. Liman

August 3, 1984 through December 14, 1984
Hourly Charges
                    Dr. Alan Greenspan $27,000.00
                    J. Mackey   2,600.00
                    Others   1,200.00
                    Expenses   125.00
                                                      $30,925.00

Trip to Washington, D.C. (12/17/84)
                    Fee $12,000.00
                    Travel Expense   240.00
                                                      $12,240.00
                    Total $43,165.00
                    Less Retainer   25,000.00
                    Balance $18,165.00

AL529-08

ACCT. No. ____653____
G/L No. ____5-8210____
POSTED ____
OK TO PAY ____   SPECIAL COUNSEL
                             EX. 209

TG000260

FIGURE 3-2. Invoice from Townsend-Greenspan & Co, Inc., dated December 20, 1984. The bill is for Alan Greenspan's services on behalf of Charles Keating and Lincoln Savings. Source: House Committee on Banking, Finance and Urban Affairs, *Preliminary Inquiry into Allegations regarding Senators Cranston, DeConcini, Glenn, McCain, and Riegle.*

one of the Keating Five) cited Greenspan's "prior endorsement" of Lincoln Savings and Loan. Greenspan reportedly said: "I was wrong about Lincoln. I was wrong about what they would ultimately do and the problems they would ultimately face." Despite these embarrassments, Woodward describes Greenspan's "private" excuse: "Privately, Greenspan believed he would do it the same way again, given the information he had in 1985. When he reviewed Keating's balance sheets, he found them both quite impressive and fiscally sound. Keating had done nothing wrong at that point, or if he had, it wasn't detectable. Greenspan just hadn't anticipated that Keating would turn out to be a scoundrel."[29]

This private excuse does not fly, according to an expert who states that information contradicting Greenspan's rosy predictions was available to Greenspan in 1985. Professor William K. Black was former deputy director of the Federal Savings and Loan Insurance Corporation and senior deputy chief counsel for the Office of Thrift Supervision in San Francisco.[30] He investigated Lincoln Savings and ACC. According to Black:

> Greenspan's letter was the principal basis for Lincoln Savings application to engage in direct investments roughly four times as large as the threshold. The Bank Board [Federal Home Loan Bank Board] adopted the direct investment rule on the basis of evidence showing that such assets caused unusually large losses in the new wave of failures . . . Mr. Greenspan's conclusions were not supported by the record of Keating's management of ACC (a failing home builder) or Lincoln Savings (a failing S&L). I researched and drafted the memorandum recommending that the Bank Board reject Mr. Keating's application. My research on ACC's performance was based on information available to Mr. Greenspan in February 1985. I reviewed ACC's securities filings. They revealed that ACC was very poorly run. It had experienced serious losses because it produced homes that consumers did not want to buy due to poor design and flawed homes that suffered water damage and led to a series of lawsuits. As a result, ACC had ceased producing homes in all but one market (AZ). Mr. Greenspan's claim that ACC had a long track record of successful management was refuted by ACC's own securities law disclosures. Note that Mr. Greenspan cites no factual support for his bare assertions.[31]

The $3 billion collapse of Lincoln became part of the huge bailout of savings and loans that cost the nation's taxpayers between $150 and $170 billion, 2.5 to 3 percent of the goods and services produced in the United States in 1993.[32]

GREENSPAN'S DIRE WARNINGS ABOUT
RECESSION IN 1989

A few months before Greenspan was nominated by President Reagan to be the new Fed chairman, Greenspan "sketched an outline of his brand of laissez-faire conservatism April 8 [1987] in a brief interview intended for use in a coming CBS television documentary."[33] The producers wanted to hear from the former chairman of the Council of Economic Advisers. After his nomination in June 1987, the network decided to play the interview on Sunday's *Face the Nation.* Concerning the next recession, Greenspan said that recessions always occur—"it's just a matter of when." He guessed the next one might be in 1989, and to a large extent the Greenspan Fed's policies would bring that guess to fruition in 1990. Greenspan sounded an alarm about the U.S. economy: if saving and investment did not increase, "we are going to fade from the scene as a huge superpower eventually."[34]

Greenspan's dire warning about investment was spectacularly wrong during the next decade, which saw an explosive increase in investment in digital information technology. Failing to specify a specific time and hiding behind the word "eventually" made his prediction immune to contradiction, sort of like a horoscope.

THE STOCK MARKET CRASH AND
MISSING FED RECORDS

Almost immediately after Greenspan became chairman of the Fed, in August 1987, he was confronted by a stock-market crash. Stock-market prices reached their peak in August, and then fell by 22.6 percent in one day, October 19, 1987. The Greenspan Fed *may* have correctly handled the liquidity problems associated with the crash. The cautionary word "may" is appropriate because the Fed reported to Congress that transcripts of eight consecutive FOMC telephone conference calls following the crash were missing (those for October 21, 22, 23, 26, 27, 28, 29, and 30).

What did the individual FOMC members advise during this period? Did their individual views reflect skill in conducting the Fed's operations? Seven years later, the Greenspan Fed, under pressure from a Gonzalez investigation and a series of hearings, sent the list of FOMC conference-call transcripts (shown in Figure 3-3) to Gonzalez. The list includes a notification of the missing transcripts.[35]

Appendix II

Inventory of Transcripts at the Federal Reserve

The Federal Reserve supplied Chairman Gonzalez with the dates of FOMC meetings at the Marriner Eccles building in Washington, D.C. and of conference calls between FOMC members since the Federal Reserve ceased releasing the Memorandum of Discussion. These are listed below. The Federal Reserve indicates it has transcripts of these meetings except as noted.

39

FOMC Telephone Conference Calls

1976
November 8

1977
May 27
October 31 (no transcript)

1978
January 5
March 10
May 5
August 8 (no transcript)

1979
January 12 (no transcript)
March 3 (no transcript)
April 27
June 27
July 17, 19
July 27 (no transcript)
September 20
October 5, 22

1980
February 22 (no transcript)
March 7
April 29
May 6
June 25
July 25
August 22
November 26
December 5, 12

1981
February 24
April 28
May 6
June 17
July 17

1982
March 2 (no transcript)
May 20 (no transcript)
July 15 (no transcript)
August 27 (no transcript)
September 24

1983
January 14, 21, 28
April 29
June 23
July 25 (no transcript)
August 8 (partial)

1984
January 11 (no transcript)
March 20 (no transcript)
October 18 (no transcript)
December 7 (no transcript)

1985
January 18
September 10 (no transcript)
September 23 (no transcript)

1986
January 17 (no transcript)
April 21 (no transcript)

1987
February 23 (no transcript)
April 29
September 8 (no transcript)
October 20
October 21 (no transcript)
October 22 (no transcript)
October 23 (no transcript)
October 26 (no transcript)
October 27 (no transcript)
October 28 (no transcript)
October 29 (no transcript)
October 30 (no transcript)

1988
January 5
May 6 (no transcript)
May 24 (no transcript)
June 22
July 19
August 5 (no transcript)
August 9 (no transcript)
October 17
November 22

1989
February 23 (no transcript)
May 31
June 5
July 26
October 16 (tape only)
October 17 (tape only)
October 18 (tape only)
November 6 (no transcript)
November 27 (no transcript)

1990
January 16 (no transcript)
April 11
August 6 (no transcript)
September 7, 17
December 7

1991
January 9
February 1
March 26
April 12, 30
May 1
June 10, 24
August 5
September 13
October 30
December 2 (tape only)
December 20

1992
January 9
March 11
July 2
December 14

1993
January 6
February 18
March 1
October 5, 15, 22

39

FIGURE 3-3. Inventory of Transcripts at the Federal Reserve of FOMC Telephone Conference Calls. The list shows that transcripts do not exist for calls made during the eight days immediately after the 1987 stock market crash. Source: Senate Select Committee on Ethics, *The Federal Reserve's 17-Year Secret*, 37, 39.

It is important for taxpayers as well as future Fed officials to know the actions and deliberations of individual members of the FOMC during this crisis. With the vote of at least five governors and its own emergency declaration, the Fed can lend billions of dollars of funds to brokerages and other private sector businesses under the Fed's emergency powers (Section 13-3 of the Federal Reserve Act). All these FOMC records missing from the same time period suggests a deliberate omission by the Greenspan Fed, an omission that shields this twelve-member committee from accountability during a critical period.

After a rapid stock-price recovery following the crash, the Greenspan Fed decided to fight rising inflation, despite Greenspan's prior prediction about a likely recession in 1989.[36] The Fed fired its monetary shotgun, pushing up interest rates and rapidly contracting the nation's money supply. The Volcker Fed had successfully fought inflation in this way, but at the cost of a double-dip recession. Volcker had fought a more rapid and more sustained inflation. Now, in 1988 and 1989, the Greenspan Fed overreacted. It fired the shotgun at a smaller target, and the economy dropped into a recession in 1990 and 1991, undermining President George H. W. Bush's reelection bid. The president's popularity dived from the high levels achieved following the victory in the first Gulf War. Like the economic policies attributed to former President Gerald Ford when Greenspan was chairman of his Council of Economic Advisers, George H. W. Bush's economic policies seemed out of touch with reality.

ECONOMIC EXPANSION, A SPECULATIVE BUBBLE IN STOCK PRICES, AND DEIFICATION

The implementation of new advances in digital information technologies, including the Internet, together with bursting optimism about the future produced a dramatic boom in investment and output in the 1990s. The excitement over the new technologies also caused a speculative bubble in stock prices in the last half of the 1990s. The nation's economic guru and sage, Greenspan, was praised unto deification for overseeing the expanding economy and the surging stock market and for keeping the rise in the prices of goods and services—inflation—low from 1992 until the end of the decade.

Many world events helped hold prices in check while Fed policy in the 1990s and early 2000s was on a roller-coaster ride. (More about the Fed's erratic monetary policy can be found in Chapter 11.) Prices were affected by competition from low-cost foreign goods and services. Huge foreign-currency crises and recessions affected prices. None of this seemed to diminish the praise for the wizard behind the curtain until the U.S. stock market began to crash in March 2000.

A reviewer of Stephen K. Beckner's *Back from the Brink: The Greenspan Years* (1996) noted in the *Financial Times:* "It has become axiomatic that the softly spoken Mr. Greenspan is the real architect of the US economy's formidable strength today. . . . It was only Mr. Greenspan's foresight and remarkable surefootedness that averted a series of events that could have sent the entire economy tumbling over the edge. In his introduction, Mr. Beckner paints a lurid picture of the nightmare scenario that might have happened [after the stock market crash in 1987] — financial collapse, bankruptcies, and mass unemployment." The review notes, somewhat cheekily, that after Greenspan was nominated by "Bush and Clinton, Presidents of rather different political views . . . saving the US economy from collapse must have seemed like a piece of cake." The reviewer concludes that the chairman was "widely called without a hint of hyperbole, the most powerful man in the world," adding, "Mr. Greenspan has already inspired a number of biographies, mostly of a hagiographical nature. But none goes quite so far as this one."[37] Hagiographies are biographies of saints.

In *Maestro* (2000), Woodward concluded: "Each of us is a character in the nation's great economic soap opera; Greenspan is both director and producer," noting as well that "Greenspan's policy of expanding openness and transparency has done more than merely increase the Fed's accountability."[38]

The claim of openness and transparency was far from reality, at least as shown by the evidence turned up in Gonzalez-led congressional investigations of the Greenspan Fed. Although some of the problems presented in this book were unavailable at the time, that evidence included Greenspan's signed replies to attempts at more transparency in 1992 and 1993, his comments on FOMC transcripts, the Fed's seventeen-year lie about the sham burial of its records, the shredding of source transcripts, and the failed attempt, engineered by Greenspan in 1993, to mislead Congress about the seventeen years of transcripts. This record evidently did not affect Woodward's assessment. Woodward and, later, a researcher called me when they were preparing *Maestro;* I offered my assistance and provided some material.

Perhaps Greenspan's speech on December 5, 1996, at the American

Enterprise Institute for Public Policy Research helped propagate his personal myth. Greenspan declared his support for transparency at the Fed: "If we are to maintain the confidence of the American people, it is vitally important that, excepting the certain areas where premature release of information could frustrate our legislated mission, the Fed must be as transparent as any agency of government. *It cannot be acceptable in a democratic society that a group of unelected individuals are vested with important responsibilities, without being open to full public scrutiny and accountability*" (emphasis added).[39] This was the same year in which unedited transcripts of Fed meetings were being destroyed, as authorized by a Greenspan-engineered unrecorded vote. This effective feint toward transparency deceived a receptive audience that could not hear the shredders humming at the Fed.

In Maestro, Woodward wrote: "Some day, in some form, the economic boom will end. Someone, an authoritative voice, is going to have to tell us the party is over . . . Who is responsible?" He asked his question just a few months too soon. The party ended when the stock market began its crash in March 2000, which was followed by a recession that ended in late 2001, which was followed by an anemic job-loss recovery. Three million jobs had been lost by 2003.[40]

President George W. Bush, running for reelection in May 2004, nominated Greenspan for a fifth four-year term as Fed chairman, saying that Greenspan's policies had "helped unleash the potential of American workers and entrepreneurs."[41]

THE CHAIRMAN TESTIFIES

From 1995 to 1998, the small hearing room (222, known as the "three deuces") at the Rayburn House Office Building was used to house some of the press waiting to cover the semiannual testimony of Fed chairman Greenspan on monetary policy in the main House chambers. These semiannual reports were required by law. The reporters were not allowed to use the telephone or leave the room after receiving a copy of Greenspan's speech to read in advance. There was an armed guard at the door, as there was in the other room containing other members of the press, who followed a similar ritual. Shortly before 10:00 A.M., when Greenspan began to speak, they were allowed to leave to rush to the toilet, to the hearings, or to call in their summary of the speech, which was immediately made public. This ritual may have evoked a bit of the Stockholm syndrome as the captives began to revere their Fed jailer, who held the key to the telephones and the toilets.

The hearings were impressive media events, with members of the press at tables along one wall, flashbulbs blinking from a swarm of still photographers crouched in front of the chairman at the beginning of the hearings, and TV cameras; the camera directly in front of the chairman was remotely controlled from the outside hallway. The Fed chairman sat alone behind a microphone, his staff contingent behind him in the first row of public seating. The committee members sauntered in slowly and sat in the tiered rows of seats behind continuous, long mahogany desks with spaced microphones. Members sat in order of seniority, starting with the longest-tenured member, who was placed next to the committee chair (not always the longest-serving member of the committee). The chairman sat top-row center. The number of members on the committee from each party was supposed to reflect the division in the full House of Representatives, but that was open to sometimes-heated negotiation between minority-party members and the House leadership. Lower rows contained members with less tenure. The newest members, whom one House Banking chairman referred to as the "babies," sat in the lower rows.

The committee has grown, reaching nearly seventy members in 2001. Before the hearing began, the Fed Chairman would go forward to speak briefly with some of the members, especially the chairman and the longest-tenured member of the minority party, the ranking member. Hearings began with opening statements from members. Because of the size of House Banking, senior members were often the only ones allowed to make opening statements. Some opening statements amounted to little more than bouquets of congratulations for the chairman; others were hard-hitting presentations of economic problems, which only infrequently could be remedied by policies over which the Fed had jurisdiction.

Following in the style of Burns, Greenspan read his long opening statements in a muffled monotone, the naive perception of a learned professor's style. They were laden with prolific economic background material, sounding like products of the large staff of economists that assist each Fed chairman. The statement might touch on many aspects of the economy but would not zero in on the effects of Fed policy. Extensive analysis of the success or failure of previous Fed policies was generally omitted. The average predictions of FOMC members about future economic activity, inflation, and employment were required to be presented. There was little or no explanation of the accuracy of previous or present observations, or of how they were related to past or future Fed policy. The result was frequently an excessively qualified mush that tasted delicious to the Fed-watchers industry, which baked them into a variety of delicious pastries.

Questions about the Fed's views of current conditions and its expected policies had to be extracted from a rapid reading of the chairman's statements and associated material, sometimes supplied to members and staff only thirty minutes before the hearing.

When the chairman stopped droning and looked forward in silence, the Banking Committee chairman would thank him for his presentation. Then came questions from members, many fewer of whom were generally present now than at the beginning of the hearing. Near the end of the hearing, the public audience had often nearly vanished, several times leaving only a visiting grade-school class on a tour of the Capitol.

Although Greenspan would assume the erudite style used by Burns, he did not adopt the same magisterial condescension when answering members' questions. Greenspan's qualified answers contained nuggets of information that fell somewhere around the question. Questions directly affecting Fed policies or operations were sometimes treated with perceptible irritation, although other subjects were discussed cordially. It was often difficult to extract a distinct reply without digging into the analysis Greenspan had offered, and this was a more rigorous style of questioning than most legislators cared to undertake or, in House Banking, could pursue in the five minutes each was allotted. Occasionally members would yield their time to another member in order to facilitate continuity via follow-up questions. These members paid a price when they forfeited TV coverage of their questioning or praising the nation's guru.

Greenspan often appeared to be going in opposite directions on partisan issues so that he would not appear to be stepping on anyone's toes, especially the toes belonging to the president. Sometimes he tripped on a contentious issue.

He opposed big deficits in 2004, which he would rather not see, but thought they were sometimes necessary during the presidency of George W. Bush, whose major economic policies emphasized income-tax reductions, which contributed to larger budget deficits. He stepped on the third rail in 2005 when his sage advice included Social Security payments, over which the Fed has no jurisdiction. Senate minority leader Harry Reid (D-NV, majority leader in 2007) called Greenspan "one of the biggest political hacks we have in Washington" after a Greenspan garblement that supported President Bush's plan to put part of taxpayers' Social Security contributions in private accounts.[42] At the same time, Greenspan continued to oppose the huge budget deficits that the privatization plan would produce. Greenspan preferred dealing with the growing deficits by cutting Social Security benefits.[43]

PLAYING CONGRESS AND THE PUBLIC

At congressional appearances, Greenspan could resort to the irrelevant detour to consume the time allotted to a legislator. With the help of Fed officials and the Fed's experienced staff, Greenspan even planned such a diversion strategy. This is shown by his statements during a 1993 conference call to FOMC members. The Fed had been in a nearly two-year fight against Gonzalez's efforts to impose greater transparency on it. Now the Fed governors and Fed Bank presidents feared being called en masse to testify. Some FOMC members turned to Greenspan for his expert assistance in producing detours away from questions. Robert McTeer, president of the Dallas Fed Bank, said: "I'm not questioning the views; [my concern] is just the way it's going to look to the people [watching] C-Span, I guess." Richard Syron, president of the Boston Fed Bank, added: "I don't know how to do it, but if there is a way, along the lines of what Bob said, of trying to raise in our testimony something about the economy, or even finding a segue between the importance of what we're doing and the [unintelligible] in some of our regions or something else to try to get somewhat off the defensive, it's worth thinking about. I'm not sure it's possible."[44]

Greenspan replied by explaining how to play committee members with a detour: "Well, that's not a bad idea, Dick, because remember: Aside from Gonzalez and a few other planted questions, this [Banking] Committee is not focused on this issue. In fact the one thing that's pretty clear is that there is a spectacular lack of interest in that Committee for these hearings. And it should be quite easy to say: *And by the way, this reminds me of an incident in 1936 in Sacramento or something like that*" (emphasis added).[45]

Another technique used by Greenspan to announce Fed policy was to use a ridiculously opaque, garbled message conveying little or no information. A bit of deception, contradiction, or falsehood in a well-written announcement might draw some criticism, but if the entire message is a big garblement, it may well go unquestioned. It is difficult to dispute an entire message that is total nonsense, especially if it is decorated with erudite jargon.

The jumbled FOMC announcement in May 2003 was interpreted as a very important message, signaling the Greenspan Fed's concern with the possibility of deflation (falling average prices of goods and services). The Greenspan Fed thought this was a terrible condition, although this was a radical change from Greenspan's prior support for zero inflation, which would require falling prices much of the time.

The muddled announcement contained contradictory statements: "over time" things should get better, "over the next few quarters" things should stay about the same, and for the "foreseeable future" things should get worse:

Release Date: May 6, 2003
For immediate release

The Federal Open Market Committee decided to keep its target for the federal funds rate unchanged at 1-¼ percent.

Recent readings on production and employment, though mostly reflecting decisions made before the conclusion of hostilities [the second Iraq war], have proven disappointing. However, the ebbing of geopolitical tensions has rolled back oil prices, bolstered consumer confidence, and strengthened debt and equity markets. These developments, along with the accommodative stance of monetary policy and ongoing growth in productivity, *should foster an improving economic climate over time.*

Although the timing and extent of that improvement remain uncertain, the Committee perceives that *over the next few quarters the upside and downside risks to the attainment of sustainable growth are roughly equal.* In contrast, *over the same period,* the probability of an *unwelcome substantial fall in inflation,* though minor, exceeds that of a pickup in inflation from its already low level. The Committee believes that, taken together, *the balance of risks to achieving its goals* [presumably to achieving full employment and price stability, as it is directed to do under 1946 legislation] *is weighted toward weakness over the foreseeable future.*

Voting for the FOMC monetary policy action were Alan Greenspan, Chairman; William J. McDonough, Vice Chairman; Ben S. Bernanke;

Susan S. Bies; J. Alfred Broaddus, Jr.; Roger W. Ferguson, Jr.; Edward M. Gramlich; Jack Guynn; Donald L. Kohn; Michael H. Moskow; Mark W. Olson; and Robert T. Parry.[46] (emphasis added)

Former Fed governor Laurence Meyer wrote in his interesting book that when the FOMC said "foreseeable future," as in this press release, it "was described as an 'elastic' concept, a period of time that depended on circumstances."[47] That ambiguity about time periods intensifies this garblement.

This important press release issued at a critical time may appear to be the work of intellectually challenged people. In fact, there were well-qualified intelligent people in this group who were simply following their leader. They adopted Greenspan's long record of success in public relations by using "what he calls 'constructive ambiguity.'"[48]

As Meyer wrote in his book about his experiences as a Fed governor, the code words used in Fed messages can be tweaked in various ways to improve their usefulness to the Fed in signaling the public.[49] These techniques, so beneficial to the health of the Fed-watchers industry, played a game with Congress, the public, and the press.

Meyer was perplexed by a public statement proposed by Greenspan at an FOMC meeting in July 1996. Meyer wondered what it had to do with the discussion of policy that he and other FOMC members had just concluded. The proposed public statement contained the following garblement: "In the context of the Committee's long-run objectives for price stability and sustainable economic growth, and giving careful consideration to economic, financial and monetary developments, *slightly greater reserve restraint* or *slightly lesser reserve restraint* would be acceptable in the intermeeting period."[50] Meyer wrote: "As I listened [to the chairman's proposed directive for the committee to vote on] I wondered what that statement had to do with the discussion we had just concluded," adding, "these decisions [at the FOMC meeting] were in the message but concealed by code."[51] Except for one dissent on policy grounds, the FOMC members approved Greenspan's garblement.

Meyer also found that another statement prepared by Greenspan and his staff before the discussion at a FOMC meeting "did not reflect a shred of the discussion just concluded."[52] This kind of manipulation by Greenspan bothered Meyer, who wrote: "The fact that the statements were prepared by the Chairman without any real input from the Committee created a degree of tension over the matter that never diminished during my term."[53]

These examples of high-handed manipulation by Greenspan apparently "created a degree of tension" but not much else. Meyer relates that during his term (June 1996 to January 2002), "no governor dissented in the vote at an FOMC meeting."[54] Thus, they were apparently tense but cowed. Meyer relates that there were occasional dissents by the Fed Bank presidents. He says that three dissents would have been seen as "open revolt with the Chairman's leadership" and would have been "disruptive." Meyer adds that he differed on occasion with the chairman but never dissented. Thus, behind the garblements, code words, and cowering, the public was shown unity. This had not been true at the Board of Governors meetings during Volcker's tenure as Fed chairman. The so-called "gang of four" won a vote on February 24, 1986, at a Board of Governors meeting, 4–3, with Volcker on the losing side.

Greenspan's positions were frequently not well defined or supported, and his vague descriptions left open a nearly free range of interpretations, something like an inkblot test. In *The Quotations of Chairman Greenspan: Words from the Man Who Can Shake the World*, Larry Kahaner records the following four headlines that appeared after Greenspan answered reporters questions during a banking conference in Seattle in 2000:

"Greenspan Sees Chance of Recession," *New York Times*
"Recession Is Unlikely, Greenspan Concludes," *Washington Post*
"Recession Risk Up, Greenspan Concludes," *Baltimore Sun*
"Fed Chairman Doesn't See Recession on the Horizon," *Wall Street Journal*"[55]

Kahaner records six additional headlines showing that Greenspan's mystique was only nourished by the continued, seemingly inconsistent interpretations of his message thirteen days later:

"Greenspan Predicts 'Modest' Recession," *Idaho Statesman*
"Greenspan: Little Risk of Recession," *USA Today*
"Greenspan Hints at Interest Rate Cut," *Nashville Banner*
"Interest Rate Cut Not on Horizon," *Los Angeles Daily News*
"Greenspan Hints Fed May Cut Interest Rates," *Washington Post*
"Greenspan: Uncertainty Abounds," *Manchester (N.H.) Union Leader*

Fed chairmen speak publicly under important constraints, as do all governmental officials. Governmental officials should not panic the public with dire economic pronouncements unless absolutely necessary. Fed chairmen, whose every utterances are thoroughly examined by the Fed-watchers industry, should not make statements that could cause depositors to run to their banks for their money. Fed chairmen cannot even visit a bank without causing great uncertainty about the bank.

Opaque and garbled statements about the policies and operations of the Fed and the state of the economy were a technique that helped Greenspan retain his position as Fed chairman through four administrations. This technique has also played a role in Greenspan's enshrinement as oracle and sage. The Fed chairman's garblements, evasions, and deceptions not only stoked mistaken praise for the undecipherable coded announcements, but also hid accountability, increased the value of inside information to the favored few, and added to economic uncertainty.

Rather than having to try to nail the chairman's custard pies to the wall or to react to the public utterances of the other eighteen Fed governors and Fed Bank presidents, the public should be allowed to read transcripts of FOMC meetings in a timely manner—no more than sixty days later. The transcripts should be lightly edited in cooperation with professional archivists from the National Archives and Records Administration, and the source records should never be destroyed.

GREENSPAN'S GARBLEMENTS LIVE ON AT THE BERNANKE FED

When Ben Bernanke succeeded Greenspan as Fed chairman, in 2006, there was hope that this capable professor would lead the Fed into a new era: one in which meaningful reports would be released to the public, and the timely release of FOMC transcripts would become a reality. Instead, the Bernanke Fed has carried on the Greenspan tradition of garblements, as evidenced by an FOMC press release in the fall of 2006. It issued a prize-winning garblement seven months after Bernanke assumed leadership, one that only the Fed-watchers industry could admire:

> *Readings on core inflation have been elevated,* and the high level of resource utilization *has the potential to sustain inflation pressures.* However, *inflation pressures seem likely to moderate* over time, reflecting reduced impetus from energy prices, contained inflation expectations, and the cumulative effects of monetary policy actions and other factors restraining aggregate demand.[56] (emphasis added)

CHAPTER 4

SPINNING MOUNTAINS INTO MOLEHILLS

The Fed's reactions to problems, especially by its chairman, provide striking public relations lessons on how to avoid significant public recriminations and accountability and to limit meaningful remedies. Greenspan trivialized mountains and deftly swept what he painted as molehills under the Fed's lumpy rug. He was called upon to deal with many problems, including nearly $500,000 stolen from the Fed's cash and vault areas—and this official amount is an underestimate; revolving-door relations between Fed bank examiners and the banks they examine; the exposure of faulty examinations of a foreign bank in Atlanta through which $5.5 billion was sent to Saddam Hussein, part of what a federal judge found to be active U.S. support for Iraq in the 1980s; meals, gifts, and sports tickets for Fed officials and examiners from banks they examine; and the Fed's bypass of the congressional appropriation process by making loans to foreign countries and by "warehousing" funds to take them off the Treasury's books.

EMBEZZLING FED MONEY AND FALSIFYING ACCOUNTING RECORDS

The Fed vault facilities are a crucial part of the nation's payment system and should be a national-security priority requiring full accountability to Congress. The Fed Banks contain uncirculated currency and coin transferred from the Bureau of Engraving and Printing. They also receive cash from banks throughout the country.

When troubling information about problems in the cash departments at some Fed Banks reached Congressman Gonzalez, he ordered an investigation in 1996. He utilized his staff and a team of auditors from the General Accounting Office (renamed the Government Accountability Office in 2004). The GAO is the legislative entity that inspects and audits governmental operations.

After requesting information from Greenspan about several major embezzlements, Gonzalez received an astounding admission of embezzlements from Fed vaults. On December 5, 1996, Greenspan replied to Gonzalez about the cash record-keeping and embezzlements from a number of the Fed's vault facilities. Greenspan attempted to reduce the importance of the thefts by comparing the amount stolen to the huge number and amount of bills the Fed handled (but failed to mention any underlying problems that the identified embezzlements revealed):

> During the ten year time frame from 1987–1996, the Federal Reserve Banks received and processed $2.7 trillion or 201 billion notes. During this time the Reserve Banks identified 21 instances of thefts or suspected thefts by Reserve Bank employees from Federal Reserve operations. The aggregate amount taken was $498,000. The large part of that amount involved two cases totaling $377,000, which have been reported in the press and which you referred to in your press release of October 1. Of the total dollars taken in all incidents approximately $279,000 was recovered and an additional $116,000 is subject to future restitution to the Federal Reserve by court order. Assuming full restitution, the net loss will be approximately $103,000.[1]

The Banking Committees that have oversight authority should have been fully notified about these thefts and the remedies that were being used to reduce or eliminate the embezzlements. Gonzalez issued an extensive press release citing the GAO study and Greenspan's information about thefts of cash by Fed employees: "Chairman Greenspan has informed me that Fed employees have lifted nearly $500,000 from the Fed's own vaults in the last ten years."[2]

Both of the larger amounts reported stolen were in connection with the processing of worn-out currency, which is destroyed. One of these employees worked at the Boston Fed Bank. A press account stated the defendant "pled guilty last summer to one-count charging him with embezzlement and theft from the Federal Reserve Bank of Boston." The defendant's lawyer explained to the judge "how the defendant managed to embezzle $70,000 from the Federal Reserve Bank of Boston, one of the most heavily guarded financial institutions in the country. According to the prosecutor," the defendant "was employed as a senior Payroll Teller and also as an Overnight Payroll Teller in the Cash Services Department of the Federal Reserve Bank in 1993, when he devised his scheme to embezzle $70,000 in cash from the Bank. During the first half of 1993," while the defendant "was working as a member of a so called 'Currency Verification and Destruction Team,'" the defendant "managed to remove $70,000 in unfit United States currency which had been hole-punched and earmarked for destruction." The defendant "then held on to this so-called 'canceled' currency until September of 1993 when he brought it back into the Bank and attempted to switch it for $70,000 in good United States currency, while working as an Overnight Payroll Teller." The defendant "attempted the switch in the following manner. On the evening of September 28, 1993," the defendant "removed $70,000 in good United States currency from a $100,000 bundle of currency in his cash drawer, 'sandwiched' the canceled currency in between the remaining $30,000 in good currency, re-bundled the bills together, and then spilled some sort of liquid on the bundle. [He then] submitted the bundle of currency to the Bank's Destruction Unit for cancellation and destruction, claiming it was unfit. . . . an alert member of the Bank's Destruction Unit discovered the $70,000 in unfit currency . . . mingled in the bundle. The case was investigated by Special Agents of the United States Secret Service."[3] The employee could have received up to thirty years in prison and $1 million in fines. The defendant received a sentence of four months incarceration to be followed by a period of community confinement and a thirty-two-month term of supervised release.

Another employee who entered a guilty plea worked at a branch of a Fed Bank and stole currency there over a reported two-year period. The total amount of discrepancies, also found in the currency-destruction operation, was $267,000, of which approximately $100,000 remained in the employee's bank account and $49,236 was recovered during a search of the employee's home, pursuant to a search warrant.[4] As Greenspan reported: The "employee stole currency during processing and falsified documentation regarding the total number of notes destroyed." The troubling part of this episode was that the theft was not detected by the Fed's security system. Greenspan added: "The FBI notified Bank management of a suspicious currency transactions report filed by a local commercial bank on an account holder, the Bank's employee."[5] The employee was sentenced to twelve months and one day in prison, the first six months to be served in a community-correction component and the remaining sentence in a prerelease component that might be called a halfway house. Confinement in a halfway house where residents may not go out at night might be especially frustrating if there was substantial stolen money that was not recovered. Again, the maximum sentence that could have been imposed was thirty years imprisonment and a fine of $1 million.

The fact that the Fed was unable to detect this currency theft that occurred over a two-year period is one reason to suspect that the officially reported amount of money stolen by Fed employees from the Fed's vaults may be substantially understated.

There are other reasons for this conclusion. Gonzalez received information—and a subsequent investigation in 1996 substantiated—grossly improper record-keeping and management-directed falsification of records at the Fed Bank branch in Los Angeles. The GAO indicated that any other Fed facilities using this type of accounting would also be suspect. Evidence included a Cash Services Department memo stating that for several months they would be "backing into" their numbers, which means they were to be arbitrarily changed to bring about an accounting balance. Gonzalez said, "The [Los Angeles Fed Branch Bank] reports were not just wrong, they were falsified *at the direction of management.* I want to know who is responsible and why."[6]

Gonzalez requested a GAO investigation, and the results indicted some outrageous practices for a central bank holding a large part the nation's supply of currency. The GAO findings were published as *Federal Reserve Banks: Inaccurate Reporting of Currency at the Los Angeles Branch.*[7] The accounting problems reported by the GAO indicated that the Fed's cash records and accountant controls were seriously flawed and incomplete. There was a severe security problem in the nonsecure manner in which the Fed Bank staff was allowed access to the general ledger of the bank, the primary record of account. The GAO team could "not find evidence that anyone at the Bank reviewed the general ledger for unposted transactions," so "certain staff could make unauthorized adjustments that could go undetected." The GAO found troubling the manner in which an $8 million mistake was handled.[8] The GAO team also found that the general ledger of the LA Branch Bank could not identity the reasons for its being out of balance. These are very serious internal security breaches for handling and storing the immense amount of currency and coin—$80 billion a year at that time in this one facility—entrusted to the nation's central bank.[9]

The problems uncovered reminded me of a past incident at the same LA Branch Bank, a branch of the San Francisco Fed Bank, which had seemed troubling. As a professor at the University of California, I had taken my MBA students on a tour of the LA Branch Bank. During the tour of the check-processing and cash departments, the initial impression was of a well-run operation with many guards, video cameras, and locked doors.

The students entered a large paper-check sorting room. It contained many rows of long mechanical sorting machines. Stacks of paper checks were placed in one end of the machines, which read the magnetic coding across the bottom of the checks and then carried each check to the slot for the Fed Bank that served the private-sector bank on which the check was drawn. Mutilated checks that could not be mechanically read were sent to employees at the end of the room, who entered the codes manually. This was part of the Fed's paper-check-clearing operations. The machines were not running, and there were no employees working at the time the students were in the room. One of the Fed managers explained that every day the Fed balanced the books with a $10 error tolerance limit. That was a good accounting control, he inferred, given the millions of checks processed each day. Just after the manager finished this statement, one of the students found a $5,000 check on the floor under one of the machines. He interrupted the presentation and asked the Fed manager how they could balance to within $10 if they overlooked this $5,000 check. The students laughed.[10]

The response was much more direct and forthright than the nearly constant diversions received from Fed officials while I assisted in investigating Fed operations as a House Banking staff economist. The Fed manager thanked the students for finding the check. Yes, they had made a mistake.

The response to the GAO audit of the LA Branch Bank some years later was very different but typical. The Fed's long-winded reply did not give forthright answers to the main concerns that the GAO investigators found: deliberate accounting errors and a poor system.[11] Where were the direct admissions of the problems found by the GAO team and the specific actions in other Fed banks that may have used similar accounting practices? Where was a complete statement of corrections for the mess that was found? What has happened to the Fed officials who ordered the accounting records to be forced?

The Fed Board of Governors had responded to the Gonzalez-GAO investigation by sending a large team to count the money in the vault, a huge task: "The Board's Washington D.C.–based financial examiners performed a 100 percent count of the currency and coin holdings of the Branch, with the assistance of the San Francisco internal audit function. . . . A total of forty examiners and auditors were used to conduct the examination. . . . The Branch's vault was sealed on Friday afternoon, September 6, [1996,] and the count continued through Monday morning, September 9. This special examination was conducted in accordance with generally accepted auditing standards."[12] The people sent by the Board presumably found little missing, since it was reported that the count agreed with the bank records under the vague phrase "generally accepted auditing standards" (GAAS). Nothing might be missing if the GAAS records were "properly adjusted," as in the deliberate falsification of the accounting records or if the type of embezzlements described above at two Fed facilities had been used.

BLAME THE PRESS AND TRIVIALIZE CORRUPT ACCOUNTING

At his Senate confirmation hearing on July 26, 1996, before Senate Banking chairman Alphonse D'Amato, Greenspan blamed the press for overstating the problem: "Unfortunately, the press coverage of this matter, in our judgment, has significantly overstated the problem." That seemed odd, since there was very little coverage, although coming from such a revered source for the Fed-watchers industry, it might have chilled any further coverage. There would be little press coverage of that part of Greenspan's statement. One reporter noted, "Greenspan also brushed aside criticism of the Los Angles branch of the San Francisco Fed regional bank for misreporting certain money supply data." He quoted Greenspan as saying, "No taxpayer money has been lost. No key decision-making has been compromised."[13]

Greenspan added that the LA Branch Bank had already discovered some problems and "was in the process of resolving them before Representative Gonzalez began his inquiry." How inconvenient that they were bothered by an investigation of what they now called "some problems." Why didn't they inform Gonzalez, his staff, and the GAO staff who were actively investigating those problems? Did any officials permanently "leave" in connection with the finding that a LA Branch Bank official ordered some cash reports to be forced into balance by deceptive entries? What responsibility does the chain of command have, and where does the buck stop?

Greenspan did not read the part of his submitted written statement in which he said that a small error, described as $178 million, had occurred at the LA vault facility, noting that it did not significantly matter because "at worst there would have been slight errors in forecasting currency demand, which could have caused a slight increase to the Federal Reserve's order to the Treasury to print new currency." He also did not discuss the widespread bookkeeping problems uncovered in the cash department by both the GAO and Gonzalez's investigation.

MEALS, GIFTS, AND SPORTS TICKETS FOR FED OFFICIALS

Fed Bank personnel examine the large private-sector bank companies in New York, some of which exceed $1 trillion dollars in assets. These banks have deposits insured by the federal government, so the collapse of one of them would require a huge bailout by U.S. taxpayers and cause massive collateral damage to banks around the country with interbank deposits in these New York banks. The task of examining these large banks with any precision is enormous. One thing should not be a problem: avoiding a conflict of interest by refusing gifts, free meals, or any form of remuneration from the regulated banks.

On April 22, 1993, Chairman Gonzalez wrote to E. Gerald Corrigan, president of the New York Fed: "I have recently received reports that both lower and higher level employees of the New York Federal Reserve Bank have engaged in the following activities with officials of private banks. The practice includes socializing with foreign and domestic bankers, accepting meals at expensive restaurants and accepting gifts from bankers."[14] On May 18, 1993, Corrigan replied: "In order to seek to comply with your request in a manner that was timely and not unduly disruptive to the workforce at the Bank, and that would avoid creating an accusatory atmosphere, we have inquired of 65 officers of the Bank . . . to determine if we could find any evidence supporting the allegations in your letter." Corrigan said the "review has not disclosed evidence of widespread socializing by Bank personnel with foreign or domestic bankers, where the costs are paid by the bankers alleged in the reports you received."[15]

He then wrote about a "limited number" of regulated-bank-paid meals for officers of the Fed Bank and a "literal handful" of tickets to sporting events, but no sign of free gifts of the type Gonzalez had mentioned. Corrigan assured Gonzalez that "the Bank has always prided itself on its independence of judgment and maintenance of high ethical standards," and that "in the context of the overall review of our policies described below, we will carefully consider whether any modifications of our policies in this area seem warranted."[16]

Anyone familiar with Gonzalez knew that you could not brush him off with platitudes and the casual response that the Fed would look into things to see if any changes should be made. Gonzalez shot back within a week (May 24, 1993): "You say to avoid an 'accusatory atmosphere' you limited your inquiry to 65 [of the 174] officers of the New York Federal Reserve Bank. I think there would be an accusatory atmosphere if you ignored legitimate allegations and lost the trust of United States citizens in their central bank." Gonzalez sharply disagreed with Corrigan that meals paid for by Fed-regulated banks were within bank guidelines because the Fed employees were conducting "bank business." He also disliked the characterizations of the complaints as "anonymous allegations": "It would have been inappropriate for me to release the names of those who made these complaints."[17]

Two months later, Corrigan ended his twenty-five-year career with the Federal Reserve System: he left his position at the New York Fed on July 18, 1993, before the end of his term. On January 3, 1994, he became a senior executive at Goldman Sachs.

William McDonough, the newly appointed president of the New York Fed, made some suggestions to the House Banking Committee that no gifts or meals should be accepted from regulated banks. On May 27, 1994, he informed Gonzalez that he was instituting a "Uniform Code of Conduct." This twenty-two-page document contained many provisions to ensure that Fed employees received no monetary advantages from regulated banks. Only gifts with a "de minimis" (trifling) value could be accepted, and only under special circumstances, such as being a "benefit available to the general public."[18] A Fed Bank employee "who ceases to be employed by the Bank should not contact the Bank concerning a particular matter in which he or she participated while employed at the Bank."[19] The rules were to be adopted by all twelve Fed Banks. Since 1998, when Gonzalez left Congress, there has apparently been no congressional oversight to determine if the provisions of this "Uniform Code of Conduct," which are critical to the unbiased, ethical regulation and examination of the nation's financial system, are being strictly observed throughout the Fed.

McDonough's work on the ethics code was a valuable service for better government. He was appointed chairman of the Public Company Accounting Oversight Board in April 2003. This board was created to avoid accounting scandals at private-sector corporations, the kind that became public after the huge stock-market decline began in March 2000.

GREENSPAN SPINS THE REVOLVING
DOOR FOR BANK EXAMINERS

Examining banks is an immense challenge that relies on examiners who earn considerably less than the officials of the banks they are examining.[20] There are excellent examiners whose primary objective is a career dedicated to serving the public interest and not to soliciting or accepting gifts or employment from the regulated banks.

Every taxpayer has a stake in these examinations, since banks hold government-insured deposits, which are ultimately a liability of the U.S. taxpayers. House Banking chairman Gonzalez had guided legislation to resolve the massive savings and loan debacle in the 1980s and early 1990s. This legislation sought to install better examination methods. He had reason to believe that some bank examiners had conflicts of interest or worse because of a "revolving door syndrome," in which examiners could be working for the Fed one day and then for a Fed-regulated bank the next. Gonzalez asked Greenspan to institute a one-year waiting period before former Fed bank examiners could accept a job with a regulated bank.[21]

Greenspan responded with a contradictory answer and a blunt refusal. He said the Fed did not routinely keep records of its bank examiners' later employment; he instead relied on the "collective memories of the Fed Reserve officials" for this information. They could only remember "one-half of one percent" of Fed bank examiners taking jobs at banks they had examined in the last five years. So it was not a significant problem according to this misty survey.[22] After thus minimizing the trouble, Greenspan noted that the revolving door has "numerous benefits" and that it was not "uncommon" for examiners to accept a job at the Fed in order to obtain a job at a bank: "We should note that it is not uncommon for examiners, given their skills, knowledge and experience, to accept employment in the banking industry; moreover, it is not unusual for many of those who enter our employ as examiners to have plans to become bankers over time. Such transitions are considered both positive and natural. Numerous benefits have been derived, by both regulators and bankers, from examiners taking employment at banking institutions."[23]

Greenspan also cited a federal law and Fed policy guidelines that do not prohibit examiners from seeking or negotiating employment "as long as the examiner does not participate in an examination or supervisory matter *once negotiations have begun*" (emphasis added). Examiners can send a "mass distribution of resumes" (a phrase used by the Fed's general counsel) even to regulated banks being examined. If employment negotiations begin with a bank official at the bank the Fed examiner is examining, Greenspan stated, the examiner is "prohibited from any further supervisory matters concerning that institution."[24]

Thus, the revolving door was protected, and a required arm's-length relationship between Fed bank examiners and banks being examined was jeopardized. According to Greenspan, the revolving door was common and beneficial, even though the "collective memories" of Fed officials did not remember it revolving very much. Gonzalez's inquiries indicated mismanagement or worse of the bank-examination functions of the nation's central bank.

The Intelligence Reform and Terrorism Prevention Act of 2004 did install a one-year postemployment restriction limited to "certain senior examiners" employed by federal regulators of depository institutions, including the Federal Reserve Banks.[25]

BILLIONS TO SADDAM HUSSEIN

On November 9, 1993, several federal marshals brought a prisoner, Christopher Drogoul, into my office at the Rayburn House Office Building. The marshals removed the manacles, and Drogoul took off his jumpsuit and changed into a shirt, tie, and business suit. He immediately looked like the manager of the Atlanta branch of Banca Nazionale del Lavoro, a government-owned Italian bank—which was, in fact, his former position.

According to a press account, Drogoul had come to testify about "a scheme prosecutors said he masterminded that funneled $5.5 billion in loans to Iraq's Hussein though BNL's Atlanta operation. Some of the loans allegedly were used to build up Iraq's military and nuclear arsenals in the years preceding the first Gulf War."[26] Drogoul's "'off book' BNL-Atlanta funding to Iraq began in 1986 as financing for products under" programs overseen by the Department of Agriculture, which allegedly authorized the loans.[27] Since Drogoul told the committee he was merely a tool in an ambitious scheme by the United States, Italy, Britain, and Germany to secretly arm Iraq in its 1980–1988 war with Iran, his testimony was politically contentious and unproven. He was sentenced in November 1993 to thirty-seven months in prison; he had served twenty months while awaiting his sentencing hearing.

U.S. District Judge Ernest Tidwell found that the United States had actively supported Iraq in the 1980s by providing it with government-guaranteed loans, even though it was not creditworthy. The judge said such policies "clearly facilitated criminal conduct."[28]

Gonzalez was drawn to Drogoul's answer about the Fed examiner who had visited his Atlanta operation:

> At the November 9, 1993 Banking Committee hearing I asked Christopher Drogoul, the convicted official of the Banca Nazionale Del Lavoro agency branch in Atlanta Georgia, how the Federal Reserve Bank examiners could miss billions of dollars of illegal loans, most of which ended up in the hands of Hussein.
> Mr. Drogoul stated:

> The task of the Fed [bank examiner] was simply to confirm that the State of Georgia audit revealed no major problems. And thus, their audit of BNL usually consisted of a one or two-day review of the state of Georgia's preliminary results, followed by a cup of espresso in the manager's office.

> The Federal Reserve bank examiner's friendly chat and cup of espresso in the manager's office at BNL is symbolic of a collegial atmosphere that may very well get in the way of proper supervision and regulation.[29]

Surely the Fed examiners should have realized whether billions of dollars were flowing to Iraq from this tiny branch of an Italian bank. Given its substantial powers and its obligation to examine and regulate foreign banks, the Fed's bank examiners should provide thorough examinations of these banks, something more than perusing a state examiner's papers.[30]

UNAUTHORIZED LOANS TO MEXICO

The power given to Congress to appropriate federal governmental funds is specified in the Constitution: "No money shall be drawn from the Treasury but in consequence of appropriations made by law" (article 1, section 9). Nevertheless, since 1962 the FOMC has voted to lend money to foreign countries and has also, in recent decades, voted to "warehouse" funds for the U.S. Treasury so that the Treasury could avoid limits on the funds available to it from congressional authorization.

Some of the members of the Board of Governors called attention to FOMC votes that could "be subject to being viewed as perhaps circumventing the Congress." They brought their concerns directly to Greenspan in then-secret FOMC meetings. W. Lee Hoskins, president of the St. Louis Fed, told Fed officials in 1989:

> And it seems to me that over time, given I think what the paper pointed out that Mexico needs $3 to $5 billion per year for the next several years, with the drying up of private resources I think we could expect more of this kind of activity. The concern is that *we would be subject to being viewed as perhaps circumventing Congress* by working more closely with Administrations down the road on this kind of activity. In that sense, I don't think it's appropriate to continue those kinds of relationships because I think it risks the political independence of this body to some extent. (emphasis added)[31]

J. Alfred Broaddus, Jr., president of the Richmond Fed, objected to making a loan to Mexico in 1994. He warned Greenspan at an FOMC meeting: "So, it seems clear to me that any loan to Mexico in the current circumstances in essence would be a fiscal action of the U.S. government. And fiscal actions—expenditures of the government—are supposed to be authorized by Congress and Congress is supposed to appropriate the funds. So, whatever the general merits may be of making loans to Mexico, *I don't think we should be involved without explicit Congressional authorization, Mr. Chairman.* So, I would oppose an increase in the swap line."[32] (The "swap line" is the general name given to the Fed's so-called "reciprocal currency transactions.")

Governor Wayne Angell called attention to violations of Congress's appropriation power when the FOMC discussed "warehousing" currency for the U.S. Treasury. The Treasury, an executive-branch department, must obtain congressional approval for most of its budget.[33] Warehousing allows it to keep funds off the books and to purchase assets that exceed its authorized budget. At an FOMC meeting in 1990 at which the warehousing of more than $40 billion in foreign currency was being discussed, Angell gave a stern warning:

> I believe the Constitution gives the Congress of the United States the power to appropriate. I believe for us to do warehousing, which in a sense

removes from Congress this appropriations power, is at best a [legally] risky proposition. . . . It eliminates the necessity for the Treasury to go to the Congress to get an appropriation, [and] I can't do that [i.e., approve more warehousing] as a matter of principle until the courts tell me that we can. . . . I do not believe that members of the Appropriations Committee understand this issue. I do not think that they know their appropriations power is being subverted by our warehousing agreement.[34]

Angell was worried that someone outside the Fed might cause political trouble: "And I believe that in that atmosphere at some point in time this is apt to become a political issue. And if it becomes a political issue, *I believe it is incumbent upon us to protect the Federal Reserve's position, which is not to go around the congressional appropriation that other warehousing would tend to do*" (emphasis added).[35]

As shown in a 1992 letter (see Figure 4-1), Greenspan told Secretary of the Treasury Nicholas Brady how eager the Fed was "to increase the size of the warehousing facility in the future, as has happened in the past, beyond its present $5 billion. I would strongly support an increase under a wide variety of possible circumstances."

The warehousing arrangement with the Treasury was increased to $20 billion in 1995 in connection with a "Mexican financial assistance package," but was reduced to $5 billion in 1999.[36] Two Fed economists reported that warehousing arrangements have been controversial since "about 1978" because they provide the Treasury "with additional funding that circumvents the congressional appropriations process and statutory limits on Federal borrowing."[37]

Thus, these warnings from Fed governors to Greenspan and other FOMC members—that by warehousing, the Fed would be circumventing the constitutional powers given Congress—produced little effect, with one possible exception. The warnings may have added some enthusiasm for a secret unrecorded vote of FOMC members to destroy three years of their source records in the 1990s, when a Fed loan to Mexico was authorized. An FOMC transcript from 1997 indicates the ease of the Greenspan Fed in circumventing the appropriation process:

> MR. BROADDUS. A point of clarification, Mr. Chairman. The authority for the warehousing is in the first vote, right?
>
> MR. TRUMAN. Yes, the authority to enter into a warehousing transaction is in the first vote.
>
> MR. BROADDUS. Okay.

BOARD OF GOVERNORS
OF THE
FEDERAL RESERVE SYSTEM
WASHINGTON, D. C. 20551

ALAN GREENSPAN
CHAIRMAN

March 24, 1992

The Honorable Nicholas F. Brady
Secretary of the Treasury
1500 Pennsylvania Avenue, NW
Washington, DC 20220

Dear Nick:

Thank you for your letter of March 20 concerning the
Federal Reserve's $5 billion warehousing facility in favor of
the Exchange Stabilization Fund and the U.S. Treasury. I
welcome your intention to undertake an advance repurchase of the
remaining $2 billion equivalent of foreign currency currently
outstanding on the facility. I also welcome your acceptance of
the proposals to adjust the terms and conditions of such
transactions in the future.

I recognize that the Treasury may feel the need to
increase the size of the warehousing facility in the future, as
has happened in the past, beyond its present $5 billion. I
would strongly support an increase under a wide variety of
possible circumstances. I am confident that the FOMC would give
full, careful and expeditious consideration to any reasonable
proposal. Needless to say, as you note, I cannot guarantee in
advance the Committee's approval of any proposal.

Sincerely,

FIGURE 4-1.

CHAIRMAN GREENSPAN. Is that satisfactory to everybody? Would
somebody like to move the first vote on the warehousing transaction
agreement?

MR. TRUMAN. Mr. Chairman, President Minehan has a question.

MS. MINEHAN. Just one small question: When we ratcheted up the
amount of the warehousing authority in the late 1980s, what was the
proximate cause for that? The Brady policy?

MR. TRUMAN. That was a period when we and the Treasury were doing
quite a lot of intervention in the markets. The Treasury essentially ran
out of dollars in the Exchange Stabilization Fund. We warehoused

some of their foreign currencies to provide them with dollars so that they could participate with us in foreign exchange operations.

MS. MINEHAN. Thank you.

CHAIRMAN GREENSPAN. Would somebody like to move the warehousing agreement?

VICE CHAIRMAN MCDONOUGH. I move the warehousing agreement, Mr. Chairman.

CHAIRMAN GREENSPAN. Seconded?

MR. KELLEY. Second.

CHAIRMAN GREENSPAN. Without objection. The next item on the agenda is boilerplate; it is the report of examination of the System Open Market Account—[38]

LENDING MONEY TO FOREIGN COUNTRIES, DECEPTIVELY

The conditions leading to the Fed's internal authorization for foreign-loan activities began in 1961 in connection with the U.S. government's gold policy. The government agreed to buy gold from foreigners (or to sell it to them) for thirty-five dollars a troy ounce.[39] This system, which regulated the issuance of money to foreigners, was the external part of a system known as the gold standard. A full gold standard would have applied to all money issued by the U.S. government: all currency would have been redeemable for gold.

The price of gold rose above thirty-five dollars an ounce in London in October 1960, and this price increase threatened the gold-standard system. As long as gold could be bought from the U.S. Treasury for thirty-five dollars an ounce and sold in London for forty dollars an ounce, U.S. dollars would flood into the Treasury to buy, and perhaps exhaust, its supply of gold. The outflow of investment funds from the U.S. in response to the London price of gold was called the "London gold rush." An official of the Bank of England warned that these events threatened "the whole structure of the exchange relationships in the western world."[40] The Kennedy administration sought to "defend the dollar" and preserve its value in terms of gold. The management of the value of the dollar in international trade, as well as the price of gold, was under the jurisdiction of the Treasury. It used a special fund, the Exchange Stabilization Fund, to support its interventions in the foreign currency markets. This fund did not have enough money to effectively operate in the foreign-exchange markets. The

Secretary of the Treasury, Douglas Dillon (1961–1965), warned against complacency, saying that the situation was "still ticklish."

Then the Fed, with its "unlimited pocketbook," entered the picture. At the inaugural meeting of the Organization for Economic Cooperation and Development, in April 1961, the U.S. team included the Fed chairman, William McChesney Martin. It became apparent early in the following year why the Fed was drawn into the international exchange problems surrounding the gold standard: As Fed Governor J. L. Robertson said (according to paraphrased transcripts) it had an "unlimited pocketbook": "Mr. Robertson inquired as to the advantages seen—aside from the Federal Reserve's 'unlimited pocketbook'—in having two agencies [the Treasury and the Fed] operating in this field instead of one, and Mr. [Charles A.] Coombs replied that he did not think there were any."[41] The need to evade congressional budgetary authority was admitted to be the basic reason for the establishment of the fund for foreign-exchange currency intervention at the Federal Reserve.[42] Robertson told the FOMC members that he opposed the operation in foreign currencies "on legal, practical, and policy grounds because it seemed to him that the only basis for the entrance of the Federal Reserve into this field would be to supplement the resources of the Stabilization Fund and because the program was being undertaken without specific congressional approval."[43]

Fed chairman Martin developed a peculiar, contradictory rationale to justify the absence of a request for formal authorization from Congress in 1962: although the Fed had received favorable opinions from its own and the administration's lawyers, it did not know exactly what it was doing, so it would not know what to ask Congress to authorize. If it truly did not know what it was doing, the pleasing approvals from the lawyers should have been suspect. This disingenuous sophistry was part of a plan to keep Congress uninformed about the Fed's circumvention of its constitutional authority to appropriate money.[44]

Still, Fed officials, mindful that someone in Congress might inquire about why it had not been notified, developed a plan to notify Congress and the public without meaningfully informing them. Public notification came from Alfred Hayes, president of the New York Fed, who referred in a speech to the possibility of the Fed undertaking foreign-currency operations.

Congressional notification consisted of a reference by Fed chairman Martin in a nine-page single-spaced statement at the meeting of the Joint Economic Committee (JEC) of Congress on January 30, 1962. This committee has no authorization to vote on legislation. Normally, it would be expected that new operations would be presented before the Banking Committees, which have legislative and oversight authority for the Fed. Martin told the JEC members that the New York Fed, acting as an agent for the Treasury, had used the Exchange Stabilization Fund for operations not previously undertaken since World War II: "As one step in such cooperation [with the Treasury], the System is now prepared in principle and accordance with its present statutory authority to consider holding for its own account varying amounts of foreign convertible securi-ties . . . [for] the primary purpose of helping to safeguard the international position of the dollar against speculative forays of funds."[45]

Alert congressman Richard Bolling (D-MO) asked Martin to explain what he meant by "As one step in such cooperation, the System is now prepared in principle and in accordance." Martin replied that the Fed was not anxious to engage in this activity, and that the Treasury had experi-mented with foreign-exchange operations in a small way in March. Then he added: "What we are aiming at is to keep the speculators from unseat-ing us."[46] This warning of a nebulous attack by "speculators" produced the desired effect, quashing questions about the Fed's grant of new powers to itself. Bolling asked one cautious question: "But I want to know what you do, within the bounds of what you should or should not say."[47] Martin replied with a short explanation of reciprocal currency transactions. That was the last question, despite the presence of Senator Paul Douglas (D-IL), a renowned economist. The Fed could breathe easy. It had cleverly notified Congress in a vague, incomplete, deceptive way that produced little immediate scrutiny. This was an early example of a Fed garblement.

The gold-standard system was completely abandoned by the United States in 1971 when the Nixon administration closed the "gold window" at the Treasury. Even though this eliminated the right to buy the Treasury's gold, and Martin's rationale for the Fed's foreign-exchange activity—to keep the "speculators from unseating us"—thus no longer applied, the Fed's reciprocal currency transactions and loan facility lived on.

SPINNING FED LOANS TO FOREIGN COUNTRIES INTO THE MIST

Thirty-two years later, in 1994, Greenspan referred to a 1962 House Banking hearing at which Henry Gonzalez had been present. As part of the Fed's claim to have the authority to carry on its foreign-exchange operations without congressional authority, Greenspan said that no one seriously objected in 1962, and that Gonzalez was there. That was incorrect. Gonzalez sent Greenspan a letter indicating that seven months after Martin had talked to the Joint Economic Committee, Congressman Henry Reuss had objected at that hearing, although further discussion was cut off by the committee chair: "I must serve notice on you right now that *I consider this an usurpation of the powers of Congress.* I don't think you are authorized to do this at all, and you give only vaguest generalizations about what kind of arrangements you are going to make with foreign Central Banks" (emphasis added).[48]

After reading this history of the Fed's deceitful announcement of its "foreign exchange network," the reader may appreciate Greenspan's 1994 denial that the Fed made loans to foreign countries.[49] Greenspan said that the Fed and the Treasury "are unique among the monetary authorities of major industrial countries in the frequency and detail in our public reports on foreign exchange operations."[50] Greenspan went on to explain part of the Fed's international currency operations called "swap drawings."[51] Greenspan said that the Fed "always seeks to assure that there are reasonable prospects of prompt repayment," and that "all drawings on this network have been repaid in full."[52] If swaps are not loans, why worry about repayment?

The Fed probably participated in swaps or loans with Mexico in 1976, 1982–1983, 1986, and 1988, and authorized a loan to Mexico in the 1990s as well.[53] The discussion at the FOMC meetings in the mid-1990s was about a loan to Mexico. Since they were involved in discussions about the collateral, they surely knew it was a loan. The mid-1990s multilateral loan facilities of $12 billion, in which the Fed participated, were clearly loans. The foreign and domestic governmental lenders that participated as well as the recipient knew this. FOMC members were worried about the collateral, which would include revenue from Mexico's oil industry. Although the Mexican peso crisis was ameliorated when the Fed authorized the loan, giving the New York Fed Bank the authority to extend it, the FOMC nonetheless authorized it without congressional approval.

Greenspan as well as former Fed chairman Martin were spinning foreign loans into a mist, and few will recognize them as foreign loans once they are labeled swaps. They are a liability of the U.S. government and the taxpayers.[54] Greenspan suggested that Congress never complained.[55] Case closed, without the bother of further congressional authorization for the Fed's loans to foreign countries and the warehousing of foreign currencies held by the Treasury.

It does not follow that foreign-exchange operations of the Fed are bad policy. The central bank should be authorized to intervene in foreign-exchange markets as long as there are appropriate checks and balances for governmental expenditures. This oversight can be done in a timely manner by the chairmen and ranking members of the House and Senate Banking Committees, provided they have high security clearances. They should have all records of these loans (including source FOMC transcripts) before the loans are made. They have the authority to introduce legislation if they think this self-authorized power by the Fed is being abused.

Foreign loans affect not only the federal budget, properly calculated, but also foreign policy. They may prop up the international value of the currency of a foreign government to assist its officials in their reelection. The political effects of Fed loans to assist the party in power apply to some Fed swaps or loans made to Mexico, especially those made immediately before an election in that country. Unelected Fed officials should not bypass congressional budget authority without timely checks and balances from Congress.

CHAPTER 5

VALUABLE SECRETS AND THE RETURN OF GREENSPAN'S "PROPHETIC TOUCH"

BILLION-DOLLAR SECRETS

Information about plans by the Federal Reserve to change interest rates could be turned into huge profits if it were known before the policy was made public. And it is wishful thinking to pretend that millions, easily billions, of dollars have not been made using just such inside information from the Fed. The Fed's secrets have been widely disseminated to its employees and the favored few. Suppose someone was able to obtain definite information that the Fed was going to lower short-term interest rates (which would translate into higher prices for short-maturity bonds—interest rates and bond prices are inversely related) and that such a change in policy was not publicly known or anticipated. He or she could buy a security in a market outside the United States, say, a security sold in Europe that entitles the holder to exchange it for a bond in the future—a bond futures contract.[1] The asset could be sold for a higher price after the Fed moves and bond prices rise. These securities may be purchased for less than half a percent of their face value in cash. A trader who purchased a large number of these securities could earn a very large profit in one day from a drop in interest rates. Rather than directly take a position in the market, a leaker or the favored leakee could sell the information to others.

It is very difficult to stop these leaks. One necessary step is to severely limit the number of people at the Fed with access to interest-rate policy information. This has not happened. Hundreds of Fed employees—over

500 of them—are directly involved in the secret meetings or in preparing the information discussed at them. Making matters worse, people not employed by the Fed, who have never had the limited background check that a new Fed employee receives, have been admitted to these secret meetings. Such visitors have included members of foreign central banks from Russia and China as well as academics from the United States.

There are two important components of this information: the loan rate—the rate at which U.S. banks can borrow money from the Fed, also called the discount rate—and the interest rate that the Fed targets in the market for short-term loans between banks, also known as the federal funds rate.[2] Both are often changed together, so knowledge of a change in one generally provides information about the other. The nine directors at each of the twelve Fed Banks (108 directors) vote on the discount rate set by the Board of Governors. There may be extended discussion at each Fed Bank by the directors, bank officers, and staff in order to convince themselves that they are doing something meaningful, not just rubber-stamping orders from Washington. Then the rubber-stamp ritual occurs, sometimes with a slight delay from some of the Fed Banks.

Even when the information discussed by the 108 directors and the Fed staffs is related to holding the current level of interest rates, it is still inside information that can be exploited for profit, especially if market partici-pants have been expecting a change in interest rates.

"WE'RE BEGINNING TO LOOK LIKE BUFFOONS"

At the FOMC meeting on December 19, 1989, Greenspan warned about the ill effects of ongoing leaks from the FOMC's supposedly secret meet-ings: "I would like to raise again a problem that continues to confront this organization with continuous damaging and corrosive effects, and that is the issue of leaks out of this Committee. We have had two extraordinary leaks, and perhaps more, in recent days: one in which John Berry at the *Washington Post* in late November had the time and content of a telephone conference; previous to that we had the *Wall Street Journal* knowing about telephone conferences and knowing a number of things that could only have come out of this Committee."[3]

Greenspan then suggested specific reporters who received the informa-tion: "I don't know whether the leaks are directly to Alan Murray, [*Wall Street Journal*] who has the clearest access, or to John Berry [*Washington*

Post] or Paul Blustein [*Los Angeles Times*]."[4] Greenspan warned about the harm to the Fed's reputation: "As best I can judge from feedback I'm getting from friends of ours, the credibility of this organization is beginning to recede and we're beginning to look like buffoons to some of them."[5]

This warning did not address the very severe problem of providing exploitable information to a select group. Similar activities at private sector corporations would be treated as crimes. Instead, during the short discussion at this meeting, Greenspan emphasized the need to keep what they said secret: "If [our discussions] start to be subject to selective leaks on content, I think we're all going to start to shut down. Frankly, I wouldn't blame anyone in the least. We wouldn't talk about very sensitive subjects. If we cannot be free and forward with our colleagues, then I think the effectiveness of this organization begins to deteriorate to a point where we will not have the ability to do what is required of us to do."[6]

Admonishing his colleagues about secrecy did not stop the leaks of inside information. Four years later he would promise to end the leaks, and there were many, and, as seen below, Greenspan was a suspect. He would try to make a case that leaks were "inadvertently provided (reporters) [to give them] enough of a sense of the policy," and hinted that even his briefings to administration officials may have produced leaks.[7] This kind of inadvertent leaking could not explain the examples given in the testimony of Anna Schwartz. She testified that the contents of the Fed's directive (containing policy instructions) from "11 FOMC meetings out of 34" that "took place between March 1989 and May 1993" were reported in the *Wall Street Journal* within a week of each FOMC meeting.[8] That sounded like blatant leaking of inside information—a direct line to one or more persons in the Fed. David Skidmore (who became a Fed employee) reported Greenspan's reply for the Associated Press:

> Greenspan said, "A deliberate premature leak of information is repugnant." However, it is possible committee members, who include the Fed's regional presidents as well as the Washington-based board "may in fact have inadvertently provided (reporters) enough of a sense of the policy considerations to allow conclusions to be drawn." He said the Fed has tightened up its precautions against leaks and vowed that the next leak will be followed "by a full investigation that will include gathering sworn statements from all attendees." . . . However, [Greenspan] acknowledged that he has briefed "members of various administrations" because they needed to know about FOMC decisions in formulating other government

policies. But that hasn't happened in the last year or so, he said, because the Fed hasn't changed its monetary policy.[9]

SELLING INFORMATION FOR $100 A MINUTE: "1-900-ANGELL?"

Wayne Angell, an economics professor at Ottawa University in Ottawa, Kansas, and a Republican legislator in the Kansas House of Representatives, was appointed by President Ronald Reagan to the Fed Board on February 7, 1986. He filled an unexpired term that ended January 31, 1994. He submitted his resignation on February 9, 1994, so that he would not remain in office until the installation of his successor.

His friendship with Chairman Greenspan and his reputation for being outspoken added to the interest in Angell's actions when he left the Federal Reserve. It was astonishing to find that Angell began selling interest-rate information a month after he officially left his position at the Fed. David Wessel and Anita Raghavan reported in a lead article in the *Wall Street Journal* on March 24, 1994, that Angell was in "hot demand" on Wall Street and was "actually charging some analysts $100 a minute for advice." They stressed that this kind of information could be very profitable: "After all, a Wall Street investment house can make — or lose — millions of dollars when the Fed moves short-term interest rates by a mere ¼ percentage point, as it did yesterday."[10]

The report also said that Angell "recently talked to a Wall Street stock analyst for 13 minutes to get his views on interest rates" and that the analyst received a bill one day later for $1,300. Another analyst, Elaine Garzarelli, an 'influential stock strategist' at Lehman Brothers, said she would "happily pay Angell $100 a minute." The *Wall Street Journal* article continued: "Ms. Garzarelli decided to talk to him one on one. She won't say what she paid, but she says it was worth it. 'He told me the Fed would probably tighten again,' she says. 'And he predicted the bond market would react favorably. And that's exactly what happened,' Ms. Garzarelli said."

Chairman Gonzalez thought this was unethical behavior and ordered an investigation. Gonzalez issued a press release asking if Fed interest-rate information could be obtained by calling 1-900-ANGELL: " 'Will I learn what happened at the last Federal Open Market Committee (FOMC) meeting if I dial 1-900-ANGELL?' Rep. Gonzalez asked. . . . 'I suggest that the Fed implement a nondisclosure agreement with employees who terminate employment with the Federal Reserve,' Rep. Gonzalez said in a letter to Federal Reserve Chairman Alan Greenspan."[11]

Gonzalez wanted to prevent inside information or what appeared to be inside information from being leaked or sold by present and former Fed officials. An inquiry indicated that laws forbidding the exploitation of inside information for profit on securities trading apply to public corporations, but apparently do not cover the Board of Governors, an executive-branch agency.

THE FED SHARES SECRETS WITH FOREIGN CENTRAL BANKERS

At a hearing on October 19, 1993, Greenspan attempted to reassure Congress on this issue: "I trust the problem of leaks is behind us."[12] But that was not the case. In 1996 the Fed reportedly called on the FBI to investigate "an embarrassing leak of inside information that churned financial markets last week and badly soiled the Fed's reputation as a paragon of bureaucratic virtue. A Fed spokesman declined to comment Monday on the reported probe."[13] Unfortunately, Bill Montague, who wrote this description in his excellent article on the Fed, was wrong about soiling the Fed's image. The severe problem of leaking exploitable information had apparently not injured the Fed's reputation. It was occurring for very basic reasons that the Fed has yet to fix. By declining to comment, the Fed once again achieved its efficient under-the-lumpy-rug sweep. There was little media follow-up. For many, the subject died and the chairman remained deified.

One year later, the House Banking Committee received information about non-Fed employees attending Fed meetings at which inside information was discussed. Congressmen Gonzalez and Maurice Hinchey (D-NY) asked Greenspan about the apparent leak of discount information and the presence of these people at Fed meetings. Greenspan was forced to admit that some non-Fed people had attended Fed meetings at which the Fed's future interest-rate policy was discussed.[14] Greenspan included a twenty-three-page enclosure listing hundreds of people at the Board of Governors in Washington, D.C., and in the twelve Fed Banks around the country who had access to at least some secret Fed information about interest-rate policy.

The list included "visiting scholars" who had attended pre-FOMC meetings at three Fed Banks. Greenspan wrote: "At the Federal Reserve Bank of Kansas City, over the 3-year period, a total of 28 foreign central bankers have attended 16 different Board of Directors meetings, including the discussion and vote on discount rates." Those attending included "central bankers from Bulgaria, China, the Czech Republic, Hungary, Poland, Romania and Russia."[15] Gonzalez presented a table showing the details of some of the foreign officials who had attended meetings at the Kansas City Fed Bank.

Following these disclosures and a letter from Gonzalez, Greenspan said the practice of allowing visitors to attend these meetings would end. There appears to have been insufficient oversight to verify whether this policy has been precisely and continually implemented.

This incident revealed a striking example of the Greenspan Fed's priorities: some of the information presented at the Fed Bank meetings attended by foreign central bankers was redacted by the Greenspan Fed before it was sent to Congress.

GREENSPAN BECOMES A PRIME SUSPECT

It is a rule of conduct at the Board of Governors that "Committee members are not to comment on monetary policy or the economic outlook" during the "blackout" period, which includes the week before an FOMC meeting "to the Friday of the week of the meeting. This means not giving speeches and not talking with reporters." So wrote Laurence Meyer, a Fed governor from June 1996 to January 2002.[16]

Meyer was surprised to see John Berry, a reporter then with the *Washington Post,* "coming out of the Chairman's office during the blackout period. I believe," Meyer continues, "that Berry and I would have been shot on the spot (perhaps by the Chairman himself) if we had been discovered together in my office during the blackout."[17]

Meyer rationalizes this kind of apparent leaking as a way of "signaling" Fed actions. The signaling can be "sanctioned" or "unsanctioned" by the FOMC members, according to Meyer: "The danger, however, is that the Chairman could prepare the markets for a move that the Committee might consider premature. That would put the Committee in the uncomfortable position of having to surprise the markets by not moving, or contradicting the signal and confusing the public. Of course, these consequences make it possible for the Chairman to occasionally use unsanctioned signaling to pressure the Committee into agreeing to a policy action when there otherwise might not be an overwhelming consensus for it."[18]

Meyer believes that unsanctioned signaling by the chairman is a "gray area." Meyer is wrong about the color. Leaking future Fed policy to the favored few, whether planned by one or more FOMC members or labeled with a euphemism like "signaling," is misconduct tinted darker than gray. Public servants who manage the central bank have an obligation to the citizens they serve to be forthright and credible stewards rather than leakers of exploitable inside information to the favored few. Meyer's observation places Greenspan on the list of suspected leakers. Meyer's description of signaling makes this incident seem like part of a broader and continuing practice at the Fed.

UNREGULATED FOREIGN CURRENCY TRADERS WITH ADVANCE INFORMATION ON THE FED'S ACTIONS

In reply to a Gonzalez inquiry in 1994, the Fed noted that in the last five years it had transacted foreign-exchange business with fifty-eight foreign and domestic institutions (including private banks and brokerages) around the world. When the Fed called these parties and told them to buy billions of dollars of a currency, say U.S. dollars, the foreign entities received very valuable information that they could exploit for enormous profits. Gonzalez wrote to Greenspan: "A large trading company could earn many millions of dollars in profits in a short time period on this inside information."[19] Earlier, Greenspan had tried to send a message that these actions were not worrisome: "Usually, these market participants *very quickly* inform the wire services." He added discordantly that even if they just dealt with "a single institution with information not generally known . . . the immediate counterparties have information on intervention *at least a couple of minutes before the entire interbank market*" (emphasis added).[20]

Would anyone have the audacity to make billions of dollars on inside information without calling the wire services? Would they be so ungrateful for their commission from the Fed that they would trade on their own account or leak the information to another trader before the Fed's trading became public? Apparently no one has come forward and telephoned the Fed about their exploitation of inside information. The remedy may well be for the Fed to simultaneously notify the media and the parties receiving orders; that way no exploitable inside information is passed to favored parties. Markets would quickly, and generally more efficiently, adapt to the Fed's actions.[21]

The legal limits barring the GAO from auditing foreign-exchange operations at the Fed should be lifted. The GAO should hire experts (not connected with the Fed) to examine these operations. Through investigations and oversight with trained experts, Congress should compel the Fed to adopt the best remedy for eliminating the dispersal of exploitable inside information.

"THE RETURN OF GREENSPAN'S PROPHETIC TOUCH"

On Thursday, November 6, 2003, Greenspan gave a speech in Florida that drew enthusiastic praise for his ability to predict the future.[22] A contribution published in the *New York Times* the following Sunday was entitled: "The Return of Greenspan's Prophetic Touch."[23] It began: "Has Alan Greenspan, the chairman of the Federal Reserve, reacquired the oracle's touch?" The *Atlanta Journal-Constitution* reported, on the day after the speech, that he had given "a carefully phrased endorsement" of optimistic predictions for the labor market: "The odds . . . increasingly favor a revival of job creation."[24] The *Los Angeles Times* reported Greenspan as being "relatively optimistic" in the short-run.[25] The *Washington Post* reported that Greenspan "in his most upbeat assessment of the U.S. economic outlook in years, said yesterday that the economy should soon start producing the kind of job growth that has been missing since the end of 2001."[26]

What was the basis for the claim of "the return of Greenspan's prophetic touch?" The day after Greenspan spoke, the U.S. Labor Department announced a turnaround in its estimates, from a decline in employment to a rise in employment. The Friday news release stated that nonfarm employment, which had fallen in the second quarter of 2003 and had been reported as falling in August and September, was now rising. August and September employment figures were revised upward to show an average increase of 85,000 jobs a month in the third quarter.[27] Although there had been a decline in the number of claims for unemployment insurance on Thursday when Greenspan spoke, the big labor market news came the following day.[28]

The Fed chairman may sometimes have sounded as though he knew the future state of employment, and he might have, although there is no direct evidence of it. Professor Alan B. Krueger wrote about confidential governmental data that are passed to the president, the Federal Reserve

Board chairman, and the Treasury secretary before they are made public. Greenspan, Krueger states, "has an agreement with the Bureau of Labor Statistics to receive monthly employment data for manufacturing, mining and public utilities two or three days early, ostensibly so the Fed can produce its industrial production statistics. . . . Surely, the chairman's reason for wanting data early is a ruse; he wants an advanced hint at where the economy is headed. Providing prerelease data makes the chairman seem omniscient and helps the Fed and Treasury outfox the markets."[29] The sharing of "business data" between governmental agencies was increased by a law passed in 2002.[30]

Perhaps Greenspan's crystal ball had a note under it from the Department of Labor, which also may have appeared when he made his famous remark about "irrational exuberance." When Greenspan described stock-market attitudes as evidence of "irrational exuberance," prices plunged on world financial markets. He included an addendum: "a drop in stock prices might not necessarily be bad for the economy." That was on Thursday night, December 5, 1996.[31]

It was bad news for investors who believed the Fed was signaling an interest-rate increase. The Associated Press reported: "Many investors were skittish ahead of the figures, fearful that news of a booming economy would lead Greenspan to tighten interest rates." His remarks on Thursday night sent stock prices falling and "contributed to the biggest drop in Japanese shares" that year. There is a question but no evidence about whether Greenspan had knowledge of the report to be issued the next day, one that would calm the financial markets.

The next morning, Friday, the Labor Department reported a smaller-than-expected rise in employment, and this news reduced concern that the Fed would raise interest rates to slow the economy. There was a recovery in prices for U.S. Treasury bonds.

By using inside information to embellish a record for accurate predictions, an official can lend undue credence to his or her other, less reliable predictions. The biased devotion of the Fed-watchers industry can increase the amount of false information and volatility in financial markets.

Senior members of the Banking Committees in the House and Senate who have security clearances should be kept informed by Fed witnesses of any confidential economic data that are coded in their testimony or responses and cannot be made public before the embargo date for their public release. No Fed official with knowledge of embargoed economic reports should manipulate the press and the public with speeches or testimony that use this inside information, unless some national emergency requires that action.

MANIPULATING THE MEDIA

Trying to persuade reporters, spinning a message, leaking a proposal to test its reception, and anonymously dumping on opponents are all common practices in politics. They are in many cases the symptoms of a vibrant democracy. Persuasion is a vital tool for successful politicians, whose re-election depends partly on their ability to persuade other legislators to support their proposals so they can establish a successful record. There are ethical and, perhaps, legal limits to such actions. These limits are especially relevant for the Fed's unelected officials.

Although Greenspan did not hold formal press conferences, he held off-the-record conferences with selected reporters. As Laurence Meyer explains, "The use of reporters as part of the Fed's signal corps is not official Board or FOMC doctrine." Although Meyer describes the practice, he notes that the public-affairs staff and Greenspan "like to pretend it doesn't happen": "He typically relies on a small group of reporters. John Berry, longtime reporter for the *Washington Post* and now at Bloomberg, is most widely recognized in this role. The *Wall Street Journal* reporter covering the Fed—it was David Wessel, then Jake Schlesinger, and most recently Greg Ip during my term—was also a regular member of the signal corps."[32] Many reporters are likely to consider their inclusion in this kind of selective access important for their employment, although exclusion awaits if their reports include criticism of the Fed.[33]

There are some pieces of vivid evidence. Jim McTague has covered the financial scene from Washington, D.C., for many years. McTague is the Washington editor of *Barron's*, one the country's most prestigious business publications. He spoke about his relationships with the Fed on national television in 2002.[34] He related that he had a one-on-one conference with Greenspan, whom he found cordial but uninformative. After he wrote a column that suggested that Fed policy had contributed to the defeat of President George H. W. Bush, he was told that he was banned from further conferences with Greenspan.

Also, McTague's report on the 1993 hearing at which Fed officials misled Congress was likely regarded as unfavorable, even intolerable, by the Fed. He compared Greenspan's congressional testimony about the tran-

BOARD OF GOVERNORS
OF THE
FEDERAL RESERVE SYSTEM

Office Correspondence

Date__December 6, 1974__

To____Chairman Burns_____   Subject:_____

From____Joe Coyne_____   _____

Concerning our conversation yesterday about Nicholas von Hoffman,
Bart Rowen thinks it would be an excellent idea for you to discuss the
matter with Katherine Graham. He said he has discussed von Hoffman on
several occasions with Ben Bradlee, the Post's executive editor. He is
certain that Mrs. Graham would approach Bradlee on the question if you
discussed it with her.

There are, of course, certain dangers in this approach. Bart,
of course, favors it strongly because you would be supporting his view
against von Hoffman. Additionally, Ben Bradlee's reaction to an approach
of this nature might be: "Washington officialdom is squirming; keep up
the good work, von Hoffman."

On balance, I don't think it would do any harm to talk to Mrs.
Graham. The reaction can't be any worse than it already is.

- 0 -

On another matter, I have learned from a friendly newsman that
Senator Proxmire is planning a Senate statement Monday morning attacking
the Federal Reserve for its "super-tight" money policy. A press release
he issued today for release in Monday afternoon papers says the recession
has been deepened by continued high interest rates caused by Federal
Reserve policy.

FIGURE 5-1. Memo from Joe Coyne to Fed chairman Burns, December 6, 1974.
Coyne urges Burns to talk to Katharine Graham, owner of the *Washington Post*.
Reporter Nicholas von Hoffman had been harshly criticizing the Fed. Source:
Arthur Burns Collection, Gerald R. Ford Presidential Library.

scripts of the Fed's meetings to an act by a double-talking comedian. Mc-
Tague told Congressman James Leach (R-IA) about his being banned.
According to McTague, Leach told him to write a letter to the Fed. A Fed
spokesman replied to McTague's letter by telling him he had never been
banned. After relating this story on national television in 2002, McTague

was called by the Fed and told he was banned again. This stick-carrot-stick attempted manipulation might have intimidated a lesser reporter. In this case it failed.

Nicholas von Hoffman was a well-known columnist for the *Washington Post* and a commentator for the "Point-Counterpoint" segment on *60 Minutes*.[35] His criticism of the Fed led to an internal Fed memo being sent to Chairman Burns (Figure 5-1), suggesting the Fed chairman contact the owner of the *Washington Post*.

In the memo, dated December 6, 1974, Joe Coyne, who handled public relations at the Fed, told Burns that he had discussed the von Hoffman matter with Bart Rowen, who was a business columnist for the *Washington Post;* that Rowen thought "it would be an excellent idea for you [Burns] to discuss the matter with Katherine [*sic,* Katharine] Graham," the owner of the *Washington Post* and the daughter of a former Fed chairman; and that Rowen had discussed the von Hoffman matter with the *Washington Post*'s famous editor, Ben Bradlee. According to Rowen, Graham would approach Bradlee about the Fed chairman's discussion of the von Hoffman matter. Coyne warned the Fed chairman that there were certain dangers: "Ben Bradlee's reaction to an approach of this nature might be: 'Washington officialdom is squirming; keep up the good work.'" Despite this caution Coyne thought the chairman of the Federal Reserve should contact the owner of the leading newspaper in the nation's capital because the "reaction can't be any worse than it already is."

There has been little media coverage of Fed operations such as those discussed in this book. After an initial story, there is little meaningful follow-up, which allows the Fed to keep brushing problems under its lumpy rug. A follow-up would invite retaliation from the Fed. A reporter wishing to meet with the Fed chairman for a lovely off-the-record chat would have disappointing news for his or her editor if a story critical of Fed operations ended this access. Nevertheless, some reporters have written important critical stories about flawed Fed operations. A few examples related to problems discussed in this book:

- Alan Abelson, "Irrational Adulation," *Barron's,* July 22, 2002.
- Stephen A. Davies, "Fed May Be Stifling Criticism by Hiring Outside Academics," *Bond Buyer,* November 4, 1994 (on Fed payments to academics).
- Gene Epstein, "No Place Like Home; Looking for Inflation, Chairman Greenspan? Have We Found Some for You!" *Barron's,* August 2, 1999 (on the need for major restructuring of the Fed).

- Jim McTague, "Greenspan Has Himself to Blame for Fervid Interest in Transcripts," *American Banker,* December 1, 1993.
- Bill Montague, "Fed under Fire; Critics Say Public Is Being Short-changed," *USA Today,* September 24, 1996 (on Fed leaks of inside information).
- Paul Starobin, "The Fed Tapes: The Revelation That the Federal Reserve's Chief Policymaking Body Has Kept Secret Records of Its Meetings Has Raised Questions about the Fed's Integrity and Accountability to Congress," *National Journal,* December 18, 1993.
- John Wilke, "Showing Its Age, Fed's Huge Empire, Set Up Years Ago, Is Costly and Inefficient," *Wall Street Journal,* September 16, 1996 (on waste and inefficiency in Fed operations).

They deserve praise for serving the public interest despite the type of retribution and attempted manipulation that the country's most powerful peacetime bureaucracy has employed.

CHAPTER 6

THE SEVENTEEN-YEAR LIE

What would happen to unelected officials in a governmental bureaucracy with immense economic powers, which include controlling the country's money supply, regulating large parts of the financial system, and making loans to foreign countries, if they perpetuated a lie for seventeen years about the existence of records of their deliberations? What would happen if, when the lie was finally uncovered, they began destroying their source records? The press and the public would be outraged and would demand that these unelected officials, who have violated the public trust in a great democracy, be, at the very least, fired.[1] They would demand an end to all these practices.

That did not happen at the Federal Open Market Committee (FOMC). When Gonzalez invited Fed officials to testify about their records in 1993, Greenspan and some Fed officials planned and participated in diversionary tactics, even if that meant misleading Congress about seventeen years' worth of secret Fed transcripts. In some cases, the statements that officials sent Congress for insertion in the hearing record were false, and they knew this before they testified.

When Gonzalez uncovered the seventeen-year lie, it drew a few press stories but no sustained coverage. The endless stream of superlatives for Greenspan continued. For seventeen years the Fed had lied, but its chairman remained deified.

EARLY REVELATIONS OF THE SECRET TRANSCRIPTS

The Fed began preparing paraphrased transcripts of FOMC meetings in 1936 for internal use.[2] Each was called a "Memorandum of Discussion" (MOD). Fed chairman William McChesney Martin threatened to end this practice in 1964. He threatened the wrong congressmen: two outspoken Democrats who would later become chairmen of the House Banking Committee.[3] Wright Patman and Henry Reuss did not blink when confronted with this threat. The House Banking subcommittee chaired by Patman voted (6 yes, 1 no, and 1 present) to demand the verbatim transcripts for 1960, 1961, 1962, and 1963. The Fed sent Congress these records and began issuing paraphrased transcripts they called the MODs, with a five-year lag. Milton Friedman and his coauthor Anna J. Schwartz believed that the publication of their classic history of U.S. monetary policy in 1963, which was very critical of the Fed, along with the congressional requests for FOMC records, induced the Fed to begin publicly issuing the MODs in 1965.[4]

Valuable information was obtained from these records, since all statements were attributed to specific individuals. An example is the questionable legality and propriety of beginning a so-called "swap" facility in 1962 by which the Fed gave itself the power to make loans to foreign governments without congressional authorization (see Chapter 4).

FIGHTING FOR LONGER DELAYS AND LESS SUNSHINE

Fourteen years later, in 1976, two attacks on Fed secrecy created high anxiety at the Fed. First, David Merrill, a law student at Georgetown University, brought a legal action challenging the forty-five-day delay in releasing the "Directive" on monetary policy. It is a short report on policy actions authorized at an FOMC meeting.[5] The federal district court agreed with Merrill. The Fed appealed up to the Supreme Court, which remanded it back to the district court. Lacking funds for further extensive adjudication, Merrill could not pursue the case. The Fed has more than all the money it needs — an "unlimited purse" — to hire private law firms and fight any legal action for a long time.[6] Adjudication of charges of alleged racial discrimination at the Board of Governors (described in Chapter 8) had been in a federal court for a decade in 2007.

The second attack on the Fed's secrecy came from the Government in the Sunshine Act, which was signed into law September 13, 1976. According to the statute: "The agency shall make promptly available to the public, in a place easily accessible to the public, the transcript, electronic recording or minutes . . . of the discussion of any item on the agenda."[7] (In this case, "agency" refers to any body in which most of the members are appointed by the president and confirmed by the Senate—like the Fed Board of Governors.) The Fed frantically tried to protect itself from such transparency and individual accountability. FOMC meeting transcripts from 1976 and other documents reveal that Fed officials devoted considerable time to preparing memoranda and discussing the dreaded timely release of their FOMC deliberations to the public. The staff reported on April 7, 1976, that they could be subject to a court order to produce part of the MODS: "*Second*, it is becoming increasingly evident that, so long as the memorandum of discussion exists, many of us will have to spend a large amount of time in the effort to comply with Court orders to make portions public."[8]

THE MOCK FUNERAL

The seventeen-year lie began. Fed chairman Arthur Burns notified House Banking chairman Wright Patman in 1974 that he could not give Congress the FOMC transcripts because "they are routinely disposed of after the Committee has formally accepted the memorandum of discussion for the meeting in question," adding, "currently we are employing a combination of note-taking and tape recording. In any event, the materials are disposed of when they have served their purpose, as noted above."[9]

Three years later, in testimony before the House Banking Committee, Burns maintained the fabrication: "In the absence of express statutory protection against premature disclosure of the memorandum, we would feel compelled to object to a proposal of returning to the practice of keeping extensively detailed minutes of FOMC meetings."[10]

The FOMC voted 10–1 to discontinue the MODS in 1976. That vote began the official seventeen-year lie. Among those voting to discontinue was the president of the New York Fed Bank, Paul Volcker, who would become Fed chairman. Philip Coldwell, president of the Dallas Fed Bank, was the only dissenting vote.[11]

The Fed's announcement of the end of the MODS produced a firestorm at House Banking. Hearings were held. Laws were proposed to restart the MODS. The chairman of the Subcommittee on Domestic Monetary Policy, Stephen L. Neal (D-SC), contacted many distinguished academics and people from the financial community, requesting their opinion concerning how FOMC meetings should be documented and made public. A preponderance of seventy respondents wanted either the transcripts or the MODs restored, and many wanted timely publication.[12] Milton Friedman, the Nobel laureate, wanted publication with only a few days' delay.

"A DEVIOUS WAY TO GET AROUND THE LAW"

Burns outfoxed some people by announcing a substitute for the transcripts. Ninety days after the FOMC meetings, the public would get something called the "Minutes of the Federal Open Market Committee." These minutes would not contain statements for attribution to FOMC members. They would not even record a member's individual views except for a very brief description of any recorded nay votes. Since the Fed tries to make the publicly recorded vote unanimous, generally little or no individual responsibility can be divined from these remnants.

Burns told Congress that the minutes recorded the votes responsibly: "The new policy record does not attribute individual opinions to committee members by name; but the record always reports the votes of the members by name and their accountability is preserved."[13] Each time the padded but anemic substitute was published, it was received with great gusto and given wide press coverage by the Fed-watchers industry. Entrails are better than a complete record for those employed to interpret them.

As Burns led the committee members to the funeral for the MODs, David Eastburn, president of the Philadelphia Fed Bank, warned, "It seemed to me that we incur certain costs in cutting out the memorandum of discussion in terms of implications to others on the outside that we're being more secretive if you want to put it that way, that *this is a devious way to get around the law*" (emphasis added). A page from the MOD containing Eastburn's remarks is shown in Figure 6-1.[14] It is less tidy than the transcripts from future periods, when computers had replaced typewriters. Notice that Chairman Burns ("CB") replied by saying, "That depends how we present it. Now I would want to present this, I would want to make a virtue of this, and never mind how we arrived at it. We were not seeking virtue for the sake of virtue."

Burns was dismissive when doubts about the lack of a full record were raised at an FOMC meeting.[15] He replied: "I think you credit individuals who follow the Federal Reserve with more knowledge than I think

'± 4/20/76   Exec. Ses.   I   -18-

                                       was
¹Eastburn   There reason I asked that question/ it seemed to me we had

incur uncertain costs in cutting out the memorandum of discussion in

terms of implications to others on the outside that we're being more secretive
subject

consider if you want x to put it that way, that this is a devious way of to

getix around the law.

CB   That depends how we present it. Now I would want to present

this, I would want to make a virtue of this, and never mind how we arrived

at it. We were not seeking virtue for the sake of virtue, I'm not going to

argue that, but if let us say we decide to drop the memorandum of discussion,
         all
wait/right than we're doing away with an instrument of secretyx retained

in the Archives for a period of 5 years. We have a policy record and that

policy record is now going to be very much fuller than it was, so the public

will be informed promptly and muchm more fully, that's another xx virtue.
                        adopt
A third as we go along with--if we dumb the second suggestion, you see,
         period
cutting the tool rate, that goes further in that direction and I would

present it as a deliberatexx attempt on the part of the Federal Reserve

to rid itself of the perenial charge of secrecy. I think that's the way
      to   it
itix/presentmd/to the public. Historically, it didn't arise that way,

that's true, but I think that is not any unfair interpretation.

many of them really have. . . . those who feel that it merely repeats that which they already know will have no difficulty skipping paragraphs or pages." Denying for the record that the minutes should be padded, he ordered more pages: "We're describing this document as an expanded policy record. . . . Now on that basis of this concept the document should be longer, you see, must be longer, and this is a formal consideration that cannot be neglected, and we need some additional pages. I'm not going to tell you how to add additional pages, and *I'm certainly not going to say that we should do anything that remotely resembles padded, but produce several additional pages*" (emphasis added).[16]

SECRECY AND VIDEOTAPES

Sixteen years later, alarm bells went off at the Fed as Gonzalez began asking about the records of FOMC meetings. During 1992 and until October 1993, officials of the Greenspan Fed answered Gonzalez's inquiries with warnings about the harmful effects of openness at the nation's central bank. The videotaping of FOMC meetings, proposed in Gonzalez's legislation (HR 28), triggered extreme irritation in Fed officials. For many of them, and for other admirers of the Fed's "independence," it was an insolent intrusion that would lead to blatant transparency and individual accountability. Fed officials said the quality of their meetings would be severely impaired. As late as 1998, Greenspan was still warning the FOMC: "If we went to the fullest extent in that direction [more information], then Henry Gonzalez's approach of live transmission of this meeting obviously would be the most ethical and most directly available source of information to the market, but it also would be the most useless."[17] He misrepresented Gonzalez's bill, which provided for a sixty-day delay before the release of the videotape of a session. The bill also prevented pulling the plug on the tape recorder when an FOMC quorum was present.[18]

    Behind the public rhetoric of disdain for the Gonzalez legislation, Greenspan and other Fed officials reached for additional political muscle.[19] The chairman of this politically powerful governmental bureaucracy traveled to Little Rock, Arkansas, in 1992 to talk with the president-elect. Reporting to the FOMC about his meeting with Bill Clinton, Greenspan interpreted Clinton's "body language and peripheral comments" as "consistent" with Fed independence.[20] (For further details, see Chapter 10.)

    During the first year of his presidency, Clinton notified all governmental agencies to comply with the Freedom of Information Act in his

"Memorandum for Heads of Departments and Agencies."[21] The Justice Department would implement this new administration policy. Greenspan reacted by warning FOMC members: "The trouble, unfortunately is . . . the Department of Justice would not under the Freedom of Information Act be on our side in the court to protect these particular transcripts and prevent [their release]."[22]

In pursuit of FOMC records, Gonzalez used the White House directive and comments from numerous scholars who had responded in 1976 to the request by Congressman Neal for their views. Many were opposed to the discontinuance of the MODS. John Kenneth Galbraith wrote: "The effort at secrecy has only one source: That is the long-standing effort of those having to do with banking and central banking to feel that they are above the procedures ordinarily required of other individuals and agencies. . . . There is no good reason why full minutes should not be published and why the obligation should not be fully on the Chairman to see that all discussion is on the record."[23]

THE FED CAN'T AFFORD IT

The statements issued by the FOMC in 1976 on why the MODS should be discontinued included the following transparently inapplicable rationale: "The decision to discontinue the memoranda [the MODS] reflected the Committee's judgment that the benefits derived from them did not justify their relatively high cost."[24]

In an FOMC conference call on October 15, 1993, Chairman Greenspan made a similar suggestion to justify eliminating a verbatim record of FOMC meetings. It cost too much. In the Fed's wasteful, bloated bureaucracy, which has an operating budget exceeding $2 billion, this rationale is a meaningless excuse for secrecy.

DOODLES AND ROUGH NOTES

Much to their assumed consternation, an impressive array of the nation's central-bank officials assembled behind a long, continuous row of tables in the Wright Patman Chambers of the House Banking Committee, with Greenspan in the middle. They looked up at Henry B. Gonzalez, House Banking chairman. Gonzalez had sent each of the twelve Fed Bank presidents and the seven members of the Board of Governors specific requests for information.[25] The letter sent to Fed governor David W. Mullins, Jr., is shown in Figure 6-2. They were directed to submit statements for the record on "any notes or records that you have made in connection with FOMC meetings" or "others have made at any FOMC meetings and the location and disposition of any such material."

According to their prearranged plan, nearly all the witnesses deferred to Greenspan, who did not disclose the most important fact concerning the FOMC records, which had seemingly shocked some of them four days earlier: the existence of FOMC transcripts from many prior years. The committee did not know that most of the witnesses had decided not to change their formally submitted written statements even after being told, four days before the hearing, that prior transcripts existed. Thus, some of them let stand written statements that misled Congress on the areas about which they had been instructed to testify.

Robert McTeer, former president of the Dallas Fed Bank, testified: "I doodle during discussions and occasionally write down a word or phrase for reference when I speak. I don't write down decisions because they are simple and easy to remember, and normally come at the end of the meeting. My doodles and notes all mixed up would be of no use to traders or journalists. I destroy them after the meeting and rely only on official documents for future reference."[26]

Did McTeer seriously think that when he was asked about FOMC records, Gonzalez would be satisfied to learn about his discarded doodles? What official documents was McTeer talking about? Greenspan testified that the FOMC kept "rough notes." These answers appeared evasive and misleading.

With artful sleight of hand, Greenspan, in his prepared statement, emphasized the temporary nature of FOMC records: "The meetings are recorded electronically by the FOMC secretariat. . . . the tapes are recorded over . . . In the process of putting together the minutes, an unedited transcript is prepared from the tapes, as are detailed notes on selected topics."[27]

Gonzalez then inquired of all the witnesses: "In the questions that I had directed, I did ask and each of you responded, as to their notes or records that you are aware of. But today's testimony by Chairman Greenspan reveals to me, at least, that the FOMC meetings are tape-recorded. . . . What I am going to ask is if any of you knew or know about these recordings being made when you submitted your written testimony for today's hearing. . . . I will be glad to hear from any of you."

As previously planned, the Fed officials let Greenspan answer. He drew

HY S. GONZALEZ, TEXAS, CHAIRMAN

FRED L. NEAL, NORTH CAROLINA
H J. LAFALCE, NEW YORK
CE F. VENTO, MINNESOTA
ALEE E SCHUMER, NEW YORK
RET FRANK, MASSACHUSETTS
L E KANJORSKI, PENNSYLVANIA
BM P. KENNEDY II, MASSACHUSETTS
FD R. FLAKE, NEW YORK
3SY MFUME, MARYLAND
UNE WATERS, CALIFORNIA
RY CARDOCO, IDAHO
ORTON, UTAH
SACCHUS, FLORIDA
BERT C. KLEIN, NEW JERSEY
OLYN B. MALONEY, NEW YORK
IR DEUTSCH, FLORIDA
I V. GUTIERREZ, ILLINOIS
BY L. NUGH, ILLINOIS
ALX ROYBAL-ALLARD, CALIFORNIA
MAE M. BARRETT, WISCONSIN
AARTH FURSE, OREGON
IA W. VELAZBULEZ, NEW YORK
ERT W. WYNN, MARYLAND
J FIELDS, LOUISIANA
VN WATT, NORTH CAROLINA
JROZ MAKONEY, NEW YORK
VIN W. DOOLEY, CALIFORNIA
ALINC, PENNSYLVANIA
FINGERHUT, OHIO

JAMES A. LEACH, IOWA
BILL McCOLLUM, FLORIDA
MARGE ROUKEMA, NEW JERSEY
DOUG BEREUTER, NEBRASKA
THOMAS RIDGE, PENNSYLVANIA
TOBY ROTH, WISCONSIN
ALFRED A. McCANDLESS, CALIFORNIA
RICHARD H. BAKER, LOUISIANA
JIM NUSSLE, IOWA
CRAIG THOMAS, WYOMING
SAM JOHNSON, TEXAS
DEBORAH PRYCE, OHIO
JOHN LINDER, GEORGIA
JOE KNOLLENBERG, MICHIGAN
RICK LAZIO, NEW YORK
ROD GRAMS, MINNESOTA
SPENCER BACHUS III, ALABAMA
MIKE HUFFINGTON, CALIFORNIA
MICHAEL CASTLE, DELAWARE
PETER KING, NEW YORK

BERNARD SANDERS, VERMONT

U.S. HOUSE OF REPRESENTATIVES

COMMITTEE ON BANKING, FINANCE AND URBAN AFFAIRS

ONE HUNDRED THIRD CONGRESS

2129 RAYBURN HOUSE OFFICE BUILDING

WASHINGTON, DC 20515-6050

September 20, 1993

CLO: #354
CCS: #93-4411
RECVD: 9/21/93

CLO · DJW

David W. Mullins, Jr.
Governor
Board of Governors of the Federal Reserve System
Constitution Avenue and 20th Street
Washington, D.C. 20551

Dear Governor Mullins:

On Tuesday October 19, 1993 the Banking Committee will hold a hearing on the "Federal Reserve System Accountability Act of 1993", HR 28, in Room 2128 Rayburn House Office Building. The hearing will focus on maintaining a record of the FOMC meetings. As a member of the FOMC your testimony is quite important as the Banking Committee deliberates whether to require a full and timely accounting of each of the FOMC meetings. I request your presence to testify at 10:00 AM on October 19, 1993.

Please prepare an opening statement presenting your own independent views on this subject and submit it to me no later than noon on October 18, 1993. Include the following information in your statement:

1.) a detailed description of any notes or records that you have made and the location and disposition of any such material,

2.) notes or records that you are aware others have made at any FOMC meetings and the location and disposition of any such material, and

3.) any information you have about the release of information by anyone employed at the Federal Reserve about FOMC meetings prior to the official release of that information by the Federal Reserve.

Due to the number of witnesses I will ask you to submit your statement for the record and to present a short summary. Your summary should include the above three areas. I look forward to your testimony.

Sincerely,

Henry B. Gonzalez
Chairman

FIGURE 6-2. Letter from Rep. Henry B. Gonzalez to Fed governor David W. Mullins, Jr., September 20, 1993, detailing the information to be brought to the House Banking hearings on FOMC records, October 19, 1993. Source: author's collection.

attention to tapes and notes rather than the existence of years of transcripts: "The FOMC staff, in the preparation of the minutes, takes a recording for purposes of getting a rough transcript, but the tapes are taped over." Greenspan then emphasized: "In other words we don't have the actual tapes themselves. We don't have electronic recordings of our meetings." Gonzalez said he was a "little bit confused here. In other words you have no tape recordings of the actual proceedings." Greenspan injected his own uncertainty about what his staff does: "We have them only—as far as I know, what the staff does is, in order to assist its presentation and preparation of the minutes, it takes recordings but then tapes over them so they are not available thereafter."[28]

Congressman Maurice Hinchey (D-NY) probed further: "And in the interim [before the minutes are issued], those tapes are taped over, so that no record exists in that way. Is that correct?" Greenspan replied: "There is no permanent electronic record, that is correct. We obviously have rough notes."[29] The neatly typed FOMC transcripts I later viewed were not rough notes.

Jim McTague, then the Washington bureau chief for *American Banker* and now the Washington editor of *Barron's*, attended the hearing. He reported: "In a performance that would have made professor Irwin Corey weep with admiration Mr. Greenspan avoided drawing attention to the existence of transcripts during appearances before the House Banking Committee on Oct. 13 and Oct. 19 to discuss FOMC record keeping."[30] Corey has famously performed as a double-talking comedian.

David Skidmore, an Associated Press reporter who was later employed at the Fed, wrote an article entitled "Greenspan Defends Secrecy Surrounding Key Central Bank Committee": "Federal Reserve Chairman Alan Greenspan warned lawmakers today that forcing central bank policy makers to operate with less secrecy would hurt the economy. . . . Disclosing the committee's directives, which are often conditioned on future economic events that may or may not happen, would cause changes in interest rates even when the panel intended no immediate change, he said."[31]

THE LIE REVEALED

Skidmore also reported that Gonzalez said: "There appears to be conflicting statements, less than forthright responses, and possibly some jointly arranged understanding with regard to the testimony."[32]

Gonzalez was not convinced that the nation's central monetary-policy committee destroyed the verbatim records of its meetings and maintained only rough notes of members' statements, as Greenspan had testified. Gonzalez ordered that letters be faxed immediately to all the witnesses, asking if they had been forthright in their testimony and demanding details of their knowledge of FOMC records.

The pressure from Gonzalez, a legislator who would not reach an "accommodation," did elicit a break in what Gonzalez called the "code of silence." In response to the post-hearing letters that Gonzalez sent to witnesses, the House Banking Committee received information regarding an FOMC conference call that had occurred four days before the hearing. David Wessel reported in the *Wall Street Journal* about this break in the Gonzalez investigation: "Fed Chairman Alan Greenspan saw this coming, according to the extraordinary notes of an hour-long Oct. 15 conference call among Fed officials: 'AG [Alan Greenspan] not as confident as previously that Fed is not at risk,' an official of the Cleveland Federal Reserve Bank recorded. '*Fed vulnerable if mishandle transcripts matter.*' The notes were obtained and released by the House Banking Committee, which has demanded unedited copies of the transcripts as well as the public release of edited transcripts older than three years" (emphasis added).[33] Pointing to the sudden change in the Fed's public stance, Wessel added: "As recently as last month, Mr. Greenspan testified that releasing a transcript of Fed deliberations 'would so seriously constrain the process of formulating policy as to render those meetings unproductive.'"

Seven days after the hearing, on October 26, the Fed liaison phoned a House Banking Committee staff member (me). He said that a courier would deliver a letter from Greenspan to Congress that would be made public in one hour. It is customary to allow the recipient member of Congress adequate time to read a letter from a governmental entity before making it public. Discourteous, preemptive disclosure may be used to jump ahead of the expected news coverage of the recipient's public reply, the news value of which would be diminished.

GREENSPAN'S MEMORY PROBLEMS AND ADMISSION

As Greenspan admitted in this letter to Congress: "Unedited transcripts exist for each regular meeting of the FOMC held after the meeting of March 15–16, 1976." Greenspan explained that he had some memory problems: "I was aware from the beginning of my tenure that the meetings were being

taped. Several years ago, staff informed me of the existence of transcripts.
. . . I gave the matter of these procedures no further thought until recently.
Indeed, until a staff member jogged my memory in the last few days, I had
been under the impression I first learned about a year ago that transcripts
were being retained."[34]

The congressional publication *The Federal Reserve's 17-Year Secret* summarized Greenspan's responses to the committee in a column of a table
labeled "Date of first knowledge of FOMC transcripts": "Knew in 1987,
then forgot. Told FOMC members on October 15, 1993 that he remembered one year ago. Several days before he sent 10/26/93 letter staff had
reminded him that he knew two years ago."[35]

Anna Schwartz, a distinguished scholar and coauthor of books with
Milton Friedman on the history of the Fed and monetary policy, was
quoted in the *Washington Post* the day after Greenspan's letter was made
public: "Whether there has been a deliberate attempt to pull the wool
over people's eyes, I don't know. But obviously they have not been truthful
all these years."[36] The mock burial was now revealed. The transcripts were
never discontinued. Transcripts did exist. The transcripts from the Burns
Fed are part of the papers Arthur Burns bequeathed to the Gerald R.
Ford Presidential Library. They have been lightly edited by archivists from
the National Archives and Records Administration.[37] In the 1980s, Fed
Chairman Volcker reportedly prevented Fed staff from destroying FOMC
transcripts that were being secretly maintained.[38]

THE SUBMISSION OF INCORRECT
TESTIMONY TO CONGRESS

Gonzalez drew attention to Fed responses that "clearly do not reveal the
existence of tape recordings or transcripts."[39] It was difficult to understand
how Fed officials did not know or forgot that they were being taped or
that FOMC transcripts were being maintained.

Meanwhile, Gonzalez asked the same group of witnesses to send any
material related to an FOMC conference call on October 15, 1993. Some of
the nineteen Fed decision makers responded. Silas Keehn, president of
the Chicago Fed Bank, admitted, "At the time of the October 15 conference call, I expressed concern about the possibility that my testimony as
then drafted might be viewed as inaccurate," adding, "Others expressed
similar views but I am unable to recall who did so or their comments in
any detail."[40]

It should be mandatory for officials of the nation's central bank to give accurate replies to Congress rather than to merely express their concerns to one another. A table from *The Federal Reserve's 17-Year Secret,* entitled "Responses of Presidents Who Refused to Submit Their Notes on the October 15, 1993 FOMC Conference Call," is shown in Figure 6-3.

The report also tabulated an interesting summary of when the Fed officials admitted they knew about the transcripts. One indicated being aware of transcripts as far back as 1989. Most indicated they had not known until immediately before the hearings.

"IF WE KEEP STONEWALLING, WE'RE IN TROUBLE"

Chairman Gonzalez demanded the transcripts of the FOMC conference call during which the Fed had planned its testimony. The Fed resisted. Gonzalez reluctantly agreed to an alternative procedure, in which congressional staff members would go to the Fed and listen to the tapes of that call.[41]

On January 13, 1994, a group of Democratic and Republican staff members from the House Banking Committee, including me, went to the Board of Governors. We listened to a tape recording of the conference call. The room was crowded with Fed and congressional staffers. Over the objection of senior Fed staffers, I turned the tape recorder off after short intervals so that the congressional staffers could make a verbatim record of the conference call.[42]

During this FOMC conference call, some FOMC members displayed an anxious tone: they had been informed that transcripts existed and that the secret might be uncovered at the hearing four days later. Robert Mc-Teer appeared to know what they were doing when he said, "If we keep stonewalling, we're in trouble."[43] A top staff person who would become Fed vice chairman, Donald Kohn, explained what Greenspan intended to do, a clear policy to mislead Congress about the written records of the FOMC, which had been specifically requested in writing: "The Chairman is not highlighting these transcripts . . . We're not waving red flags."[44] Greenspan said he took some solace from his recent testimony experience, on October 13, before House Banking: "I would say Fed-1, House-0. We were on very safe ground earlier this year, and presumed threats to the Federal Reserve System were considerably far less six to nine months ago . . . We can become very vulnerable if this is not handled properly."

Appendix VII

Responses of Presidents Who Refused to Submit Their Notes on the October 15, 1993 FOMC Conference Call

Richard Syron, Boston	"My staff and I have some brief, handwritten notes on the disclosure issue, some of which are from the conference call." [notes not sent]
Edward Boehne, Philadelphia	"I did not take notes during the call. Richard Lang, who was not present for the entire call, took incomplete, handwritten notes. The appropriate procedure for obtaining FOMC-related material not regularly released is to make the request through the office of the Chairman of the FOMC." [refusal to send notes]
J. Alfred Broaddus, Richmond	"This question directs me to provide an extraordinary disclosure of internal deliberative documents and information. I feel obliged to decline to provide such deliberative information at this time, particularly information that may involve individuals whom you have asked me not to consult and that could affect their rights and interests or that would involve otherwise privileged communications. I hope you will understand that my reluctance to release details of internal Federal Reserve conversations unilaterally without the opportunity to consult others affected does not arise from any disrespect for you or your Committee, but from a sense of fairness and obligation to the Federal Reserve System and its officials. As a matter of information, I will tell you that we have no tape-recording of this meeting or memoranda regarding it." [refusal to send notes]
Thomas Melzer, St. Louis	"There were no tape-recordings or memoranda that were prepared by me or my staff regarding the October 15 conference call. I made a few brief notes solely for my personal use; presumably my staff did the same." [notes not sent]
Gary Stern, Minneapolis	"Preston Miller, of our staff, made notes but I am not at liberty to disclose them because they are regarded as information of the FOMC and are subject to restrictions on the disclosure of FOMC information contained in the Committee's Rules Regarding Availability of Information, 12 CAR 271 (Rules)." [refusal to send notes]
Robert D. McTeer, Dallas	"While I do not believe that I have any information that will add to what I've already related, I respectfully urge you to deal with Chairman Greenspan as the spokesman for the FOMC on the questions of releasing internal documents after the FOMC has had a chance to deliberate." [refusal to send notes]

FIGURE 6-3. Appendix VII: Responses of Presidents Who Refused to Submit Their Notes on the October 15, 1993 Conference Call. Note Fed governor Broaddus's claim that "we have no tape-recording of this meeting or memoranda regarding it," although a twenty-four-page transcript of the call was eventually released. Source: House Committee on Banking, Finance and Urban Affairs, *The Federal Reserve's 17-Year Secret*, 46.

Virgil Mattingly, general counsel for the Fed, tried to soften the idea of possible public disclosure of the transcripts: "Well, I don't know what the Justice Department would say, but my suspicion is that they would probably say that we are fully able to put a disclaimer on those transcripts saying that they are rough and unedited and they may or may not reflect what the person actually said." Greenspan replied: "You know, that's like taking the National Enquirer and putting that on the front of it. [Laughter]" Governor Wayne Angell added: "And every newspaper that quoted it would run the full disclosure as the lead!"[45]

A Fed Bank president inquired whether Gonzalez knew about the transcripts or leaks of information. A Fed congressional liaison replied: "I don't have any sense that they have any knowledge whatever of what we've been talking about."[46]

A Fed Bank president stated that some Fed officials had submitted false written statements to Congress: "Some members of the FOMC who happen to be members of the Board of Governors knew about the transcripts. Other members who happen to be Reserve Bank Presidents didn't know and now have submitted to Washington statements saying that they didn't know. And that's going to come out on Tuesday [at the hearing] and that's awkward."[47] Although "awkward" is a gross understatement for describing the submission of false written statements to Congress, Greenspan did not see a problem.[48] His reply bypassed the whole issue of sending knowingly false written statements to Congress.

Edward Boehne, president of the Philadelphia Fed Bank, confirmed the Fed's seventeen-year lie:

Let me just [say], since I may be one of the few people who was around when the Memorandum [of Discussion] was still being done and when the change was made, that to the very best of my recollection I don't believe that Chairman Burns or his successors ever indicated to the Committee as a group that these written transcripts were being kept. What Chairman Burns did indicate at the time when the Memorandum was discontinued was that the meeting was being recorded and the recording was done for the purpose of preparing what we now call the minutes but that it would be recorded over at subsequent meetings. So there was never any indication that there would be a permanent, written record of a transcript nature. And I think that—[49]

Virgil Mattingly added, "That accurately describes what Chairman Burns told the Congress."

"I HOPE THEY DIDN'T THINK THAT WHEN THE GREEN LIGHT WENT ON IT MEANT RAISE INTEREST RATES"

The congressional staff members examined the meeting room used for FOMC and Board meetings. The recording systems were extensive. A voice-activated green light before each member who sat at the large conference table was part of the recording system. An adjacent room contained recording equipment. During FOMC meetings, a cable extended from this adjacent room to a string of microphones that were placed along one wall to make a backup recording. A staff member seated at the head of the conference table next to Greenspan assisted in operating the recording system. Just around the corner of the L-shaped hallway passage from the offices of Greenspan and the other governors was an office with a secretary and a file cabinet containing the FOMC verbatim transcripts.

This array of recoding equipment raised questions. How could any of the nineteen decision makers who had attended many meetings in this meeting room fail to know they were being recorded? How could any of them, including Greenspan, fail to comprehend that the recordings were being carefully typed and stored in an office around the corner from the conference room? How could any of them in carrying out their extremely important decision making, which affected the economic welfare of the nation, fail to ask the Fed staff if the transcripts were being retained?

At a later Banking Committee hearing, Chairman Gonzalez asked one FOMC member, William McDonough, these questions. He had submitted a statement that declared that he did not know he was being recorded at FOMC meetings. Gonzalez quipped: "I hope they didn't think that when the green light went on it meant raise interest rates."[50]

Governor Wayne Angell testified at this later hearing about Greenspan's memory problems: "He said he [Greenspan] forgot about the transcripts. He never forgot about the recording. . . . And I want you to know that in my view, Chairman Greenspan is one of [the] world's most accurate people; and he would never, ever want someone to believe what wasn't the case."[51] That did not seem to explain the memory problems Greenspan said he had, as described in the congressional report.

SHREDDING FED RECORDS AND TURNING
OFF THE TAPE RECORDER

Obviously, Chairman Greenspan's memory of the unedited transcripts was acute when he orchestrated an unrecorded vote to shred them. When, as a result of the Gonzalez hearings and investigations, the transcripts of the FOMC meetings from 1995 were placed on the Fed's Web site in 2001, it was astounding to find that the Fed officials had voted to destroy the unedited transcripts. As a professor of public affairs at the University of Texas, I wrote to Chairman Greenspan on September 3, 2001, praising him for his admission that transparency had not impaired their deliberations. Greenspan had acknowledged at a 1995 FOMC meeting that any prior reluctance to publish the transcripts was ill founded: "I believe there was some strong support within this Committee a year or so ago, mainly on the grounds that we thought the taping inhibited the deliberative process . . . I think the conclusion, with perhaps a qualification [a subpoena for early release of the transcript] . . . is that there is very little evidence that the quality of our discussions have been reduced."[52]

My letter also contained some specific questions. A timely reply was not expected, because the terrorist attacks of September 11, 2001, occurred eight days after the letter was sent. However, Greenspan's senior staff member, Donald Kohn, who became a Fed governor in 2002 and vice chairman in 2006, replied in a letter to me on November 1, 2001. He confirmed that the FOMC members had voted to destroy their unedited transcripts for 1994, 1995, and 1996.

FOMC members were told in 1995 that even though they were "not permitted" to discard "raw transcripts" of meetings before 1994, future unedited transcripts would be "thrown out," and only transcripts edited by the Fed would be retained. FOMC members were also told to move some discussions to the lunch period, when "the tape is not on."[53]

The 1995 transcripts also revealed that FOMC members agreed to pull the plug on the taping system used at their meetings without agreeing on the subjects that should be "off the tape." The term "organizational subjects" was suggested for off-the-tape discussions, although there was little consensus on what that constituted. A subcommittee of the FOMC reported on its deliberations. The subcommittee chair, Governor Alan Blinder, characterized the discussion at the FOMC meeting: "I did not hear any consensus—maybe someone else heard a consensus. Maybe we should just have a vote on whether there should be an 'off the tape' portion. Do you agree?"[54] Greenspan replied: "I agree." He later added: "I am not going to record these votes because we do not have to. There is no legal requirement."[55] The vote was taken without recording members' names. Greenspan announced: "The 'Ayes' have it."[56]

Greenspan's anonymous voting scheme removed the Fed officials' individual fingerprints from the vote to pull the plug on the recording of their meetings for undefined reasons—which means whenever they wanted to block the public or anyone else from finding out what they were saying.[57]

"UNREDACTED" DOES NOT MEAN
"UNEDITED AND UNREDACTED"

A final deceptive practice on shredding Fed records should be emphasized for the interpretation of Greenspan Fed records. Future Fed governor Kohn indicated in his 2001 letter to me that the Fed had notified Congress in 1995 that it would destroy the unedited FOMC transcripts, noting that the Fed "is not obligated to retain draft transcripts." He said that the minutes of the meeting held on January 31–February 1, 1995:

> reads as follows: "As permitted by the National records Act, the recordings and unedited transcripts will be discarded after all the participants at the meeting have reviewed and corrected, as necessary, the transcripts prepared by the Secretariat." In keeping with the National records Act and with the concurrence of officials at the National Archives, the FOMC is not obligated to retain draft transcripts or any meeting recordings used in their preparation. *What must be retained are the edited transcripts, i.e., those that incorporate member corrections in both their redacted and unredacted versions.* The redacted versions are released to the public after five years; the unredacted versions will be sent to the National Archives after 30 years. (emphasis added)[58]

Notice the word "incorporate," which is emphasized. The law, according to the letter, says "incorporate" not "shred." The corrected page from the FOMC MOD of April 20, 1976 (Figure 6-1), from the Burns Fed, was lightly edited by archivists at the National Archives. It is very different from the destruction of source FOMC transcripts, which the FOMC approved in a nonrecorded vote in 1995. Regardless of how the law cited above can be interpreted or twisted or even broken without consequence, Fed officials, who are unelected agents serving the public, should diligently preserve their source records for full accountability. That did not happen in the 1990s, and the practice may be continuing.

Kohn also said that Greenspan had sent a letter to six members of Congress in 1995 with this information. This congressional notification was in a class with the previously discussed 1962 Fed plan for using an obscure announcement that would not be fully perceived or properly understood to notify Congress about the new foreign-exchange operations it was undertaking.[59] This was how the deception worked in 1995. A 1995 Greenspan letter looked as if it heralded the new procedures for openness at the Fed, but there was a terrible caveat: "I [Greenspan] am writing to bring to your attention recent decisions of the Federal Open Market Committee (FOMC) on disclosure of its policy and deliberations. As may be seen in the enclosed press release of February 2, 1995, the FOMC has formalized the procedures for greater openness in policy making that it has been using for the past year. We believe these procedures will make our policy intent as transparent as possible to market participants without losing our flexibility or undermining our deliberative process."[60]

Greenspan announced the implementation of a formal practice that would require FOMC transcripts to be released after a five-year lag. This appeared to be the Fed's formal statement of its transparency rules. Then Greenspan used sleight of hand. With the shredding card up his sleeve, he held up the transparency card: "A complete, unredacted version of the transcripts of each FOMC meeting" would be retained, and then turned over to the National Archives after thirty years. Hail the rules for transparency: they will continue a policy of retaining the unedited transcripts!

No, that is wrong. On the second page of his letter, Greenspan states that unedited transcripts will be discarded: "As permitted by the National Records Act, the tapes [recordings of FOMC meetings] and unedited transcripts will be discarded when all the participants at the meeting have approved the lightly edited written transcript." So the Greenspan Fed is really shredding the unedited FOMC transcripts. A new distinction has been added to the vocabulary of deceptive record shredders: "unredacted" does not mean "unedited and unredacted."

Transparency, accountability, and trust are sharply curtailed by this practice, cleverly hidden by Greenspan, who publicly displayed his strong support for transparency and accountability: "It cannot be acceptable in a democratic society that a group of individuals are vested with important responsibilities, without being open to full public scrutiny and accountability."[61]

CHAPTER 7

CORRUPTED AIRPLANES
AND COMPUTER MICE

"FED PRICING SYSTEM FLOUTS PRIVATE
SECTOR—AS USUAL"

Allegations of breaking the law are an informative introduction to the Fed's airplane fleet. The headline "Fed Pricing System Flouts Private Sector—As Usual" appeared in an article in the *American Banker* in 2002.[1] The authors, Gilbert Schwartz and Robert G. Ballen, held that the Fed was flagrantly violating the Monetary Control Act of 1980: the Fed itself announced that its revenues would not cover its costs of clearing checks.[2] The Fed was still operating its check-clearing operations at a loss in 2004, as shown in the press release reproduced as Figure 7-1. The Fed was subsidizing the check-clearing services it sold to private-sector banks, resulting in lower prices for the Fed services.[3] It is not difficult to see that the subsidy would impair the Fed's actual or potential private-sector competitors if it allowed the Fed to undercut them, a condition that clearly violated the spirit, though maybe not the letter, of the Monetary Control Act.[4]

Another serious problem was the corrupt operation of the Fed's airplane fleet. Henry B. Gonzalez had carried out investigations of the Fed's approximately fifty contracted airplanes in 1995. Congresswoman Carolyn Maloney, (D-NY) who worked with Gonzalez, carried on additional oversight. Maloney was responsible for obtaining Fed witnesses for congressional hearings, including the manager of the Fed airplane operations, the accountant for those operations, and another member of the small staff that supervised the operations, all employed at the Boston Fed Bank. They testified in 1997. These three witnesses as well as other information obtained in the Gonzalez investigation blew the whistle on the Fed's corrupt

Federal Reserve Release

Press Release

November 4, 2004

Release Date:

For immediate release

The Federal Reserve Board on Thursday approved fee schedules for Federal Reserve Bank payment services for depository institutions (priced services), effective January 3, 2005.

The Reserve Banks project that they will recover 100.1 percent of all their priced services costs in 2005 and estimate that **they will recover 94.6 percent of these costs in 2004.**

From 1994 to 2003, the Reserve Banks recovered 97.8 percent of priced services costs, including operating costs, imputed costs, and targeted return on equity (ROE, or net income), which amounts to a ten-year total net income of slightly less than $500 million.

FIGURE 7-1. Federal Reserve press release, November 4, 2004. The Fed admits that in 2004 it sold its services at subsidized prices, in apparent violation of the Monetary Control Act of 1980 (emphasis added). Source: Federal Reserve Web site, http://www.federalreserve.gov/Boarddocs/Press/other/2004/20041104/default.htm.

bookkeeping. There was some scrambling at the Fed. The Fed closed the office at the Boston Fed Bank where these courageous federal witnesses were employed.

Few showed an interest in pursing the problems, least of all the inspector general of the Fed or the Justice Department, led by Janet Reno. Both had been contacted. Even banks and private firms competing with the Fed for check-clearing services were reluctant to complain. They had to suffer in silence, and some were even intimidated into praising the powerful governmental regulator that had the power to approve or stop trillion-dollar bank mergers and acquisitions, and to impair the use of modern technology with regulations. Consumers have been and are significantly affected by the Fed's apparent violation of the intended purpose of the 1980 law. Hopefully, the description presented here will arouse some public interest as well as oversight and legal remedies by the congressional Banking Committees. In the meantime, modern digital technology—the attack of computer mice—caused immense changes after 2003, when the Fed finally supported a past-due effort to feed paper checks to the mice.

THE PONY EXPRESS AND PAPER CHECKS

The United States central bank's fleet of approximately fifty airplanes, which still haul cancelled paper checks around the country in the twenty-first century, should be depicted next to an exhibit in the Postal Building of the Smithsonian Institution Museum. Artifacts from the Pony Express, which delivered the mail in the nineteenth century, are displayed there. The Pony Express was gradually discontinued after the first telegram was sent to California, in 1861.

The Fed started its telegraphic funds-transfer service in 1918. It is now called Fedwire. Together with a private wire-transfer system, CHIPS, it transmitted $2 trillion in electronic payments daily in 2002.[5] The Fed has electronically processed payroll transactions for private businesses through its automatic clearinghouse (ACH) since 1972.[6] Given the availability of electronic methods for transferring payment information, how was it possible in the early twenty-first century that paper-check usage by U.S. consumers substantially exceeded usage in many other developed countries?[7] There are many reasons for this discrepancy. The most inexcusable reasons have been the Fed's own policies.[8]

The condition of the payment system in the United States in the early 1980s may appear to today's Internet surfers to be from antiquity. In 1984,

Senate Banking chairman Jake Garn complained to the Fed about the long time it took to return a paper check that had bounced for insufficient funds. It had to be returned to the bank where it had been initially deposited. Garn asked: "Is it true that it may take the participants in a check collection as long as two weeks to return a check to the bank of first deposit, even when each of the participants have [*sic*] acted timely under the Uniform Commercial Code? How is this possible?"[9] The Fed replied with a description that seems like something out of the stagecoach era:

> Under the Uniform Commercial Code (u.c.c), each institution has until midnight of the banking day following the banking day it received the check to make timely return. . . . Furthermore, it takes additional time to transport the check physically between each of the institutions in the original collection chain. Consequently, depending upon the extent to which the U.S. mail is used for transportation, the number of institutions involved in the collection of the check, the intervening weekends and holidays, and the geographic location of the institutions, *it may take as long as two weeks* [after] the payor institution has dishonored the check [for it] to be returned to the institution of first deposit. (emphasis added)[10]

The Fed may as well have said: "Saddle up the horses. We'll be riding into Dallas with the bad check at the next full moon."

A CHECK KITER'S DREAM: THE WONDERFUL
WORLD OF FLOAT

The slow clearing of checks was a gift to kiters. Kiters pay their bills with checks drawn on insufficient funds. When it took two or three weeks for an out-of-state check to clear, kiters could cover an incoming check with a check drawn on another account with insufficient funds. With the proper timing, they could continue to play that game and make purchases while having net cash balances of zero. Passing bad checks, which occurs in this kiting scheme, is illegal. If the banks suspect kiting, they may place the depositor on a "collections basis," which means the bank withholds crediting a deposit until the check clears.

Banks were making money on "bank float": the time between when a check is deposited and when its value is subtracted from the account it is drawn on. The Fed would credit a bank for a deposited check before collecting its value. This time interval allowed two banks—the bank the check was drawn on and the bank of deposit—to use the funds as part of their reserves. Both banks could buy interest-earning assets with the reserves.

Crediting a bank for a deposited check one day before the check is collected is equivalent to making a one-day zero-interest loan to the depositing bank. The Fed was required in 1980 to price this kind of float as if it were a loan at a particular rate of interest.[11]

The Fed made an effort to reduce float in the 1980s. One step was the reorganization of the office that managed its airplane fleet, the Interdistrict Transportation System (ITS). Unfortunately, the story of the ITS related below reveals how bank float was reduced at the expense of encouraging corrupt practices and subsidized prices that impaired the implementation of modern technology. The Fed and private-sector banks were further induced to reduce float by a 1990 law enacted to help consumers get timely credit for their deposits. Since 1990, nonlocal checks have been required to be available to depositors by the fifth business day after they are deposited.[12]

THE INEFFICIENCY OF PAPER CHECKS

If, in 1995, someone wrote a ten-dollar check for lunch in a Los Angeles restaurant, and the check was drawn on a bank account in New York City, the check would first be deposited at the restaurant's LA bank. If the bank used the Fed's services, the check would be driven to the Los Angeles branch of the San Francisco Fed Bank. The LA Fed Branch would have the check driven to an airport facility, where a Fed airplane would pick it up near midnight and fly it to an airport at a Fed hub city, probably Midway Airport, in Chicago, since that airport and Love Field Airport, in Dallas, would be the closest of the Fed's five hubs.[13] The check would be put on another Fed airplane and flown to another hub facility, Teterboro Airport, in New Jersey. Barring bad weather or problems with the aircraft, the check would arrive early in the morning, then be driven to the New York Fed Bank. From there it would be driven to the New York bank on which it was drawn. The Learjet 35 and Learjet 25 (each with a speed of 500 mph, and payloads of 3,500 and 3,000 pounds, respectively) were the primary carriers on cross-country flights. Smaller, propeller aircraft were generally used for transportation from the Fed's hub sites.

The process of paying for that lunch—involving a 2,800-mile nighttime airplane ride, various truck deliveries, and sorting costs—was expensive compared to electronic clearing. According to some estimates, the cost of a paper-check payment compared to some systems of digital payments was over $2.50.[14] If the paper check bounced, it would be physically returned to the restaurant through the same convoluted system.

Rather than using the Fed to clear paper checks, a major private competitor, AirNet Systems, Inc. (formerly known as US Check), which had more airplanes than the Fed, offered bank-to-bank clearing of paper checks. AirNet currently operates more than 120 aircraft, including 35 Learjets. It is a small-package shipper and has customers in more than 100 "major markets" nationwide, according to its Web site in 2007, a period when computer mice were taking big bites out of AirNet's business, as described below.[15]

Few people realize how critical the payment system is to the functioning of a market society. Its collapse could shut down much of the economy and create chaotic conditions, since people and businesses would not be able to receive payments or access funds to make payments. Bad weather and events such as the September 11, 2001, terrorist attacks delay air transportation of paper checks, substantially increase float, and impair the entire payment system.

The national emergency following the September 11, 2001, attacks included the closing of all airports. There was a crisis in the payment system. The Fed's outmoded paper-check-clearing system included its fifty-three contracted airplanes, which were now grounded. Credit cards, ATM networks, and debit cards could function normally, since these systems operated with electronic communication.

The Fed justifiably put a good face on its personnel's rapid response to the crisis: "Unlike the Y2K scare it was the lack of air transportation that impaired the payments system, as every weeknight the Fed relies on this system to move about 43,000 pounds of checks among the 45 Fed processing sites." By evening of the day of the attacks (Tuesday), "the Fed dispatched several hundred check-filled trucks, via ground hub and spoke network. On that and the following nights, the Fed delivered about 75 percent of its normal volume by truck." It received help from the "FAA and U.S. Air force to resume flights of courier planes, and by late Wednesday, these jets returned to the air, even though commercial airports were not yet open. On Thursday, the Fed began working with various check transportation vendors, and through the weekend patched together a network of Fed and charter flights that represented what one Fed employee described as a 'whirlwind of improvisation.'"[16]

The slow delivery of transaction information caused the Fed to absorb "billions of dollars of float during the days it continued to provide credit to depositing banks on money that had not been collected." These were interest-free loans to the banks and an invitation to pass bad checks and drawn on balances that had yet to clear (kiting). On September 12, the Fed lent the banks "$45.5 billion, up from $99 million the Wednesday before."[17] According to one official of the Richmond Fed Bank: "The Federal Reserve at one point injected more than $100 billion in additional liquidity, an unprecedented sum."[18]

THE UNITED STATES FELL BEHIND

In the 1990s, nearly all developed economies, including most in Europe, were more advanced than that of the United States in switching from paper checks to the electronic processing of transactions. A 1999 survey showed that paper checks were a substantially smaller proportion of transactions in Canada, Great Britain, Sweden, Italy, Belgium, Germany, the Netherlands, and Switzerland than in the United States.[19] These substantial differences (68.56 percent of payments by paper checks in the United States versus 31.48 percent in Canada, which had the next-highest percentage) were not because of the unavailability of more advanced technologies. There had been an explosion in the implementation of new technologies for electronic processing since the 1980s.[20]

The Fed was very slow to advocate changing state and federal laws to allow for the rapid implementation of electronic processing. It imposed regulations for the presentment of transactions (called settlement times), protecting its paper-check-clearing operations. These regulations set the time of day when a Fed Bank would accept payments to be credited or debited from a private bank's account. The Fed's actions threw sand in the gears of technological change, the expected inertia of a governmental bureaucracy with substantial resources dedicated to clearing paper checks.

THE INVESTIGATION OF THE FED'S AIRPLANE FLEET

In 1995, the House Banking Committee received information about the Federal Reserve's contracted airplane fleet, which was managed by ITS at the Federal Reserve Bank of Boston (FRBB, or the Boston Fed Bank). Gonzalez ordered an investigation. He sent me to Boston to visit the Boston Fed Bank; I was accompanied by the Banking Committee's minority counsel, Armando Falcon, and an expert from the Federal Aviation Administration (FAA).

When we arrived at the Boston Fed Bank in 1995 to interview employees, officials of the Boston Fed Bank decided on a preferred method for this congressional investigation. They did not want us to interview Fed employees in private. Formal interviews would be done with the full knowledge of the Fed, and all written questions to employees and their written answers would be sent to the Boston Fed Bank and to the Board of Governors, mainly to Fed chairman Greenspan.

The extensive documentation from the Boston Fed Bank and interviews with Fed employees were the basis for the report from Congressman Gonzalez, *Waste and Abuse in the Federal Reserve's Payment System*. A large number of outrageous problems were found, including paying for airplanes that did not exist—one was called the "phantom" aircraft by personnel at the Teterboro airport. The Fed's bidding procedures for vendor services were severely flawed. One vendor had been receiving multimillion-dollar contracts without competitive bidding since 1987 for an operation in which more than 80 percent of the work involved unskilled labor loading and unloading Fed aircraft. The Fed paid two vendors for the same airplane services, although it knew that the FAA had permanently grounded one of the vendor's aircraft.[21] The Fed's accountant did not want to pay the false charges. The Fed competed against private vendors while offering subsidized prices, yet it overcharged the U.S. Treasury to transport its cancelled checks.

Two persons from the Board of Governors read the final report at the office of the House Banking Committee's minority staff director, Kelsay Meek, in 1996. Meek asked them to read the report, and they spent substantial time looking at it in the office. They did not indicate that there were any factually incorrect statements. Selections from the report are included in an appendix to this book; they reveal abusive management practices and corrupted bookkeeping at the Greenspan Fed.

JUSTICE PASSES TO THE IG

After substantial evidence was collected, Gonzalez asked Attorney General Janet Reno to investigate and determine if any laws had been broken. The Justice Department told Congressman Gonzalez to take the matter to the Fed inspector general (IG). This was a foolish diversion from investigating serious charges against a powerful governmental bureaucracy.

Justice must have known that the Fed IG is the only IG of a major governmental bureaucracy who can be fired by the leaders of the bureaucracy: "The Chairman can prohibit the Inspector General from carrying out or completing an audit or investigation, or from issuing a subpoena, if the Chairman determines 'that sensitive information is involved.'"[22] Furthermore, the Fed's Office of the Inspector General must receive its financing from the Board (see Chapter 12 for a recommendation to change this authority). The IG produces nicely bound reports, sometimes marked "confidential," which seemingly enhances their contents. He can suggest a few improvements. The IG's budget ($7.8 million in 2002–2003) can be removed by the governors he might investigate; nevertheless they supply the Office of the Inspector General with rooms, furniture, personnel, paper, report covers, and salaries—all the stage props of an investigative, independent IG.

Regarding the investigation of the Fed's airplane fleet, the Fed IG informed me that he was uncertain whether he had jurisdiction over the Fed Banks, including the one in Boston. How quaint. The *Washington Post* reported: "Federal Reserve officials say they have seen nothing to warrant a criminal investigation," although they will "change some procedures as a result of his [Gonzalez's] inquiry."[23]

The Fed made some changes after the report was made public. For example, the report identified no-bid contracts for a company called Santa Express.[24] In response, the Fed hired employees to replace contracted employees from Santa Express. These personnel loaded and unloaded bags of checks at the Fed's facilities at its five hub airports. The Fed closed its hub facility at the Teterboro Airport, where the employees had recalled the phantom plane. It opened a new facility at the Philadelphia International Airport.

John Martin wanted to record some video of the new facilities for a segment called "Your Money" on *ABC World News Tonight* with Peter Jennings. Martin called the Boston Fed Bank, and officials there were extremely cordial and said they wanted to cooperate. Calls went back and forth, but the Fed failed to authorize Martin and his camera crew to film at the new Fed facilities in Philadelphia. Finally, after more than a month, Martin gave up trying to get permission from Fed officials. It seemed ridiculous for them to refuse permission for the U.S. media to visit an international airport to see cancelled paper checks being loaded on airplanes. Martin finally entered the airport through another entrance. Pictures of the Fed's operations at the Philadelphia hub appeared on *ABC News* on August 13, 1997. They did not show a well-organized operation.

Some of the fifty-pound bags of cancelled checks were dropped on the tarmac and then retrieved by Fed employees as they brought them out to the airplane. Martin also broadcast some of the findings from the congressional report, and Congresswoman Maloney spoke about the Fed's check-clearing problems.

Fed officials had successfully waved off the serious allegations of abusive practices with inane comments or with no comment at all. The daily trade paper of the banking industry captured the Fed's attitude: "'What we regard most of the report to be are honest differences of opinion about management decisions,' said Paul M. Connolly, the first vice president of the Federal Reserve Bank of Boston responsible for the check transport system."[25]

Fed officials shamelessly offered the most extravagantly absurd excuses for their mismanagement. The Fed said that its contract for a warm standby jet at Teterboro was fulfilled even when the airplane was not there. The Fed claimed that its mere existence, somewhere, maybe in maintenance, was sufficient. This lame excuse for corrupt practices is symptomatic of the lack of transparency and accountability in the Fed's operations.

Greenspan also took the occasion of his 1996 confirmation hearings to trivialize the findings regarding the Fed's airplane fleet. He labeled payments for nonexistent airplanes, no-bid contracts, falsified accounting records, and other practices as simply the products of management decisions. Greenspan said that the Fed airplane fleet "requires Federal Reserve management to make numerous, and complex decisions every day, constantly balancing efforts to improve service, reduce float, and operating costs. In hindsight are there some decisions that should have been made differently? Almost surely. But from a broad perspective, ITS had been managed effectively in our judgment."[26]

The only other witness was Ralph Nader, who asked that a copy of the congressional report on the investigation of the Fed's airplane fleet be placed in the record. Nader spoke to a nearly empty chamber, since the reporters and most of the public audience and senators had left after Greenspan testified. Greenspan was being hailed as a major reason for U.S. prosperity of the 1990s, so his dismissive statements stifled inquiries.

GREENSPAN AND RIVLIN: FABULISTS

The ITS manager, the accountant, and the other courageous employees who had spent many years running ITS attempted to correct some of the

information the Fed had sent to Congress. One example of this information was supplied to the House Banking Committee under a cover letter
from Greenspan. Gonzalez replied to Greenspan: "*The Central Bank of the
United States is heavily subsidizing its canceled paper check transportation network, ITS, in an effort to increase its share of business:* In your [Greenspan's]
May 16, 1996 letter the Board Staff states: 'For the period January through
March 1996, the commercial check component of ITS recovered 86 percent of its costs'" (original emphasis).[27] Gonzalez also called Greenspan's
attention to statements by "the ITS staffer who calculated cost/match-
ing at ITS: 'My preliminary estimate of costs recovered from commercial checks for the period January through March is 59%.'"[28] This meant
that the prices that the Fed charged banks to transport their checks were
heavily subsidized.

Problems raised in the congressional report should have been in full
view at the House Banking subcommittee hearing held on September 16,
1997. Congresswoman Maloney had requested a hearing at which some of
these ITS employees could testify, and subcommittee chairman Michael
Castle (R-DE) agreed.

The night before the hearing, when the Fed knew its employees would
appear and radically contradict Boston Fed Bank documents sent to Congress, Congresswoman Maloney received a letter from Greenspan. It contained a weird and classic Greenspan garblement. Finally, caught in an expected outpouring of truth, he was forced to admit what had been found
in the Gonzalez investigation. Because of the way the Fed was operating
the airplane fleet, the amount it charged for airplane services did not cover
the costs. These were subsidized services. Unlike his memory problems
regarding the FOMC transcripts, this Greenspan admission was weirdly
disguised as being imaginary: "The loss on ITS is really a fiction because
the value it creates to accomplish broader efficiency in check services far
exceeds the amount that our internal records reflect as a loss."[29]

Greenspan, an ardent advocate for capitalism and free markets, also
claimed in the letter that the government could operate the Fed's aircraft fleet less expensively than a private-sector company. This was a plea
for continued nationalization of the management of a substantial part of
the nation's check-clearing system: "Some observers believe that the ITS
network could be replicated by private-sector couriers at a lower cost. It
must be noted, however, that the Federal Reserve contracts with private-
sector couriers to operate the ITS network and awards contracts based
on competitive bids. We are unaware of any vendors who can meet the
stringent delivery schedules to provide funds availability at a cost less

than we currently expend."[30] Had Greenspan forgotten about the Fed subsidies? Greenspan's reference to competitive bidding overlooked or disregarded the evidence presented in the Gonzalez report about abusive bidding practices and no-bid contracts. That evidence had been sent to Greenspan and other Fed officials.

The next day, the press left the hearing room after the fanciful testimony of Vice Chair Alice Rivlin, a former director of the Office of Management and Budget. She said, among other things, "A loss is not necessarily a subsidy" and "We cover the marginal costs when that network is used." "That network is used" seven days a week, counting the contracted service on the weekends, and what about covering total costs?[31]

Three long-term ITS employees, including the ITS manager, testified in the mostly empty chambers. The ITS employee who for many years had been in charge of calculating cost-recovery data testified that there had been a 25 to 30 percent subsidy at ITS, and that data had been manipulated "to give us a more favorable position" in calculating cost recovery. The testimony supported the contention that the Fed had sent Congress falsified reports.

SHIELDING THE WHISTLE-BLOWERS

These three longtime ITS employees were informed that their office at the Boston Fed Bank would be closed. A new air-transportation management office named Check Relay was opened at the Atlanta Federal Reserve Bank. The Fed's actions indicated that these courageous Fed employees needed protection. Congressman Robert Ney (R-OH) and Congresswoman Carolyn Maloney notified Greenspan that the employees were federal witnesses and that there should be no retaliation. The employees were retained at the Boston Fed Bank, but transferred to jobs that did not draw on their long experience running the Fed's airplane fleet. Some later retired. They honorably served the public interest.

RAIDING THE PENSION FUND

In the 1990s, the Greenspan Fed used a "pension cost credit" from its employees' pension fund to meet the legal requirement that it cover the costs of its check-clearing services. The pension fund's stock investments rose in value during the 1990s. In 1995, a consulting firm hired by the Fed found the retirement plan to be overfunded—it contained more than the actuarial value needed to pay expected future benefits—by $1.3 billion, or 45 percent of its assets.[32] How convenient! The Fed's excuse for dipping into the pension fund was that it was following financial accounting standards.[33] This explanation led to a bizarre pricing policy: the Fed could price its services below those offered by private-sector competitors that had not done as well in the stock market. And why were employees' premiums not reduced if the pension fund had excess money?

The use of employee pension funds to subsidize the check-clearing services would have been prohibited by a version of the Bank Modernization Bill (S 900) that a Senate-House conference committee was considering. Section 317 of that bill was suggested by Senator Harry Reid and placed in an amendment by Senate Banking Committee chairman Phil Gramm (R-TX). It required full cost recovery for each of the services the Fed sold, "excluding the effect of any pension cost credit."

Greenspan notified Jim Leach (R-IA) in a strongly worded letter (dated June 24, 1999) that the Federal Reserve Board was opposed to the amendment. The amendment was killed behind the scenes, almost certainly by Greenspan, who was using his formidable political muscle to lobby for the Financial Services Modernization Act, as it was grandly called.[34] This amendment might have exposed the Fed to a charge of budgetary chicanery for using its employees' pension fund this way. That had to be stopped during the march to financial "modernization."

THE FED'S SELF-FULFILLING ROAD-SHOW INQUIRY

The Fed organized its own committee, chaired by Rivlin, which traveled around the country "to receive the views of representatives from over 450 institutions." The committee posed a rhetorical question: would there be considerable disruption if the Fed withdrew from the ACH system? Of course there will be disruption if the Fed pulls the rug out from under a major part of the payment system. As expected, when the chief regulators interviewed the regulated bankers, the responses were very satisfying to the Fed. Surely, many bankers were somewhat intimidated about appearing before their regulators. Would they dare to suggest changes detrimental to the power of the governmental bureaucracy that rules on the mergers and acquisitions affecting the profitability of their banks?

Patrick K. Barron, the retail payments product director at the Atlanta Fed, commented on the Rivlin committee study: "Many of us began to dust off our resumes . . . However, we quickly put them away as the results of the study confirmed a desire by banks for the Fed to remain active in the payments system as an operator, even a leader, and facilitator for change as well as an 'enlightened' regulator."[35] The Fed's self-fulfilling road-show inquiry did not change the reality of the dire effects that advances in information technology and innovative private-sector competitors were having on much of the Fed bureaucracy.

The final Rivlin committee report includes a cryptic conclusion about the subsidies for check clearing. The committee could "find no evidence to suggest that the Reserve Banks subsidize check collection services. Over the last decade, the check service met its cost recovery goals and earned profits that exceeded $200 million after recovering its actual and imputed costs. (see attachment 2) In addition, the Federal Reserve's cost accounting methodologies have been reviewed and were deemed reasonable and appropriate by outside auditors."[36] Attachment 2, "Check Service Pro Forma Income Statement," was scrubbed of important details: five lines on revenue and expense. Cost recovery is said to average 99.5 percent of revenue. There is no mention of money taken from the employee pension funds to cover the costs.

A Fed Board governor ran up the banner for preserving the Fed's bureaucracy, essentially issuing a warning to "keep your hands off our check-clearing operations," as reported by *Wall Street Journal* reporter John Wilke: "In Washington, Fed officials reject the suggestion they should leave check-clearing to private companies. 'That's how the Fed banks make their living,' says Edward Kelley, the Fed governor who oversees many Fed bank activities and is leading an effort to improve planning and efficiency. 'We'll be in that business until checks disappear or the Congress takes us out of it.'"[37]

THE ATTACK OF THE COMPUTER MICE

The Fed estimated that "roughly 42 billion checks were written in the United States in 2000, down from 50 billion in 1995."[38] With money transactions only a mouse click away, modern digital-information technology was attacking the Fed and its chief private-sector competitor, Air-Net. One estimate in 2000 of the savings to the U.S. economy of switching from paper checks to electronic processing was $100 billion.[39]

Long after the technology train had left the station and long after the Fed tried to throw sand in its gears with its subsidies for paper checks and its check-settlement rules, the Fed ran to get onboard. In 2003 the Fed proposed the Check Truncation Act of 2003, also known as the Check 21 Act, which would make electronic check images a legal substitute for paper checks starting in October 2004: "Substitute checks are printed reproductions made from digital images of the original paper check. The legal status of substitute checks will facilitate the truncation of checks and greater use of electronic check processing."[40] Truncation meant that paper checks could be converted to digital images. The images would be sent to the bank on which the checks were drawn; the paper check no longer had to be physically transported by ground and air transportation.

Check 21 had rapid effects on the Fed bureaucracy. The Fed had plans in 2004 to reduce the number of its check-clearing operations from forty-five to twenty-three by 2006. In 2004 the Fed stated that 4,300 of its approximately 23,000 employees "work in the check function."[41]

AirNet was bitten harshly by computer mice. On September 28, 2006, the Dow Jones Newswires reported: "AirNet Systems, 3 Bank Customers to End Some Services. These customers accounted for $500,000 to $1 million in bank-services revenue during the company's last quarter."[42]

HACKERS, PHISHERS, BLACKOUTS, AND E-BOMB DETONATIONS

The attack of the computer mice comes with serious national-security concerns. By substituting a digital image for paper checks, the safeguards of watermarks and original signatures are removed. If truncation causes banks to destroy paper checks and maintain only their images, it will be more difficult to trace forged or imitation checks. Phishing, a term that denotes practices such as e-mailing official-looking documents from a bank to obtain passwords or account numbers, can occur. Hackers will be busy trying to get into bank or customer computers to steal information. Banks should retain paper checks for substantial periods or return them to depositors, unless sophisticated identification procedures are used when the checks are accepted for deposit or payment.

Those are relatively small problems compared to the disruption of digital transmissions and electric power. The massive power outage that blacked out the northeastern United States and parts of Canada on August 14, 2003, closed down much of the retail payment system, including ATMs. It did not cause sustained disruptions, since it was short-lived and was not a terrorist attack. Many banks and the Fed have backup power generators and distant backup facilities.

There is a more damaging potential threat to the payment system, which should not be ignored: an electromagnetic pulse (EMP) from a device called an E-bomb. If one were exploded in the atmosphere 200 miles above Kansas, it "could propagate an EMP enveloping the entire United States. Electrical systems connected to things that can conduct current, like wires, antennas, and metal objects, will suffer significant damage" with "irreparable damage to microcircuits, and even disabling of satellites. Fortunately, electronic equipment that is turned off is less likely to be damaged."[43] There is a need to prepare for the explosion of an E-bomb even at lower heights, such as over a metropolitan area. An E-bomb "can today easily [be constructed] . . . using 1940s technology for only $400."[44] Metallic shielding of auxiliary communication systems might be appropriate. That will depend on experts' advice and governmental action.

For national-security reasons, the Fed should retain some paper-check facilities as backups. The Fed or some more inclusive federal entity, perhaps the Homeland Security Department, must impose and continually improve required multiple backups and other protections for the digital payment system. There will be a continual fight to keep digital systems safe from criminal intrusions.

Federal deposit insurance regulators have imposed regulatory requirements on insured banks to inhibit theft, embezzlement, and bank takeovers from old-fashioned gun-wielding criminals. Evolving hacking technologies operating within a digital payment system will breed unseen criminals with more effective methods. A modern regulatory entity for the nation's digital payment system, independent of the banks it regulates, is needed.

Chapter 8

Standing in the Door Against Civil Rights

IT WAS AS IF THE INSTITUTION HAD SLEPT THROUGH THE 1960S AND 1970S

The Federal Reserve's almost emotional insistence on total independence often leads the Fed into some dark corners. Under Greenspan, the Federal Reserve Board had great difficulty coming to grips with the civil rights revolution. It was as if the institution had slept through the 1960s and 1970s. Alabama governor George C. Wallace's stand in the schoolhouse door in 1963 seems almost enlightened in the face of the Fed's claim of not even being covered by the Civil Rights Act of 1964.

The Greenspan Fed consistently said that it was not covered by this law because of a technicality that, even if true, the Fed did nothing to correct. The Greenspan Fed affirmed that it "subscribes fully to the basic goals and the spirit of the Civil Rights Act of 1964," as shown in a 1995 letter from the director of the Fed's in-house Equal Employment Opportunity Programs Office (Figure 8-1).

Greenspan repeated this assertion to Gonzalez in 1996: "While the Board is technically not subject to the Equal Opportunity Act, the Board long ago decided that it should act in strict conformity with the precepts of the Act, which implements national policy."[1] That was pleasing rhetoric.

Congressmen Gonzalez and Jesse Jackson, Jr. (D-IL), in a press release and letter to Greenspan in 1997, cited recent legal actions against the Fed for racial discrimination, including one in which the verdict went against the Fed (described below). Contrary to Greenspan's position, they noted: "The EEOC informed the General Counsel of the House Banking commit-

BOARD OF GOVERNORS
OF THE
FEDERAL RESERVE SYSTEM
WASHINGTON, D.C. 20551

EQUAL EMPLOYMENT
OPPORTUNITY PROGRAMS
OFFICE

October 27, 1995

Mr. Robert Walker
The Equal Employment Opportunity
    Commission
Office of Federal Operations
Federal Sector Programs
1801 L Street, N.W.
Washington, D.C. 20507

Dear Mr. Walker:

        The Federal Reserve Board's annual statistical report of
discrimination complaints is enclosed for your information.

        The data entered on EEOC form 462 does not accurately
reflect the Federal Reserve Board's system of recordkeeping on EEO
counseling and complaint activity because the Board operates on a
calendar rather than a fiscal year basis. In order to provide you
with information on our activity for the period of October 1, 1994
to September 30, 1995, this office combined and reported its
fourth quarter 1994 thru third quarter 1995 data.

        While the Board of Governors of the Federal Reserve
System has taken the position that is not subject to the Civil
Rights Act of 1964, as amended, and its associated executive
orders and regulations, it subscribes fully to their basic goals
and spirit. The Board has an effective counseling and complaint
process governed by established internal regulations and
procedures found in our Rules Regarding Equal Opportunity at 12
CFR Part 268.

        If we may be of further assistance, please contact me at
452-2883 or Dorothea Thompson on 452-2077.

                            Sincerely,

                            Sheila Clark
                            EEO Programs Director

Enclosure

FIGURE 8-1. Letter from Sheila Clark, director of Equal Employment Opportunity Programs at the Fed, to Robert Walker at the EEOC, October 27, 1995. Ms. Clark repeats the Fed party line on racial discrimination: "While the Board of Governors of the Federal Reserve System has taken the position that it is not subject to the Civil Rights Act of 1964 . . . it subscribes fully to their basic goals and spirit." Source: author's collection.

tee in 1989: 'It is the EEOC's position that Title VII applies to the Board of Governors of the Federal Reserve System.'"[2]

One month later, Greenspan, while still waving the Fed's independence flag, made a suggestion for amending a section of the 1964 Civil Rights Act so that it would cover the Fed: "The amendment would not affect the Board's statutory independence from other laws respecting federal employment. Accordingly, this proposed change is not inconsistent with the important principle of central bank independence within the federal government."[3] If this is what he wanted to do, he should have publicly supported Jackson's legislation that is described below.

The Greenspan Fed's artful dance was all the more incongruous given that the Federal Reserve was charged with enforcing laws to eliminate discrimination in lending by the nation's banks. Not only was the Fed Bank supposed to be a model for diversity in the banking system that it regulates, but it was charged with enforcing specific laws against discriminatory loan practices: the Equal Credit Opportunity Act (ECOA), which "ensures that all consumers are given an equal chance to obtain credit"; the Community Reinvestment Act (CRA); the Home Mortgage Disclosure Acts; and the Fair Housing Acts.[4]

For the Federal Reserve, the issue was more than academic and more than a simple case of once again intoning the Fed's independence mantra. A number of civil rights cases have been brought against the Federal Reserve, and several were pending in courts. President Lyndon Baines Johnson and a series of House Banking chairmen had taken actions to bring diversity to the Fed and to end gender and racial bias there in the 1960s and 1970s. Those efforts did not seem to extend into the 1990s. New, abusive management actions—including firing black female employees who sued for racial discrimination problems—emerged at the Greenspan Fed.

LBJ, SISTER GENEROSE GERVAIS, AND JEAN CROCKETT

President Johnson made an important move toward diversity at the Fed in 1966. He nominated the first black member to serve on the Board of Governors: Andrew Brimmer, a distinguished economist with a PhD in economics from Harvard. He served for eight and a half years. This established a precedent for having a permanent minority member on the Board.

A study of the boards of directors of the Fed Banks was begun by

House Banking chairman Wright Patman and published in 1976 by his successor, Henry Reuss (see Chapter 2). It found that there were few women or minorities, and little diversity in affiliation, among the 108 directors at the Fed Banks.[5] Its findings of racial and gender diversity were close to zero: "Women are ignored totally in the selection of district bank directors and only six women are among the 161 branch directors. Minorities are given little more than token representation."[6] Reuss emphasized the clear gender bias at the Fed by comparing its record with another governmental regulatory entity: "The Home Loan Bank Board has appointed six women directors since 1974, while *the Fed has never had a woman among the 1,042 directors in its 62-year history*" (emphasis added).[7] Burns had a catch-22 rationale for the Fed's difficulty in finding qualified women or minorities: few had served on boards of directors in banking and big business, and thus few had the skills needed to serve on the Fed's boards of directors. Reuss retorted: "I must once again disagree with your contention that the talents needed for these boards of directors can come only from banking and big business. . . . I cannot accept the idea that there have been no women capable of meeting your criteria for service on the boards of directors of these Federal Reserve Banks."[8]

The banking industry was well known for its exclusion of women and minorities from all but lower-level jobs. True, it may have been difficult to find women and minorities who had impressive resumes of higher-level jobs in that industry. High-level jobs in the banking industry were not a prerequisite for Fed service: Fed chairman Burns had been an academic. There were female and minority academics who studied central banking, a subject that many who are proficient in private-sector bank management find arcane.

Reuss's leadership and persistence in trying to remedy this problem, spurred on by Burns's seeming determination to preserve the bureaucracy's form of discrimination, led to the writing of one section of the Federal Reserve Reform Act of 1977. That section was directed at the three Class C directors on each of the nine-member boards of directors at the twelve Fed Banks. Unlike the other six members on each of the boards of directors, these three members were selected by the Board of Governors, which essentially meant by Burns. The intent was to direct with the force of law that these Class C directors were to be selected "without discrimination on the basis of sex or race, creed, color, or national origin, and with due but not exclusive consideration to the interests of agriculture, industry, services, labor and consumers."

This part of the act had an immediate effect on the insular leaders of the Fed. The late Jean Andrus Crockett served as a director of the Philadelphia Fed Bank from 1977 to 1982, when she was appointed chairperson, the first woman to hold that position at that Fed Bank. She had been a staff researcher for a statistical commission at the University of Chicago, a full professor at the Wharton School (of business) at the University of Pennsylvania, and chairperson of the Wharton Finance Department in 1966. Also, Sister Generose Gervais, a well-known Catholic nun, was appointed to the board of directors at the Minneapolis Fed Bank in 1979.[9]

Since 1977, Class C directors have included women as well as professionals who had not been officers of businesses or banks.

1990: GREENSPAN AT THE DOOR THAT GONZALEZ IS TRYING TO OPEN

Soon after Henry Gonzalez became House Banking chairman, he ordered a comprehensive study of diversity at the Fed. The results filled more than 3,200 pages in three books.[10] It was clear that the central bank had serious problems. When it came to the boards of directors of the Fed Banks, Gonzalez concluded that there was "a decided lack of minorities and women" and that the Fed "simply ignored those parts of the law which require consumer and labor representatives on the Federal Reserve Boards [of directors]." He said that the "appalling lack of diversity among the 277 [including boards of directors in branches of Fed Banks] directors of the Federal Reserve Banks" was primarily caused by "the Federal Reserve's practice of cultivating a supportive constituency in the banking industry and among big business."[11] The Fed Banks were not good models for the nation's banking industry.

Neither was the Fed headquarters. Gonzalez had asked Greenspan for a breakdown of all Board of Governors personnel earning more than $125,000 a year. Out of nearly two thousand employees, the governors had placed only one woman and one minority person in a top paid position. This is shown in a table sent by Greenspan in 1993 (Table 8-1).

A Fed Bank president told his board of directors that the conclusion of the Gonzalez report—that women and minorities were underrepresented in decision-making positions at the Fed Banks—"appears to be biased and not representative."[12] This criticism was uncovered in 1992 during a Gonzalez-led investigation of the minutes of boards of directors meetings in Fed Banks. When Gonzalez inquired about diversity, he found an

TABLE 8-1. A SECTION OF THE FED EMPLOYMENT CHART (AS OF MARCH 1, 1993) THAT GREENSPAN SENT TO GONZALEZ IN 1993*

Base Salary Range ($000)	No. of Emp.	Cash Awards 1992/1993		Occupational Area					No. of Emp. by Gender		No. of Emp. by Race	
		No.	Range ($0000)	Legal	Econ.	Opers./Mgt.	Auto-mation	Fin. Anal./Bk. Exam.	Male	Female	Min.	Non. Min.
160.1–161.6	12	1		1	3	6		2	12			12
155.1–160	0											
150.1–155	3				1		1	1	3			3
145.1–150	3	1			2			1	3			3
140.1–145	4				1	1		2	4			4
135.1–140	4	1			2	1		1	4		1	3
130.1–135	4	1		1	1	1	1		4			4
125.1–130	5		5	1	1	1	1		4	1		5
Total	35	4	3–5	3	11	10	3	7	34	1	1	34

Note: Officers at $151,600 average 21 years of service with a range of 10 to 29 years

**Author's note:* Approximately 2.9 percent of the higher executives at the Fed were women, and an equal number were minorities.

Source: author's collection.

absurd rationale from a Fed Bank president in the minutes of a board of directors meeting, and then cited it in a press release on October 30, 1992: "It is sometimes difficult to find qualified consumer and labor prospects *who are not politically active. We find that minorities we wish to recruit are often serving on commercial bank boards which precludes them from serving on a reserve Bank Board*" (emphasis was added when the material was quoted in the press release).[13] The contention that eligible blacks, Hispanics, and other minorities were already on bank boards, and that qualified consumer and labor prospects were all politically active and therefore ineligible, drew a reaction from Gonzalez that might be called strongly negative: "This is sheer nonsense." He said that the Fed Banks "should stop hiding behind *code words* such as 'politically active' and admit that they don't want to rock the boat by elevating more women and minorities including persons with a consumer and labor orientation, to decision-making posts" (emphasis added).[14]

The Fed could not silence or intimidate Gonzalez. Greenspan and his staff of lobbyists were making the rounds in Congress. Greenspan notified Gonzalez that the Fed had better representation among women and minorities at salary levels below, rather than above, the $125,000 cutoff in Gonzalez's survey. This was an especially poor argument to send to Gonzalez, who would not take lobbying calls or visits from Greenspan unless appropriate action had been taken beforehand. Greenspan, accompanied by several other Fed personnel, lobbied members of the House Banking Committee, explaining the Fed's desire to comply with the spirit of the Civil Rights Act of 1964. He did not publicly support any efforts to eliminate the technicality, such as the corrective legislation described below.

The Greenspan Fed had to endure some uncomfortable publicity, and it made some changes. Gonzalez commended the Fed "for some improvement" in 1996, when diversity had improved, but added, "the record is still far from adequate."[15] There were then seventy-two employees earning more than $125,000, and the top twelve earned $174,100. Eleven women and five employees classified as "minority" were in this group.

$163,800 FOR THE SUPPORT SERVICE DIRECTOR, $148,400 FOR THE SECRETARY OF DEFENSE

The Greenspan Fed made a bizarre move to elevate an employee into Gonzalez's top salary tier. The Fed increased the pay of what it referred to as the "support services director," whom some others derisively called "the janitor."[16] This employee's pay was raised to $163,800, definitely putting him or her among the highest-paid employees at the Fed. This person now made more than a cabinet secretary, who then earned $148,400. Greenspan then drew a salary of $133,600; forty-eight employees earned more than he did.

Asked by an Associated Press reporter why the support services director, who is in charge of maintenance workers at several buildings at the Fed's headquarters, earns more than the secretary of defense, the Fed's spokesman said: "He's got a lot under his wing."[17] The Fed spokesman also said that the support services director was far more than a maintenance chief; he oversaw several hundred employees.

COVERING UP REDLINING

Redlining is a practice of discriminating against some loan customers by signaling with a red line drawn under their name in the bank records. With this practice, lenders systematically deny loans to minorities and women. Although actual red lines are probably seldom if ever used now because of antidiscrimination laws, redlining has become a generic name for any type of signaling meant to discriminate financially on the basis of race or gender.

In March 1994, Gonzalez announced some grave allegations about the Fed's examination of banks for bias in lending:

> One brave person, knowing of the work I have been doing on the Fed, has approached me with chilling details about unethical conduct taking place at the Federal Reserve. This person is a former Federal Reserve bank examiner who has volunteered to expose gross unethical conduct in the Federal Reserve examination process. The situation had gotten so bad that the examiner decided to quit working at the FED rather than stomach the unethical behavior.
>
> This is a very serious situation which, if system-wide, raises serious questions about the Federal Reserve's commitment to enforcing the Community Reinvestment Act and policing for bias in lending practices.
>
> The examiner said a team of bank examiners documented evidence of violations of the Community Reinvestment Act and bias in lending. The examiner's original report was critical of lending to low-income and minority populations and had noted discriminatory remarks from bank employees about redlining.

The supervisors then replaced the criticism with contrived examples of the bank's eagerness to comply with consumer lending laws.[18]

THE FED IS SUED FOR RACIAL
DISCRIMINATION, REPEATEDLY

In 1994, the Federal Reserve lost a jury trial brought by an African American employee who charged that she had been repeatedly denied promotion because of racial bias. The employee had worked for the Federal Reserve Board of Governors as a senior statistical assistant, providing support to economists. She had been employed at the Fed for more than twenty years. She had sought a promotion to the next category, research assistant, for twelve years. As Gonzalez and Jesse Jackson, Jr., wrote to Greenspan: "She performed many of the same job assignments carried out by research assistants, the main difference being the higher pay of research assistants. Two supervisors testified that she had performed her work better than some of the research assistants who had worked for them."[19] Her attorney, William A. H. Briggs, Jr., of Ross, Dixon and Masback in Washington, D.C., reported that she was told by Fed officials that she could not be promoted because she did not have a college degree.[20] For seven years she went to night school while working full-time and raising six children as a single parent, and obtained a degree in accounting in 1989.

Again she asked to be given the job of research assistant; but according to Briggs, "she was told that even though she had a degree, she had not taken the right courses." She filed a racial discrimination charge with the Fed's in-house Equal Opportunity Office (EEO). A settlement was reached that "essentially provided her with a list of courses she had to complete."[21]

When she "re-applied for the same position in 1992, she was interviewed by a woman who was named in her first EEO-complaint. She was again turned down for the job as she was told that others were better-qualified for the position, even though she already preformed many of a research assistant's duties."[22] The Fed's runaround, including the farce with the Fed's EEO, ended when she sued again.

She won the case when "a federal jury in Washington found that she was denied the promotion because of her race and then retaliated against for filing an EEO complaint."[23] Federal District Judge Ricardo Urbina ordered Greenspan to retroactively promote the employee and to give her back pay and $150,000 in compensatory damages. Attorney fees were paid out of the $150,000.

About sixteen African American women filed a class action suit in 1998 against the Federal Reserve, charging discrimination in promotions and salaries. This was a continuation of a case originally filed in 1995 and later dismissed without prejudice. The Fed hired an outside law firm to handle the case. The case wandered on for years through mounds of motions filed by the Fed's attorneys. A continuation of the case was still in the courts in 2007.

Some of the women were "invited" to resign with a payout that the Fed dubbed "career transition pay." Congressman Jesse Jackson, Jr., said; "I have received information that six of these women have left the Board of Governors and were given 'career transition pay' consisting of two years' salary provided they do not return to employment at the Board of Governors."[24]

At a seminar at the National Press Club on January 7, 2001, televised on C-SPAN, I interviewed two longtime Fed employees, one of whom was a secretary to Virgil Mattingly, general counsel to the Board and the Federal Open Market Committee until his retirement in 2004. The employees had sued the Fed for racial discrimination. One of these women said she had been called into an office, informed of her career transition pay, and told to sign a resignation letter. She said that "the minute you sign the agreement," you are told to leave, even though the resignation letter is postdated. She added: "They pay you for not coming to work."

Despite this altruistic-sounding name—career transition pay—this compensation amounts to nothing more than a bribe in exchange for an employee's signature on a resignation letter or possibly for an employee's dropping of a lawsuit. The Department of Justice and the courts should determine if these Fed actions regarding plaintiffs suing for racial discrimination are legal. Did the Fed chairman's words to Gonzalez in 1997 cover the longtime Fed employees whose career transition was to the street outside the Fed: "Of course, under the Board's well-established policy, persons who participate in any administration or judicial proceeding relating to allegations of unlawful discrimination in employment must not be subject to retaliation."[25] Similar racial discrimination cases were filed against the Chicago Fed Bank. In 1998 it was reported that: "Eight present and former employees of the Chicago Fed Bank sued. They charged that they had been subjected intentionally to unequal and discriminatory treatment because of their race and color."[26]

A minority person who was a former vice president at the Chicago Fed Bank filed a lawsuit claiming she had been asked to investigate problems concerning minorities at the Fed Bank and that she had come back with the "wrong" answers. It appeared that the Fed Bank's minority personnel had some valid complaints. The investigator evidently did not use the Fed's usual sweep-under-the-rug technique while waving the independence banner. She was allegedly given the equivalent of a demotion, causing her to sue the bank. The Chicago Fed Bank settled with her for an undisclosed amount. The case did not go to trial, and the Chicago Fed Bank was no longer burdened with a bank official who reported problems with minorities.

The costs to the Fed and the nation's taxpayers of this type of settlement to employees and payments to private law firms should be clearly specified in a detailed and clear budget that can be examined by the House and Senate Banking Committees. Congress should request the Fed to show where in the Chicago Fed Bank's accounting records the settlement is specifically identified. The amount should be public, so taxpayers can see where their money goes.[27] The Banking Committees should also be given the original report of the former Fed official.

STOPPING THE FEDERAL RESERVE CIVIL RIGHTS COMPLIANCE ACT OF 1999

Despite some court findings, Greenspan continued to contend that the Federal Reserve was not subject to the Civil Rights Act of 1964. Angered by the Fed's repeated denials of discrimination, which flew in the face of trial records and the continuing cases brought by employees, Congressman Jesse Jackson, Jr., introduced legislation mandating that the Federal Reserve post signs to notify its employees of "applicable provisions of Title VII of the Civil Rights Act of 1964" legislation.[28] Jackson immediately gained twenty-four cosponsors for the legislation, but then the power and political muscle of the Greenspan Fed came into play. Greenspan's lobbyists descended on Capitol Hill.

One source described the reaction in Congress.[29] The recruiting of cosigners slowed, and then the chairman of House Banking [now called the Financial Services Committee]—Jim Leach—did not sign on to Jackson's legislation. And John LaFalce, who had just replaced Henry Gonzalez as ranking Democrat on the committee, declined to cosponsor. When asked about the failure to sign Jackson's legislation, Leach reportedly said he had "no plan to investigate the Federal Reserve's personnel practices while the cases were pending in Federal courts."[30] LaFalce simply declined to respond to inquiries. In the Senate, neither Banking chairman Phil Gramm nor ranking Democrat Paul Sarbanes (D-MD) appeared interested in Jackson's legislation or the Fed's repeated claims of being exempt from the Civil Rights Act.

THE GREENSPAN FED IN WONDERLAND

The Greenspan Fed's denial of the applicability of the Civil Rights Act to itself may have seemed harmful, but the Fed's retreat on fair lending on December 23, 1996, also damaged equal rights. While everyone was preoccupied with the holidays, the Greenspan Fed took a giant step back on fair lending. At issue was a proposed rule to end the Fed's longstanding ban on the collection of data on the race and gender of applicants for small-business and consumer loans. The data, community and civil rights groups contended, were critical for revealing discriminatory lending patterns and for enforcing the Equal Credit Opportunity Act (ECOA). But the Greenspan Fed turned its back on this issue, justifying its inaction with a garblement that was in a class with its monetary-policy announcements:

> Ultimately, there is no easy way to measure the extent to which discrimination occurs in credit transactions, nor the effect the rule has had on the incidence of discrimination. It is impossible to know precisely how, if at all, lifting the prohibition and making these data available would affect creditors' actions. On the one hand, it is likely that the prohibition has helped to prevent discrimination in at least some credit transactions. On the other hand, creditors have collected data in connection with mortgage loan applications for nearly twenty years, and there is no indication from this experience that data collection increases the potential for discrimination.[31]

Every governmental agency involved in loan programs—the Small Business Administration, the Department of Housing and Urban Development, the Agriculture Department, to name just a few—collects data on race and gender as an important tool in making certain that there is equal access. More to the point, the Federal Reserve was already required to collect race and gender data on loan applications under the Home

Mortgage Disclosure Act (HMDA). These data have proven invaluable in efforts to spotlight discriminatory lending and enforce the ECOA.

APPEARING WITH CIVIL RIGHTS LEADERS

Although the media had largely ignored the racial discrimination lawsuits and a federal jury in Washington "found that [a Fed employee] was denied the promotion because of her race and then retaliated against for filing an EEO complaint," Greenspan deserved and received favorable civil rights coverage for his actions in 1998. Greenspan walked with Congresswoman Maxine Waters, chair of the Congressional Black Caucus, through her district in South Central Los Angeles. Several days later, Greenspan and other celebrities appeared with the Reverend Jesse Jackson, who was promoting an effort to bring greater diversity to financial firms, at a three-day conference on Wall Street.[32] Greenspan's appearances were certainly helpful in bringing attention to the need for investment in South Central Los Angeles and for shining a spotlight on the need for diversity in Wall Street firms.

CHAPTER 9

WHEN FIVE HUNDRED ECONOMISTS ARE NOT ENOUGH

GETTING PRESSED DURING PRE-WASH

The first-floor lobby of the Fed Bank in Kansas City has the cavernous, cold appearance of a classic, old-time bank lobby. In the mid-1970s, a ceremony was held there to honor the retiring president of the Kansas City Fed Bank. Most of the bank's employees gathered behind the bank's officers. The officers included vice presidents and assistant vice presidents, all smiling proudly in front of a larger, more restrained crowd of Fed employees, who were thankful for this entertaining break from work.

The incoming and outgoing presidents of the Fed Bank faced the group. At the end of a laudatory speech about the contributions of the retiring president, a high school chorus broke into hallelujahs as the new president pulled the sheet off of a statue. On top of a large cutout of Superman's body was a picture of the head of the retiring president. There were applause and laughter.

The retiring president was a very amiable man with long executive experience at a large private-sector company. He had looked and acted quite lost when it came to officiating at the "pre-Wash meeting," which was held on the Thursday or Friday before the Federal Open Market Committee (FOMC) meeting, on Tuesday, at the Board of Governors in Washington, D.C. At the pre-Wash meeting, the president, his chief economist (the senior vice president in charge of the research department), and the staff of economists would file into a conference room. There was heightened interest and intensity because the president had been rotated into his one-year voting membership on the FOMC. (Four FOMC seats are rotated among eleven Fed Bank presidents; the New York Fed Bank president is a permanent member of the committee.)

At the pre-Wash meeting, the president might tell a story about the experience of a relative in a store with high prices. Mostly, he would say nothing. At one of these meetings he read a poem that he had written and then delivered at the last FOMC meeting. He bragged that Fed chairman Arthur Burns had specifically complimented him on his fine poem. Those in attendance at the pre-Wash meeting assumed frozen smiles as he eagerly recited something like "The money supply went up the staircase so fast that we all knew it would not last. Down, down it came back to run just where it started from." Then the awkward silence was interrupted by the chief economist, who asked the staff for their selection of policies.

Before the pre-Wash meeting, the Board of Governors would send out the menu, which consisted of three choices for money growth and an associated band of short-term interest-rate targets.[1] Each economist could say *a*, *b*, or *c* and offer supporting comments. Nearly all economists selected option *b* because that looked like the one most agreeable to management and would not cause a fuss in Washington by appearing to support "extreme" views. As a staff economist at the Kansas City Fed Bank, I decided not to play the game at one pre-Wash meeting in the mid-1970s, and suggested a different policy, which I called *d*. I presented reasons for this policy. An officer of the bank immediately asked me to accompany him out of the room. We had a very friendly discussion about my wife and young child. The officer advised me that if I wanted to continue to be able to pay the mortgage on our newly purchased house, I should be a team player.[2]

WHO DETERMINES MONETARY POLICY?

Many of the 500-plus economists at the Fed perform similarly as advisers on domestic monetary policy. Their role is to enter mahogany-paneled conference rooms en masse and chime in during serious discussions of monetary policy with Fed Bank officials a day or two before FOMC meetings.

On the following Tuesday, the FOMC convenes in Washington. FOMC members gather around a large conference table. They enter through one set of doors, and the Fed chairman enters through a door from his adjoining office. They speak into microphones with voice-activated green lights that indicate the recording of their utterances. As described in Chapter 6, some members claimed not to know what the green light indicated. If true, it was not a good sign, given the skill level desired in FOMC members. In other seats, away from the conference table, sit employees of the Board of Governors and the twelve district banks.

Greenspan's dominance over the Fed governors appears to have been nearly complete, according to the description given by former governor Laurence Meyer. Meyer reports that Greenspan "would meet individually with the other governors during the week before FOMC meetings."[3] He "would sit down and explain his views on the outlook and his 'leaning' with respect to policy decisions that would be considered by the Committee at the upcoming meeting. . . . Some governors found this rather offputting." Given Meyer's view that the "Chairman is expected to resign if the Committee rejects his policy recommendation," "offputting" would be an understatement for describing the process imposed by Greenspan. "After a while," Meyer reports, Greenspan "abandoned the private talks" and instead gave his views one day before the FOMC meetings to the governors at a Board meeting. Meyer also reports that during his term as governor, no governor dissented from Greenspan's views, and there was "an implicit commitment to support the Chairman." Meyer also describes FOMC meetings as being "more about structured presentations than discussions and exchanges."[4] In this picture, Greenspan's dominance of the process reduced the other governors' contributions to Fed policy to a triviality. Meyer draws a very different picture from what occurred at the Volcker Fed with the "gang of four" (described in Chapter 10).

The Board staff also sets the tone at FOMC meetings with their analyses. Their reports serve as the vehicle for much of the discussion about monetary policy. The staff reports generally support the chairman's views, for obvious reasons.

Members' opposing views could potentially change policy. If such views come from the subservient Fed Bank presidents, pressure from the Board of Governors can affect their peace of mind as well as their salaries and tenure, since at their next yearly review the Fed chairman can lower the hammer. Unlike governors, who can be removed only by congressional impeachment, Fed Bank presidents can be fired or their contracts not renewed for another five-year term. Fed Bank presidents have left in the middle of their five-year terms with an official announcement of voluntary departure.

All but the occasional recalcitrant official will vote in conformity with the chairman; Meyer reports three dissents by Fed Bank presidents during his term. A few principled presidents withstood the substantial pressure to conform, most notably the late Darryl R. Francis, the former president of the St. Louis Fed Bank. He may have lasted for two terms—ten years—because he had well-known outside support and had assembled a skilled and renowned research department.[5]

The chairman heads the large staff at the Board of Governors. He is in close contact with the president of the United States. He meets frequently with the secretary of the treasury, and the Fed staff is in contact with Treasury staff. Many members of Congress seek the Fed chairman's advice and try to be seen on television with him at hearings, since he is the face of the Fed and sometimes, as in the cases of Burns and Greenspan, the country's enshrined economic sage.

HOW MUCH SHOULD CENTRAL BANKERS KNOW ABOUT CENTRAL BANKING?

Many FOMC members have been either trained economists or people who became very knowledgeable about central banking through their work experience. The economic welfare of hundreds of millions of people can be threatened when some of the voting members of the FOMC are completely or nearly ignorant about central-bank functions and their effects on the economy. They may be unable to determine which staff suggestions or media stories have merit. Even worse, economic analysis produced by the Fed's huge staff of economists—full of "aggregates," "indexes," and "high order filters"—could be impenetrably confusing. Untrained members can become rubber stamps for the chairman's views. An FOMC member can maintain this neutered stance at meetings and still participate for the record by reciting anecdotal events and imprecise descriptions of the economy, and then vote for whatever the chairman wants.

FOMC transcripts show that the staff reports presented to the committee are often primitive, lacking an analytical framework as well as even modestly sophisticated statistical evidence. The top staff of the Board of Governors delivers policy in a form suitable to the chairman.

This description does not automatically mean that only well-credentialed economists should be appointed to the Board. Many well-credentialed economists, in think tanks and on academic faculties, would be ill suited for these decision-making positions. Many are partially or completely tone deaf with respect to politics, a desirable trait when conducting research projects that seek answers in a world without political constraints. But an apolitical sensibility can be a shortcoming for public service, especially in anyone who will have a hand in setting Federal Reserve policy. Congress can involve a Fed official in days of painful testimony in front of committee members who are often delighted to play to the television cameras by toying with a politically inept foil.

Milton Friedman, the Nobel laureate who devoted much of his research to studying monetary policy, emphasized the quandary about expert knowledge when he compared former Fed chairman William McChesney Martin, Jr., who served in that position for nineteen years (1951–1970), with former Fed chairman Arthur Burns, who served eight years (1970–1978). Burns was an economics professor from Columbia University. Friedman had been his student at Rutgers University, and they were friends, although Burns's advocacy of faster money growth and price controls put a strain on their relations.

Martin became the first paid president of the New York Stock Exchange, the "boy wonder of Wall Street." According to his obituary in the *New York Times,* he was well aware of his limited knowledge of central banking: "When he took office, Mr. Martin said he had told himself: 'My gracious, here I am the new Chairman of the Fed, and I'm not the brightest fellow in the world but I'm working hard on this—and I haven't the faintest idea of how you figure the money supply. Yet everybody thinks I have it at my fingertips.'"[6]

Friedman wrote to me: "It is not clear to me that competence about monetary policy will necessarily lead to better monetary policy. I offer you the example of the contrast between Martin and Burns. I am sure that both you and I would agree that in any academic sense Burns was far more competent, understood the operation of monetary policy far better than Martin. Yet I suspect that you and I will both agree that monetary policy was better under Martin than it was under Burns."[7]

This assessment is consistent with the lower average rate of inflation during the Martin years (2.1 percent) and the much more rapid average rate of inflation during the 1970s (6.5 percent) when Burns was Fed chairman.[8] Nevertheless, dismissing the need to know what you are doing is alarming, given the powers that are placed in the hands of Fed officials.[9] A serious mistake in managing the money supply can cause an explosion of inflation, which would wipe out much of the purchasing power of millions of people. Likewise, a rapid sustained contraction of the money supply can cause a recession, leading to millions of people losing their jobs.

DOES IT MATTER IF FED OFFICIALS ARE UNABLE
TO EXPLAIN THEIR JOBS?

To illustrate the problem of Fed officials' inability to explain what they are doing, consider the example of an esteemed former manager of the New York Fed Bank's open-market desk. He had the important task of overseeing the daily auctions that are central to the Fed's management of the nation's money supply. He came to a seminar held by Milton Friedman at the University of Chicago in the 1960s. This famous weekly seminar was called "The Money and Banking Workshop." The small group of attendees consisted of scholars from around the world and PhD students whom Friedman had admitted to the workshop. The procedure required each invited speaker to submit a paper in advance. The speaker was not to read the paper to the group, since that would be redundant. Friedman would begin by calling out: "Page one." That was the signal for any member of the workshop to ask the speaker a question about something on page one of the paper. The questioning was intense but very productive—that is, until Friedman invited this retiring manager of the New York Fed Bank's open-market desk.

This speaker broke precedent by not submitting a paper in advance. Friedman began by asking him how he conducted open-market operations: What precisely did he use as signals? How precisely did he use various variables in determining his actions? He could not answer any of these questions except with generalities that produced frowns on workshop members. Friedman continued to search for some kind of specific answer. He asked the Fed official what he would tell his successor to do in handling various situations. The Fed official said there were no specifics about that; each situation was different. Friedman did not end the workshop as he had a previous meeting: when someone complained that the paper being presented was so poor as to be a waste of time, Friedman adjourned the meeting. Since the Fed official was obviously not an academic researcher or a scholar, the seminar ended courteously.

The Fed's open-market manager was an able official and had had a successful career. Like many successful private-sector traders, he could not present a clear description or analysis of his methods. Despite his successes or failures at the Fed, his inability to describe what he had done meant that his experience and knowledge were not passed on to future open-market managers.

TABLE 9-1.

Type	Board	Fed. Banks	Total
Officers	27	95	122
Economists	189	171	360
Statisticians	7	4	11
Total officers, economists, and statisticians	223	270	493
Professional support staff	89	148	237
Total			730

Source: This table is from an attachment to a letter dated September 15, 1993, from Fed chairman Greenspan to Rep. Gonzalez. The note on the table reads: "This table covers all formal positions involved in economic research/management activities. For Reserve Bank only filled positions are counted, but vacancies are included in the Board count." Author's collection.

WHEN MORE THAN 500 ECONOMISTS ARE NOT ENOUGH

Although many of the excellent economists at the Fed appear to have little effect on monetary policy, they produce some good papers. They write articles for the Fed's extensive publications, many of which have been moved onto Fed Bank Web sites. Many are useful summaries of economic topics. Other economists are officials in management positions at Fed Banks. How many economists are employed at the Fed? A reasonable estimate is that more than 500 economists were employed at the Fed in 1993. Greenspan responded to an inquiry from House Banking chairman Gonzalez by verifying that the Fed employed 360 economists in its research departments, as shown in Table 9-1.[10] In addition, 122 officers in research departments were presumably economists, making a total of 482. This figure did not take into account the economists employed in other parts of the Fed. This makes the Fed one of the largest U.S. employers of economists. In 2000, the Department of Labor employed 1,076 economists, and the Department of Agriculture had 525.[11]

The Fed also extends contracts to economists in academia. A Gonzalez-led investigation collected information on the Fed's use of outside contracts for academics. During the thirty-six months ending October 1994, the Board and the twelve Fed Banks awarded 305 contracts to 209 professors, virtually all of whom were economists. The total payments on contracts in this period amounted to nearly $3 million, an average of $81,091.14

a month.[12] Thirty-eight economists had contracts that paid more than $20,000. Many of the economists had multiple contracts, generally from different Fed Banks or the Board. One economist had six contracts, three had five, four had four, and fifteen had three.[13]

These payments were not extravagant, and probably attractive to professors who were not well paid compared to their business-world counterparts. There was no evidence that these outside consultants failed to provide useful advice or research efforts for the Fed. Questions may be asked about the multiple Fed Bank contracts.

According to an article by Stephen Davies: "The New York Fed, which has the largest staff of economists outside of the Federal Reserve Board because of its role in executing monetary policy and watching financial markets, listed only a handful of outside economists. By contrast, the Federal Reserve Bank of Minneapolis has what is by far the most ambitious program of hiring outside researchers. Records show that the bank signed 105 contracts [from January 1, 1991 to June 30, 1993] with academics, including a number from universities outside the United States. Many were one-time deals to write papers for the bank."[14]

There are problems associated with the Fed's employing or contracting with large numbers of economists. The problems arise when these economists testify as witnesses at legislative hearings or as experts at judicial proceedings, and when they publish their research and views on Fed policies, including in Fed publications.

In 1992, roughly 968 members of the American Economic Association (the largest association for economists in the United States) designated "domestic monetary and financial theory and institutions" as their primary field, and 717 designated it as their secondary field. If a significant percentage of these people either work directly for the Fed or contract with the Fed, there can be consequences, as Milton Friedman described in 1993, first in a letter to me and then to Reuters: "I cannot disagree with you that having something like 500 economists is extremely unhealthy. As you say, it is not conducive to independent, objective research. You and I know there has been censorship of the material published. Equally important, the location of the economists in the Federal Reserve has had a significant influence on the kind of research they do, biasing that research toward noncontroversial technical papers on method as opposed to substantive papers on policy and results."[15] Reuters reported Friedman's statements in an interview: "The Fed's relatively enhanced standing among the public has been aided 'by the fact that the Fed has always paid a great deal of attention to soothing the people in the media and buying up its most likely critics.' Recognizing that the Fed employs 'probably half of the monetary economists in the U.S. and has visiting appointments for two-thirds of the rest,' he [Friedman] saw few among the academic community who were prepared to criticize the Fed policy."[16]

SOME PERSONAL EXPERIENCE WITH CENSORSHIP
AND NONDISCLOSURE AGREEMENTS

The working conditions for some economists at the Fed are excellent. When I was hired at the Kansas City Fed Bank in the mid-1970s, I doubled the salary I had made as an assistant professor. I was shown a spacious, mahogany-paneled office with a large, impressive desk, situated along a corridor of other economists' offices. I was told that I would have access to several programmers for statistical research and that all the newspapers and journals that I wanted would be delivered to me. Best of all, I could spend 90 percent of my time on my own research and use the other 10 percent for developing reports for the bank.

Only one caution from the Fed Bank officer who headed this research-department group seemed a bit awkward, a sign of the bureaucratic rules that foster regimental conformity. I was told that security at the bank required me not to wander around. I was to stay in my office except to go to the men's room, to the cafeteria for lunch, or on official business, such as a meeting. It was the equivalent of being told to knock before coming out of my office. The cachet of the splendid office faded. I began to miss the freedom of the small bare-walled furniture-deprived office I had left in academia. Nevertheless, many first-rate well-trained economists are attracted to the Fed by the salary and the perks. Some who oppose the Fed's policies bear this burden with some pain. They learn how to mentally ignore or minimize the restrictions that this bureaucracy imposes.

For an economist who spent many years earning a PhD and believed in the production of unbiased contributions to knowledge, censorship could be difficult to ignore, a bureaucratic sliver under the fingernail. Articles intended for Fed publications had to be sent to the Board in Washington for editing and approval. Because of this, the publications should indicate that the material has been emended to comply with Fed policies — something along the lines of "EDITED BY THE FEDERAL RESERVE FOR GENERAL CONFORMITY WITH ITS VIEWS AND POLICIES." Without this sort of label, Fed publications appear to be unbiased products of its huge think tank.

One type of censorship could have more immediate effects on the Fed's monetary policy. Each of the twelve Fed Banks prepares several reports designated by color: the Beige Book is about economic conditions, and the Red Book is about banking conditions, including any problems at banks in the district. Those books are available to the FOMC members at their meetings, and, presumably, the contents affect their decision making.

Assigned to help compile the Red Book, I began calling the CEOs of the banks in the 10th District (Wyoming, Colorado, Kansas, Nebraska, Oklahoma, and parts of Missouri and New Mexico). It became immediately apparent that there was trouble. A popular anchor on one of the heavily watched morning news programs had announced that the Fed Banks were selling Treasury securities in denominations as small as $1,000. This information by itself was correct, but $1,000 was not the market price at which these securities could be purchased; it was the final return in three months. The market price was determined by an auction. The interest on three-month Treasury bills was attractive to many savers because banks were then paying zero interest on checking accounts. The three-month Treasury-bill rate had averaged 6.23 percent in 1974, 1975, and 1976.

There was a stampede to some of the private-sector banks in the 10th District to buy these securities, as well as some chaos because of incorrect information about their market price. There were long lines of customers at many of the banks in the district. They did not have the personnel to explain the pricing policies of these government securities to the insistent customers who had "heard it on TV." The bankers issued almost frantic appeals for help in advising citizens about the mistake. That should have concerned the Fed, since its clients, the U.S. public and the private-sector banks, were having trouble.[17]

I dutifully summarized the problem and included it in a report for the next Red Book. The head of the research department called me into his office and told me to take the problem out of the report. He was told that everything was fine in the 10th District. I left, humming quietly "Everything's Up to Date in Kansas City" (from *Oklahoma!*). Unfortunately, it was no joke to realize that information sent to the Board was censored to avoid admitting any problems existed. This type of cover-up is expected in any large bureaucracy. However, the muddled organization of the Fed makes it much more difficult to enforce uniform rules across all twelve district facilities.

An insightful example of limitations for an economist doing unbiased research is the nondisclosure statement (officially labeled "Nondisclosure Clause") that contracted economists signed before obtaining consulting jobs with the Board of Governors. According to the story by Stephen Davies mentioned earlier, "in the case of the Federal Reserve Board all contractors are required to sign a non-disclosure statement promising to keep all information confidential. The statement is broadly worded to prohibit the release of any information 'relating to past, present, or future activities' that can be considered 'damaging to the Board.'"[18] An economist who is doing research on monetary policy and wants to be critical of the Fed's policies should not be limited by such nondisclosure clauses; an economist testifying before Congress must not be. At the beginning of any testimony concerning Fed policies, congressional witnesses should provide information about any such limitations, especially nondisclosure agreements with the Fed, and any money they have received from the Fed for contracted services. Disclosure forms are required (as of 2003) for witnesses before the House Banking Committee. Nondisclosure clauses signed by academic economists who have been under contract at the Fed should also be revealed.

A number of economists interviewed by Steve Davies, including those with contracts with the Fed, applauded the contracts. They said that consulting was an opportunity for the best minds in academia to lend their expertise to the Fed and that it was mutually beneficial. They said they did not bias their research. Several economists reportedly told Davies that they talked to Fed staff members about statistical models and not about what they thought "interest rates are going to be"; some stated that they did not "comment on current policy" because they were not experts "on what's happening at the moment."[19]

Compare these answers with the call I received at Congress in the 1970s from the late Arthur Okun, an esteemed economist who was certainly very honest and who had been chairman of the Council of Economic Advisers in the Johnson administration (1968–1969). He said he would like to comply with the committee's request that he testify. However, he was receiving a check each year for $3,000 from the Federal Reserve, and he simply did not want to testify without stating this fact, which would be a potential conflict of interest. When asked what he did to receive this payment, he replied that the Fed probably wanted to call on him for his views, but no required work was involved. It was a small payment, and Okun evidently knew that it might not be considered payment for his advice, which he probably would have been happy to provide to the Fed free.

Of course, the Fed would reject these criticisms. It does, however, mention the existence of "bureaucratic restraints" in its Web site solicitation for economists (as it appeared in January 2003): "The Board offers a work environment that minimizes bureaucratic constraints, encourages creative thought, and stimulates the lively and free exchange of ideas." A "little" bureaucratic restraint never hurt anything, except possibly unbiased research about the operations and policies of this powerful governmental bureaucracy.

The above censorship warning should appear on any Fed material distributed to high school teachers and college professors. In 2005 the Fed began publishing its message on "economic and personal education" with the help of *USA Today*.

> www.FederalReserveEducation.org
> The Federal Reserve System is committed to economic and personal financial education.
>
> USA TODAY and the Federal Reserve are working together to introduce students and educators to the wide variety of instructional resources available through the Federal Reserve Education website and especially the new FED 101 website.
>
> The Federal Reserve Education website provides links to instructional materials and tools that can increase student understanding of the Federal Reserve, economics and financial education. All of the Fed websites, curriculum, newsletters, booklets and other resources are free.

As the Fed belatedly moved from relying on hard-copy mass mailings to exploiting the Internet, the New York Fed Bank advertised its new Web site in 2006: "The Research Group recently launched *Course Readings for University Educators*, a new website that highlights the value of the Bank's research publications as teaching tools. The site's key element is a directory of recommended readings organized by course title and level of mathematical complexity. Finance and economics professors can select a course and then link to articles from our principal research series that might be assigned to students in that course."[20]

ENTERTAINING POTENTIAL CONGRESSIONAL WITNESSES

The House Banking Committee received information about a three-day Fed conference on financial derivatives to be held in Coconut Grove, Florida, on February 24–26, 1994. It happened that the committee was planning to hold hearings on financial derivatives. Coincidence?

The information received by the committee indicated that participants at the Fed conference were told to bring their golf clubs. The preliminary program showed the conference would adjourn at one thirty on the second day, after a noon speech by Greenspan, and except for a reception "with spouses" at seven that night, would not reconvene until a "continental breakfast" scheduled for nine the next morning, and it would then adjourn again at one thirty in the afternoon. Why was the Fed using taxpayers' money to entertain economists who might well be called as congressional witnesses? At least one economist understood what was happening. As Gonzalez later put it: "The purpose of the early adjournment is to allow time to examine and explore the local golf terrain, according to one prominent economist who was invited to attend and was advised to bring his golf clubs. . . . This may all look like small potatoes to individuals with good jobs. But to American taxpayers who are paying their bills and to the 2.3 million civilian governmental employees who fear that many of them will be shown the door in the name of efficiency and eliminating waste, the Federal Reserve is throwing a little Miami Beach sand in their faces."[21]

On behalf of House Banking, I called the Atlanta Fed Bank, which was sponsoring the conference, to ask why a conference was being held at a resort where the Fed would be paying $325 a day for each attendee's room, when the Atlanta Fed Bank had adequate meeting space. Displeased with the inquiry, the Fed Bank president informed me that even Fed chairman Greenspan would be in attendance. I said that made matters worse, since it would increase the cost of the conference. The Fed Bank president then complained in writing to me. Gonzalez thanked me for the work I was doing and said the letter was proof of the arrogance of the Fed and the need for oversight.[22]

CHAPTER 10

THE MYTH OF
POLITICAL VIRGINITY

RECITING THE POLITICAL VIRGINITY PLEDGE

Fed officials have reason to relish the holy grail of independence. By claiming it, they can repudiate any call for individual public accountability as a violation of their independence from politics. Of course, they still affirm their intention to serve the public interest. Yet Fed chairmen tend to bring out the holy grail of independence from politics rarely, lest a determined member of Congress extract the confession that democratic government—politics in its best sense—should in fact reach all the way down to Fed headquarters, where the chairman and his colleagues are knee-deep in the old-fashioned variety.

A new and inexperienced Fed chairman once gave such enthusiastic responses to questions about Fed independence that he undermined the concept. Chairman G. William Miller was questioned by Iowa congressman Charles Grassley in 1978 before the House Banking Committee.[1]

Miller, who was short, wished to stand during his testimony. An appropriately sized podium was not available. Instead, the dapper gray-haired former CEO stood behind a small podium that was normally used on top of a table. The podium was mounted on the two chairs and some thick books, giving it the appearance of a somewhat contrived prop in a low-budget play. Despite the poorly rigged podium, the TV cameras recorded a stately and sincere witness who went skillfully through the drill without showing any awareness of its obvious contradictions. The performance could have been an operatic duet entitled "Preserving Independence with Close and Continual Contact."[2]

MR. GRASSLEY: Mr. Miller, I have a general question or two dealing with the independence of the Fed. I think the independence of the Federal Reserve System is very closely connected with maintenance of a sound monetary policy in this country, so you understand then what direction I am coming from. Previous Fed chairmen and previous administrations usually met to discuss general matters, at breakfast, or at other meetings, particularly with the Secretary of the Treasury of those administrations. My first question to you is: What kind, how often and in what environment do you have discussions with administration officials; and are these discussions any compromise of the principle of independence of the Fed?

MR. MILLER: I will answer in reverse order. I think there is no compromise of independence of the Fed in carrying out discussions with other officials in the Government who are interested in economic policy. There is none because we continue to use these discussions only as a basis for considering matters of mutual interest and policies of mutual concern. I do meet with the Secretary of the Treasury once a week if we are both in town. Out staffs tend to meet once a week. These meetings may not involve me; they may just involve some of our staff working on technical aspects or coordination of our activities. We act as a fiscal agent for the Treasury and do a lot of other things with the Treasury. I usually meet periodically with the chairman of the Council of Economic Advisers. And I also meet occasionally with the officials in other agencies of the government who are dealing with economic issues. As you probably know, on occasion the President asks for a number of us to come in and sit down with him and discuss economic matters; that may, I think, be a continuing procedure.

MR. GRASSLEY: From that standpoint, I would detect that your relationship with the administration doesn't depart too much from what we have been told have been the patterns of previous administrations and previous chairmen.

MR. MILLER: I know of no difference. I have really picked up the agenda that was established by Dr. Burns.

MR. GRASSLEY: Are you taking any new and/or different actions to insure the independence of the Fed as it might be within your power to so do?

MR. MILLER: I don't know of any action that is necessary. Our commitment to independence is absolute. I think there is no one in the Federal Reserve who is not fully committed to the concept of independence.

I detect, in the arrangements that have been made since I succeeded Dr. Burns, no evidence of efforts to subvert that independence. I do not think our discussions entangle us or require us to become silent supporters of something in which we don't believe. So I haven't found any forces at work that seem to require a new initiative as far as independence.

MR. GRASSLEY: The final question would probably give you an opportunity to sum up what you have previously said. But is the independence of the Fed in any danger from either political pressure from the administration or from the Congress?

MR. MILLER: I don't detect it at this time. The President has stated over and over again that he believes in the independence of the Fed. He has stated that, at the time I was nominated and at the time I was sworn in. There was a slight slip when I was sworn in giving us constitutional blessing, but I know it is only the Congress that has created the Fed, not the Constitution — although perhaps that is an amendment we should look into (laughter).

One year and four months later, in August 1979, President Carter replaced Secretary of the Treasury W. Michael Blumenthal, who had assumed office in 1977, with G. William Miller, ostensibly because Blumenthal had been acting too independently.

PRESIDENTS AND MONETARY POLICY

Politics affects monetary policy. First consider how the Fed formerly managed the nation's money supply. When did the Fed pump money into circulation at a fast rate (which may stimulate the economy and inflation), and when did it slow down the growth of the money supply (which may reduce economic activity and inflation)? From 1951 until around 1984, the answer generally depended more on who was president of the United States than on who was Fed chairman. The Fed shifted the course of monetary policy — changing the money-supply growth rate — in 1953, 1961, 1969, 1971, 1974, and 1977, all years in which the presidency changed. Except for the change from Kennedy to Johnson, those were the only years a new president assumed office between 1953 and 1977.[3] Carter changed policy in midterm during the 1970s inflation. He appointed Paul Volcker, who changed policy and stopped rapid inflation. The changes in money-supply growth after the early 1980s are described in Chapter 11.

REAGAN AND REGAN'S DEMANDS FOR FASTER
AND SLOWER MONEY GROWTH

Because of sharp internal disagreements, the first Reagan administration leaned heavily on the Fed to produce both faster and slower money-
growth policies. On one side were several slow-growth advocates, including Beryl Sprinkel, the undersecretary for monetary affairs.[4] They feared
that the recovery projected by the administration would not occur, and
yet were careful not to accelerate the rate of inflation, which had hit 13.15
percent in February 1981.

Treasury secretary Donald Regan, Sprinkel's boss, took a number of
different public positions. First, he called for faster money growth because
of fears of the second dip in the double-dip recession. He also wanted
very fast short-term money growth in order to meet the target for money
growth set by the Fed. This appeared excessive to many inside the administration. Perhaps his haste to hit the target in one month was due to a
mistake in his arithmetic, although he was getting good economic briefing papers.[5] Although the Fed's immediate spurt of fast money growth
could be viewed as an attempt to catch up to its own targets for money
growth, it certainly looked as though Fed officials knew who was the secretary and who was the undersecretary. The Fed accelerated money growth
until early in 1982, when President Reagan "criticized the Federal Reserve
Board because of the recent spurt in the nation's money supply."[6]

Inside the administration, the disagreements became public when the
Washington Post published a statement from Reagan administration officials, contradicting Regan: "Meanwhile, in Washington, sources said that
a group of four top administration economists—Lawrence Kudlow in the
Office of Management and Budget, Jerry Jordan of the Council of Economic Advisers and Treasury Undersecretaries Norman Ture and Beryl
Sprinkel—drafted a statement Tuesday, for use by White House spokes-
men, that essentially backed the Federal Reserve's policy of keeping slow,
steady growth in money."[7]

Congressman Jack Kemp, who coauthored the Kemp-Roth tax-rate-
reduction legislation that Reagan strongly advocated and signed into law,
was hostile to a policy of slower money growth.[8] Kemp called for Volcker's
resignation. When asked about this, President Reagan said that the Fed
is "autonomous" and that "there is no way I can comment on that." That
lack of endorsement of his Fed chairman sounded like a slap across the
chairman's knuckles. Counteracting this perception, "David Gergen, the

senior White House spokesman, said that the President was not intend-
ing to avoid an endorsement of Mr. Volcker. 'It was strictly a statement of
neutrality.'"[9] What does that mean?

By that time, 1982, the country was suffering from a harsh recession: officially, 10.8 percent of the nation's workforce was unemployed in
December 1982. Business failures went up drastically.[10] The administration
sent a new message: it would be desirable for the Fed to provide faster
money growth. Reagan and Regan's different messages created confusion,
as reported in the *New York Times:* "The statements today by Mr. Reagan
and his aides added to the general confusion about the Administration's
stand on monetary policy. Since last summer, the Administration has
criticized the Federal Reserve for being both too tight and too easy in its
control of the money supply—on both occasions attributing high interest
rates to these factors."[11]

Near the end of the year, the chairman of the Council of Economic
Advisers, Martin Feldstein, supported faster money growth. He stated
this position on the television program *Meet the Press:* "I think looking at
the broadest measures of the money supply and looking more generally at
what is happening in the financial markets and credit markets gives one
no reason to be concerned about the Fed's expanding too quickly."[12]

By the end of Volcker's term, a combination of retirements and resig-
nations allowed President Reagan to appoint all seven members of the
Board of Governors. That appeared to give him substantial influence at
the Fed. President Reagan was preoccupied with many issues (including
an Iranian arms scandal that erupted at the end of 1986). The new secretary of the treasury, James A. Baker III, became the dominant voice for
monetary policy in the administration.

HOW A PRESIDENT CAN LEAN ON AND
THEN REMOVE A FED CHAIRMAN

Although administration spokesman Marlin Fitzwater reportedly told reporters that Reagan had asked Fed chairman Volcker to remain, Fitzwater
was apparently contradicted by Treasury Secretary Baker, who reportedly
"confirmed that President Reagan did not ask Volcker to remain for a
third term."[13] According to another report, Volcker resigned because the
Reagan administration had sent a clear message when it "made no serious
attempt to urge him to remain."[14] Replacing federal governmental officials in this way is, of course, usual. The difference during the last years of

Volcker's tenure was the technique allegedly used by the administration to influence the Fed's policies and to get rid of Volcker.

Shortly before Governor Wayne Angell left the Fed, on February 9, 1994, Hobart Rowen, writing in the *Washington Post,* described him as a member of the "gang of four": "And despite his constant anti-inflation commitment, what may be Angell's most significant contribution as a member of the board goes in the other direction, when as a brand-new member, he helped lead a 1986 revolt by a 'Gang of Four' against Chairman Paul A. Volcker for his stubborn refusal to lower interest rates."[15] The four rebels were reported to be Board vice chairman Preston Martin and Governors Martha Seger, Manuel Johnson, and Wayne Angell. As new members, Johnson and Angell reportedly were part of the rebels who, at a Board of Governors meeting on February 24, 1986, had forced a vote to cut a Fed interest rate; they won the vote, 4-3. This vote changed the discount rate, the rate of interest that banks pay on loans from the Fed. These Reagan appointees were said to follow the more stimulative approach favored by the Reagan administration. Rowen said they did not wish to humiliate Volcker, so they offered him a deal that required an immediate, coordinated reduction in rates in Germany and Japan. Volcker acquiesced, and ten days later the three nations lowered their rates. The gang of four leaked their actions to the newspapers: "The 'Gang of Four' Reagan appointees at the Fed—Preston Martin, Martha Seger, Wayne Angell, and Manuel Johnson—took control of the seven-person board only last month. They have wasted no time in publicly humiliating Mr. Volcker by first forcing him to accept a cut in the discount rate against his better judgment and then leaking a detailed account of the incident to the newspapers."[16]

The FOMC transcripts from February 11-12 and April 1, 1986, contain no evidence of hostility or serious disagreement between Volcker and the so-called rebels. This strongly suggests that the 4-3 vote was the result of a coordinated behind-the-scenes revolt.

President Reagan put the customary pretty ribbon around the pink slip when he made "a short appearance at the White House briefing room" to say that he had accepted Volcker's decision "with great reluctance and regret."[17]

GREENSPAN READS CLINTON'S BODY LANGUAGE

Fed chairmen Greenspan, Miller, and Burns were astute politicians who sought to interact closely with presidential administrations. The Fed strives to avoid promoting any policies that clearly oppose the administration's. However, more than monetary policy was involved in a 1992 meeting between Greenspan and president-elect Bill Clinton. A bill pending in Congress threatened Fed officials with making FOMC meetings almost completely transparent.

Greenspan traveled to Little Rock to visit with president-elect Clinton who had requested the meeting. This was a time of great uncertainty for the Fed. Not only were Fed officials unsure of Clinton, but they were also unnerved—or more pointedly, freaked out—by the legislation Gonzalez had proposed. This legislation would authorize the videotaping of FOMC meetings and the publication of the transcripts. The Greenspan Fed sent Gonzalez letters saying that publishing any such transcripts or recordings would inhibit discussion and impair monetary policy—and, in general, that the sky would fall.

As reported in the transcript of an FOMC conference call, Greenspan brought back good news from the future president: "If I read his body language and peripheral comments [correctly], his views were clearly favorable as best I can judge." Note that in the FOMC transcript, Greenspan refers to Edward (Mike) Kelley as "someone brought up in that arena," apparently meaning a Texan, like Gonzalez:

Transcript of Federal Open Market Committee Conference Call
December 14, 1992
CHAIRMAN GREENSPAN. Let me start off by briefly reviewing the meeting I had with President-elect Clinton in Little Rock ten days ago. I had about 24 hours' notice but a choice of days on which to go down and visit. It was fairly apparent that the basic purpose of the meeting was to indicate a desire to work with the Federal Reserve. . . . but obviously the main purpose of this call is the update I indicated we would have following our discussion about Henry Gonzalez's letters. But before I call on Don Kohn to brief us on his review of the detailed minutes of our last meeting on that particular subject, does anyone have a desire [to discuss] anything further on my meeting with Mr. Clinton?
MR. BOEHNE. Did you get any impressions about how he views the Fed as an institution and our role in the public policy structure?
CHAIRMAN GREENSPAN. Ed, we didn't discuss that directly but if I read his body language and peripheral comments [correctly], his views were clearly favorable as best I can judge. We had a very short break after about 2 hours into the meeting when he apparently spoke to Mr. Stefanopoulous

[*sic*], and in discussing the content of our meeting apparently made a special point about the importance of maintaining the independence of the Federal Reserve System. I must say that everything I heard in our meeting was consistent with that and I gained no indication of any concerns about the Federal Reserve, its policy or structure, or the nature of the Fed as an institution.[18]

MR. BOEHNE. Do you have any impressions about how the new Secretary of the Treasury might view some of those issues?

CHAIRMAN GREENSPAN. Well, I know of no reason to believe that his views would be otherwise. He certainly would not be expected to be supportive of Chairman Gonzalez because I don't think he ever has been to my knowledge. But we do have somebody who was brought up in that arena, and I thought Mike Kelley might inform us as to his insights.

MR. KELLEY. Well. I don't have any special insights but, as I said to the Chairman when he asked me the other day, I can't imagine in my wildest dreams that Lloyd Bentsen [a former U.S. senator from Texas] is going to go out of his way to support an initiative by Henry Gonzalez. It would indeed be revolutionary in his career at this late date.

CHAIRMAN GREENSPAN. That's what I like about Mike. He doesn't come to the point! Does anybody else want to pursue anything further on this? If not, why don't I call on Don Kohn to brief us on what he sees as the central focus or the nature of our rather random discussion relating to the two letters that we received from Chairman Gonzalez.[19]

Although Gonzalez's bill, which had twenty-three sponsors, did not pass, it was the beginning of a successful effort that resulted in publication of the Fed's transcripts (described in Chapter 6).

THE GREENSPAN FED'S QUARTERBACK SNEAK

Greenspan indicated that politics was the primary consideration in deciding whether to tell Congress and the public about the Fed's policies. In 1991 he said it would be best not to "signal" the Fed's planned "disinflationary" policies because of political problems that could arise from pending legislation that might be ornamented with undesirable amendments: "I'm not sure there's anything to be gained in the short run in signaling a tightening for '92 this far in advance. I don't think we need it. All that will do is galvanize some anti-Fed actions which, since the Banking bill is still open and under negotiation, can create an inadvertent problem for us because amendments on the floor of the House and Senate can be particularly ill-informed and still pass."[20]

It is not difficult to understand Greenspan's reluctance to "signal" Congress and the public about a policy to fight inflation, since the economy had just hit the bottom (the trough) of the 1990–1991 recession. Many Members of Congress might legitimately object to an action likely to raise interest rates. The Greenspan Fed opted for a quarterback sneak. The damage from using the sneak included the spreading of false information, rumors, and leaks, which filled the gap between the need to know and the planned deception by the Fed.

THE FED LOBBIES CONGRESS USING PUBLIC FUNDS

The Fed's use of public funds for lobbying purposes is particularly disturbing for a governmental entity with such immense economic power and enshrined leaders. Evidence comes from the minutes of the board of directors meetings that were obtained by House Banking chairman Henry Reuss in 1976 (described in Chapter 2). Reuss's floor speech in the House, "What the Secret Minutes of the Federal Reserve Banks Meetings Disclose," documented how the Fed used its funds—public monies—to organize the bankers it regulates to lobby Congress. He revealed that Fed officials used taxpayers' money to fly to Fed Banks and instruct the directors to organize private-sector bankers to lobby against bills that would bring outside auditors and public accountability to the Fed:[21]

In 1974 and 1975 the Congress was the subject of a barrage of lobbying by the commercial banks against two bills affecting the Federal Reserve— both bills that have been badly needed in the public interest.

One bill, approved by the House Banking committee on July 10, 1975, would have authorized an audit of the Federal Reserve System by the General Accounting Office. The bill specifically exempted from the audit both monetary policy and foreign transactions.

The second bill, the so-called "Government in the Sunshine" Act, required generally that meetings in which the public interest is decided be open to public scrutiny. The bill passed, but with substantial exemptions for the Federal Reserve.

A reading of the minutes of the Reserve Bank boards of directors meetings demonstrate that the Fed has gone well beyond the bounds of propriety to generate lobbying against these bills. With the Federal Reserve Board in Washington serving as the command center, a well-orchestrated lobbying campaign was mounted, using the members of the boards of directors as the point men. They would indeed be valuable operators in any lobbying campaign. The bankers and businessmen who make up the majority of these boards of directors are men with powerful ties into the board rooms of banks and corporations all over the country. They also enjoy strong ties into the most powerful trade associations. It is no wonder, from what we see in these minutes, that such organizations as the Business Roundtable and the American Bankers Association geared up for an all-out defense of the Federal Reserve.

Let us look at some of the lobbying efforts against these two pieces of legislation, as revealed by the directors meetings.

On February 19, 1974, President Frank E. Morris of the Boston Federal Reserve Bank called on his board of directors to contact the members of Congress to promote the Federal Reserve's position on an earlier version of the GAO audit bill.

The official minutes of this meeting state—page 95 of Federal Reserve Bank of Boston directors' minutes 1972, 1974, 1975, as delivered to the House Banking Committee:

> Mr. Morris also called attention to the Fact that H.R. 10265, which would provide for a G.A.O. audit of the Federal Reserve System had not died in the House Rules committee but was expected to reach the floor of the House of Representatives on or about March 5. He indicated that the System's position was to support an amendment, to be proposed by Rep. Ashley (Democrat, Ohio), which would limit the scope of the audit so as to exclude monetary policy actions, but to continue to oppose the bill, even if amended, on the final vote. *The directors were encouraged to let Members of the house know their views on the bill.* (Emphasis added.)[22]

The following colloquy of January 21, 1975, occurred at hearings before the Subcommittee on Financial Institutions Supervision, Regulation and Insurance of the Committee on Banking, Currency and Housing, House of Representatives, 94th Congress, first and second session, page 2006:

> CHAIRMAN REUSS. Chairman Burns, let me now get into the area of politics, which you brought up several times this morning in connection with the audit bill for the Fed. On October 1, 1975, the American Banker carried an interesting story on your Reserve Bank chairman in Richmond, Robert L. Lawson.

The headline was, "Federal Reserve Board Official Hails Bank Role in Killing GAO audit of the Fed." And then it went on to describe his speech to a bankers group, in which he said: "Banks played a key role in blocking a congressional audit of the Federal Reserve Board. The bankers in our district and elsewhere did a tremendous job in helping to defeat the GAO bill. It shows what can be done when the bankers of the country get together."

My question is: If you get the support of the banks on an issue which is of great concern to you, whether Congress has the right to audit your books or not, are they not likely to expect in return kind treatment from you as a regulator? They would not get it, of course, but are they not likely to expect it?

DR. BURNS. As for Mr. Lawson's statement, let me merely remind you that, as I indicated in my testimony, we have in the System 269 directors, and neither I nor the Board can be responsible for what individual directors may or may not say.

CHAIRMAN REUSS. Did not the Federal Reserve people, to your knowledge, communicate with the banks about bank lobbying against the audit bill?

DR. BURNS. I played no part in this activity at all, not because I would consider it wrong, but because I did not have time.

CHAIRMAN REUSS. My question was, with respect to people at the Fed, was there not a little communication there?

DR. BURNS. Yes. That is to say there was some communication between our various directors, not with bankers as such, but with bankers, journalists, business people. I do not know whom they contacted. And that, I think, is an entirely legitimate activity. After all, do not Members of the Congress want to hear from their constituents?

[Reuss continued:]

Think what would happen if the Federal Power Commission enlisted the executives of the oil and gas companies it regulates to lobby Congress on legislation of concern to the FPC. Congress would be outraged. And it would be clearly illegal.

It is a fine line to draw between the intent of this section of the criminal code, which prohibits the use of appropriated funds for lobbying, and the Fed's use of funds which would otherwise be paid into the Federal Treasury. It is all in reality, the taxpayers' money. In fact, in other instances the Fed itself has argued that Federal Reserve System funds are in fact

Government funds. The Office of Management and Budget recently issued "Guidelines for Reducing Public Reporting to Federal Agencies" which said: "Federal agencies are not to engage in any data collection activities which are not financed wholly by Federal funds."

In a letter to Senator Lee Metcalf, chairman of the Governmental Affairs Subcommittee on Reports, Accounting and Management, Dr. Burns stated: "We believe that System funds may be viewed as 'Federal funds,' as distinguished from private funds, within the limited context of the provision of the OMB guideline in question.

In other words, when it suits its purpose, the Fed claims that it is no different from other government agencies simply because its funds are not appropriated.

Congress, therefore, should remove this distinction between the Fed and other agencies by applying to the Fed the same restrictions on lobbying that govern other agencies.[23]

The Fed-orchestrated lobby helped keep the audit bills considered in the House Banking Committee from reaching the full House for a vote. The bill was then considered in another committee, the Government Reform Committee. The Fed successfully lobbied for limitations on audits both by the General Accounting Office (GAO) and private accounting firms. The final audit law, the Federal Banking Agency Audit Act of 1978, placed the Fed's monetary and international-exchange activities off-limits for outside auditors. Those limitations may be stretched to cover many Fed operations, and they remain in force, severely curtailing audits of the Fed.[24]

House Banking chairman Henry Gonzalez obtained minutes of the board of directors meetings from the twelve Fed Banks in the 1990s. After reading the minutes from a meeting that had been held on August 8, 1991, he made the following observations, in a press release dated October 30, 1992: "Contrary to the Federal Reserve's oft repeated claim that it is politically independent, some of the regional Federal Reserve Bank Boards *are* politically active." The directors discussed the "Senator Paul S. Sarbanes/Representative Lee H. Hamilton" bills to reorganize the Fed. The minutes recorded that directors asked to be advised if their "help would be appropriate at some point." Remembering that the "Federal Reserve organized bankers through their Reserve Bank boards of directors to lobby the Congress to exempt the Federal Reserve from a GAO audit of its monetary policy functions," Gonzalez said he knew "what it means when the Federal Reserve offers to 'help.'" So Gonzalez asked a Fed Bank president what the directors meant by the word "help." The Fed Bank president indicated "that a number of the Reserve Bank's directors were 'extremely critical of the measure' (the bills to reorganize the Federal Reserve) and that 'One director volunteered that he would like to discuss his views of the legislation with one or more members of Congress.'" The Fed Bank president informed Gonzalez: "The Bank's General Counsel advised against a deliberate or coordinated effort by directors to influence legislation."

Using Fed board of directors meetings to organize "deliberate or coordinated" lobbying efforts by banks and financial institutions regulated by the Fed is difficult to stop, especially if there is no strenuous congressional oversight or GAO auditing of the Fed.

TRILLION-DOLLAR MERGERS AND POLITICAL POWER

Large banks have a huge incentive to become part of and to cultivate favor with the Fed, which can approve or deny their billion-dollar mergers and acquisitions. This raises a central question about bank regulation. Does the Fed give priority to the public interest when judging the effects of allowing a handful of huge financial holding companies and the banks they own to dominate the financial system in the United States? According to a Fed report in 2000: "The U.S. banking industry has experienced an unprecedented, persistent merger movement since 1980, with nearly 8,000 mergers and about $2.4 trillion in acquired assets. . . . Concentration of control over aggregate U.S. bank deposits among the largest banks increased substantially, with the share of the 100 largest rising from about 47 percent to 71 percent and the share of the 10 largest rising from around 19 percent to 37 percent, the latter rise occurred mostly after 1990."[25] This was during the period of the Greenspan Fed. Another Fed study points to a very severe problem in large metropolitan areas, where concentration has increased substantially.[26]

In 1994, some limits were placed on mergers during a House-Senate conference committee chaired by Gonzalez. The Riegle-Neal bill was negotiated and signed into law. It limited a bank's overall concentration to 10 percent of domestic deposits in the country and not more than 30 percent in a state. The law specifically limited the ability of the Fed's Board of Governors to approve mergers and acquisitions if doing so would cause the cap to be exceeded.[27]

The second-largest bank in the United States, Bank of America, was close to the cap in 2004. In 2005, Bank of America bought a large New England banking group, FleetBoston, for (reportedly) $48 billion. The new conglomerate was too close to the 10 percent cap to allow it much room to grow, since growth would be very likely to require additional Fed approvals for mergers and acquisitions.[28] The combined entity would reportedly control the largest percentage of U.S. bank domestic deposits.

The three banks with the largest share of domestic deposits on September 30, 2006, were Bank of America, 9 percent; J. P. Morgan Chase, 6.9 percent; and Wachovia, 5.8 percent.[29] These banks had had much smaller percentages of the deposits twelve years earlier. Bank of America then had 4 percent.

The 10 percent cap could be avoided by buying financial firms not involved with bank deposits. In January 2004, J. P. Morgan Chase was reported to be buying Bank One for $58 billion.[30] (The sale went through that July.) During 2005, Bank of America announced it would purchase the largest U.S. independent credit card issuer, MBNA. This (reportedly) $35 billion purchase made Bank of America the world's largest credit card issuer.[31] The trillion-dollar financial conglomerates provide widespread services, such as huge ATM networks.

The cost to the public of the formation of larger financial conglomerates includes those firms' immense political power, exercised through lobbying, largesse, and the revolving doors between business and government. This increase in political power can tip and bend the regulatory apparatus.[32]

The 10 percent deposit cap would not go unchallenged for long. In 2004, a Bank of America "spokeswoman" reportedly did not want to remove the cap.[33] That appeared to be a political statement to tamp down adverse reaction to the bank's recent expansion, not a submission to a ceiling on future growth. And so it was that in 2007, Bank of America argued "that U.S. banks are artificially small and vulnerable to foreign acquirers," and so it had "begun a quiet push to raise the regulatory cap ... that would give it more than 10% of the nation's total deposits."[34] The "push" was not quiet enough to keep the story from appearing on page 1 of the *Wall Street Journal*. Legislators seem to face a dilemma: limit the banking operations of large foreign banks in the United States, or remove the cap and allow more deposits to be concentrated in a few large U.S. banks. Lawmakers should look into the large literature on competition in industries dominated by a few large firms.[35]

What about the Fed and Congress? Will they fight to hold the cap at 10 percent? Under the present organization of the Fed, two-thirds of the directors of Fed banks are voted in by bankers, meaning that banks to a large extent are the Fed. Some members of Congress may oppose increasing or removing the cap. Congressman Barney Frank, who became chairman of House Banking in 2007, declared in 2004 that "the rules regulators use to judge merger and acquisition deals should be toughened."[36] With the resources of trillion-dollar financial conglomerates, these obstacles may be overcome.

GREENSPAN, RUBIN, CALIO, THE WORLD'S BIGGEST BANKING CONGLOMERATE, AND THE "WALL STREET FIX"

Those who dreamed of an umbrella bank, a "superbank," a place for one-stop shopping for every kind of financial service from a single firm, surely heralded the appointment of Greenspan as Fed chairman, in 1987.[37] Apparently, Greenspan and the Board of Governors favored the repeal of the Glass-Steagall Act, the 1930s law that prevented banks from combining with other financial firms.[38]

The law stood in the way of the giant conglomerate Citigroup, which had been put together in 1998 under the leadership of Sanford I. Weill. He was appointed chief executive of Commercial Credit Company, a troubled Baltimore finance company, in 1986, and then used this company as a base for acquiring a number of major businesses, leading to the formation of Citigroup in 1998. The conglomerate included the country's largest bank, Citibank; the second-largest retail brokerage, Salomon Smith Barney; and a large insurance company, Travelers Life and Annuity.[39] The Glass-Steagall Act, still in effect in 1998, prohibited the formation of this conglomerate. If Citigroup were to survive in its 1998 form, Glass-Steagall would have to be repealed.[40]

A bill with a name that focus groups would like, the Financial Services Modernization Bill (the Gramm-Leach-Bliley Act), was signed into law on November 12, 1999. The law, which was needed to legalize Citigroup's formation, authorized the organization of conglomerates of financial businesses, to be called "financial holding companies." It removed Glass-Steagall's restriction barring banks from being underwriters (issuers) of new stock offerings. Commercial banks in the United States were generally limited to traditional banking activities, albeit with many exceptions granted by the regulators.[41] The law gave the Fed substantial new powers. It could decide which private firms would be allowed in the new conglomerates.

Robert Rubin, President Clinton's secretary of the treasury, played a central role for the administration in the development of the law. Rubin was a highly effective and well-regarded secretary. He acknowledged the existence of serious concerns that "these large aggregations [created by the legislation] could present competitive problems in the initial stages, and then subsequently, if small banks are not able to compete, then you can have other kinds of pricing mechanisms develop once they're gone."[42] The Clinton administration subsequently supported the legislation.

Robert Rubin left his position on July 2, 1999. Within four months (October 26, 1999), he took a top-level position with Citigroup, one month before the Modernization Bill was signed into law. Rubin's subordinate, the comptroller of the currency, who regulates banks with national charters, is barred from taking a position with a bank for one year after leaving office, but can take a position with a bank holding company, a loophole that eviscerates the restriction. Rules restricting employment after leaving office are used to reduce conflicts of interest in decision making and to help prevent regulators from being bought by the parties being regulated.

On September 22, 2002, Senator John McCain blasted an official of the Federal Election Commission for lobbying Congress on measures affecting his supposedly independent agency. McCain said on *Meet the Press*, "I've never seen so much corruption" by a member of an independent agency.

As an official of another supposedly independent governmental entity, Chairman Greenspan, may have used his position to help pass the Financial Services Modernization Bill. Sitting in a room near where the House-Senate conference committee was meeting on the bill, he could conveniently lobby members who sought his highly regarded advice on why they should vote for the bill.

In 2002 and 2003, investigations by Eliot Spitzer, attorney general of New York, revealed allegedly fraudulent practices at leading financial firms. Ten banks reached a $1.4 billion settlement with Spitzer in a civil action against them for "fundamentally corrupt" actions, including giving false information to the public about the stock of companies that were its customers. Much of the corruption centered around the rise and fall of a giant company, WorldCom, and its CEO, Bernard Ebbers, who was convicted and sentenced to twenty-five years in prison in 2005. He was convicted of an $11 billion accounting fraud. He personally received millions of dollars from underpriced initial public offerings (issuances of stock).

Twenty thousand employees of his company lost their jobs. The stockholders, which included thousands of small investors as well as large institutional investors, such as pension funds, lost billions of dollars. World-Com stock was worth about $180 billion at it peak, in 1999. According to Hedrick Smith, WorldCom's collapse showed "how brokers and analysts shaped and hyped the telecom boom, pocketed enormous profits and then took millions of ordinary investors on a catastrophic ride, $2 trillion in losses on WorldCom and other telecom stocks."[43]

The story of these scandals also included a stock analyst, Jack Grubman, who worked at Salomon Smith Barney, part of Citigroup, with Sanford Weill, the leader of Citigroup. Grubman continued to make favorable comments about WorldCom stock even as the company was collapsing. Citigroup made large fees for handling much of the financing of the buyouts that transformed WorldCom into a giant company.[44] But Citigroup's involvement in the corruption surrounding WorldCom went further: "Travelers [part of Citigroup] gave WorldCom CEO, Bernie Ebbers, a personal mortgage for $1 billion. Ebbers would use the loan to build a personal business empire by purchasing a half million acres of timberlands in Mississippi, Alabama, and Tennessee. In addition, Citibank [the bank owned by Citigroup] gave Ebbers another loan that he used to finance ownership of a 500,000-acre ranch in Canada—a loan that attorneys representing irate stockholders charge was backed by 2.3 million shares of Ebbers' WorldCom stock."[45]

Eliot Spitzer was asked an underlying question:

FRONTLINE: So you're saying the repeal of Glass-Steagall and the permission for these huge superbanks is one of the proximate causes of the corruption on Wall Street?

ELIOT SPITZER: Absolutely. There's no question about it. On that day I announced the global settlement, on Dec. 20 [2002], I began saying that problem at its root is a flawed business model, and that business model is the product of a government regulatory decision to repeal Glass-Steagall administratively and legislatively, and to seek this tremendous concentration of power, and the abuse of that power by investment houses.

But it was that effort to create these full-service banks, and that was the proximate cause for all of this.[46]

Under attack, Citigroup turned to the government for help. Nick Calio, the head of the White House Office of Legislative Affairs during the George W. Bush administration, quit his job in the middle of the president's first term (January 2003) and went to work as a lobbyist for Citigroup. This job change—allowing for the ethics rule prohibiting lobbying the White House for one year—is another demonstration of the importance of governmental officials to large government-regulated banks and financial conglomerates. Arianna Huffington wrote: "Earlier this month Calio left the White House to become chief lobbyist for Citigroup. The hire couldn't have come at a better time for the embattled banking behemoth, which has been under fire from state and federal regulators—and has just agreed to pay $300 million in fines to settle claims that its stock analysts intentionally misled investors."[47]

Not to worry—the nation's primary regulator of financial holding companies in New York, the New York Fed Bank, is on the job. What kind of job were its officials doing? Whose side were they on? Two-thirds of its directors were elected by the banks in the New York district. Sanford Weill, chairman of Citigroup, was elected to the board of directors of the New York Fed Bank in 2001. He was reelected for a three-year term beginning January 2004.

What has this primary regulator of financial holding companies, the Fed, done to police financial holding companies such as Citigroup? What safeguards are in place for federally insured deposits, largely a liability of the nation's taxpayers? Is it time to take bank regulation away from a governmental bureaucracy that is managed largely by the bankers it regulates? It is long past time to end the pretense of independence and political virginity at the Fed.

CHAPTER 11

PRICKING THE STOCK MARKET BUBBLE AND OTHER GREENSPAN POLICIES

TURNING ON THE FOG LIGHTS

It was clear that the value of many peoples' incomes and wealth was shrinking fast as prices shot skyward in the 1970s. Prices rose by over 13 percent in 1979 and then by more than 12 percent in 1980. The Volcker Fed's policies applied the brakes to this untenable rapid inflation, but at the cost of a double-dip recession. The rapid inflation rates of the 1970s and 1980 did not return during 1987–2006, although inflation rates rose over 3 percent in eight of those years (calculated separately). The Greenspan Fed years included two recessions, a bubble, a collapse of stock prices, and slow economic recoveries. The period also saw the implementation of digital technology and the rise of the Internet, and both altered the effects of the Fed's primary economic tool, changing the money supply. In addition, the intent of the Greenspan Fed's policies was fogged over by its chairman's deceptive announcements in the mid-1990s. The fog lights that cut through this deception were an article in *Barron's* and a congressional hearing in 2000.

"WE LET A LOT OF AIR OUT OF THE TIRE"

The Fed began to double its short-term interest-rate target (called the federal funds target) in February 1994.[1] What was the Fed's policy? Inflation fell from 6.2 percent in 1990 to 2.6 in 1994, a slow recovery from a recession was underway, and unemployment still topped 6 percent, yet the Fed was raising interest rates.[2] Why?

Greenspan said the move was a preemptive strike against inflation. That was difficult to believe, especially because Greenspan and a few others had warned that the measurement of inflation was too high. Taking their suggested error into account, the inflation rate was heading to nearly zero.

In March 1994, the press reported the preemptive attack on inflation as well as Greenspan's meeting with President Clinton at which he reportedly explained the policy: "The Fed is boosting rates to cool the economy as a pre-emptive strike against inflation. . . . The president, who met Friday with Fed Chairman Alan Greenspan at the White House, said he was told a further increase in short-term rates should help to lower long-term rates by convincing investors that the central bank was being vigilant against inflation."[3] At least, Greenspan reportedly mentioned "investors," hinting at what he was really doing. Perhaps he said more. The administration was not completely passive. President Clinton nominated Alan Blinder to be vice chairman of the Board of Governors. Blinder sent this reminder to the public and his new colleagues: "Alan Blinder, recently appointed vice chairman of the Federal Reserve Board by President Clinton, called last week for the Fed to use monetary policy to bring down unemployment from temporarily high levels. That prescription put him at odds with Chairman Alan Greenspan's testimony to Congress that the Fed cannot control employment and ought to focus only on inflation."[4]

The announcement of a preemptive policy to stop inflation turned out to be misleading, incomplete, or false.[5] Transcripts of FOMC meetings from 1994, released over five years later, revealed that Greenspan was using monetary policy to "prick the bubble" in the stock market.

If Greenspan had testified that the Fed was pricking the "stock market bubble" or "letting the air out of the tire," there would have been a stampede of reporters to communicate that information. On an FOMC conference call in February 1994, Greenspan stated his view of the effect of Fed policy: "I think we partially broke the back of an emerging speculation in equities . . . We pricked that bubble [in bond markets] as well . . . We also have created a degree of uncertainty; if we were looking at the emergence of speculative forces, which clearly were evident in very early stages, then I think we had a desirable effect."[6]

Greenspan had expected that by raising interest rates the Fed would reduce stock prices. He told the FOMC in March 1994: "When we moved on February 4th, I think our expectation was that we would prick the bubble in the equity markets. . . . So what has occurred is that while this capital gains bubble in all financial assets had to come down, instead of the decline being concentrated in the stock area, it shifted over into the bond area. But the effects are the same."[7]

On an FOMC conference call in April 1994, Greenspan heralded a decrease in the financial markets' bubble: "Secondly, the sharp declines in both stock and bond prices since our last meeting, I think, have defused a significant part of the bubble which had been previously built up. We let a lot of air out of the tire, so to speak." He thought the dangers of precipitating a significant stock-market crash had diminished: "The dangers of breaking the surface tension of the markets clearly are less than they were at the time of the last meeting. . . . The problem, as I've argued in recent meetings, is that we have to be careful about breaking this so-called surface tension of the market and . . . selling begetting selling. That is potentially quite dangerous."[8]

In May 1994, Greenspan declared that the Fed had "taken a significant amount of air out of the bubble" but that "there's still a lot of bubble around": "We have taken a very significant amount of air out of the bubble. . . . And I think what we have reached in conclusion at this particular point is the defusion of a good part of the bubble. I think there's still a lot of bubble around; we have not completely eliminated it. Nonetheless, we have the capability I would say at this stage to move more strongly than we usually do without the risk of cracking the system."[9]

In November 1994, Philadelphia Fed Bank president Edward Boehne (a nonvoting participant in that FOMC meeting) summed up the Fed's actions in raising interest rates to deflate the bubble: "I think you argued rather persuasively, Mr. Chairman, that we had a bubble in financial markets and that we had to deflate that rather slowly. Otherwise, we could take a big hit. In hindsight, I think that was wise."[10]

Five years later at a congressional hearing before a subcommittee of House Banking, Representative Maxine Waters asked Greenspan about my article in *Barron's* (July 24, 2000) that stated Greenspan had consistently advocated targeting stock-market prices in 1994. Greenspan said it was an important question, and he replied with an admission: "And it's my judgment as of today [not to target stock prices], and, indeed, it has been my judgment for the last two or three years. It was not my judgment in the earlier period, and indeed, it was not my judgment in 1994."[11] Representative Carolyn Maloney continued examining Greenspan's admission that he had targeted stock prices:

MALONEY: Earlier, Mr. Chairman, you responded . . . to questions of Congressman [Barney] Frank and Congresswoman Waters and you said that the Fed does not target stock markets. I think that is a substantial statement, and I would like to place in the record the article that they both referred to. It is in *Barron's* this week. And I think that it is important to note and that prior to 1994, because in this article they quote the minutes from the meetings, you felt that monetary policy could target the stock market and that is basically what was quoted in here. So I would ask—

GREENSPAN: As I indicated in my response, at that time I thought it might be appropriate and, indeed, on occasion, thought it was. I've since changed my mind on that issue.

MALONEY: Well, I think that is a substantial statement and I just wanted to make sure that this was in the record.[12]

STOCK PRICES AND MONEY RIDE THE FED'S ROLLER COASTER

The nation's money supply and stock-market prices were on a roller coaster ride from the late 1980s through the 1990s and into 2000. As seen in Figure 11-1, the average growth rates for both money and stock prices dropped for a number of years.[13] That was the initial ride downward on the roller coaster, to near zero growth in 1994; growth in both areas then rose rapidly in the last half of the 1990s. Stock prices shot up an average of 35 percent a year from 1995 to 1999, and some hot sectors, such as technology stocks, did much better.[14] Many delirious stock buyers had dreamed of such large paper gains, and they could not resist buying more.[15]

The Greenspan Fed did not initiate the bubble, but it did help finance it in the last half of the 1990s by adding over a trillion dollars to the supply of money from 1996 to 2000. Fed officials paid little attention to money growth. The growth in the money supply during the stock-market bubble was a by-product of the Fed's policy to target interest rates.[16]

The finding that stock prices were related to money growth in the 1990s, as suggested by Figure 11-1, is similar to evidence presented by Milton Friedman in 2005. He showed how monetary growth affects economic activity and stock prices during periods of rapid economic growth "in response to rapid technological change: the booms of the 1920s in the United States, the 1980s in Japan and the 1990s in the United States."[17] This was only part of the story.

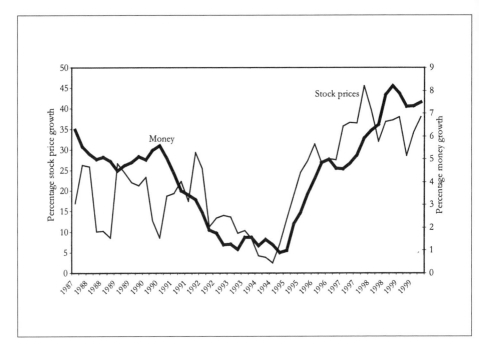

FIGURE 11-1. Money and stock price growth rates, 1987–2000. Both growth rates (six-quarter moving averages) fell from 1992 to 1995 and then dramatically changed course in 1996. The simultaneous trillion-dollar rise in the money supply, which grew at nearly 9 percent in 1998, and the more than doubling of stock prices from 1996 to 2000 suggest that the Greenspan Fed played a role in financing the stock-market bubble with the government printing press.

It was a two-way street. Not only did the Fed's policy help finance the stock market bubble, Fed policy was also based to a small but significant extent on previous changes in stock prices. I found evidence of this when I worked at the Fed, and I published the findings in one of its publications.[18] The effect of this two-way causation complicates statistical testing and indicates a more interconnected relationship than is apparent in Figure 11-1.

The last thing Fed officials would be happy to admit is that their policy funded the stock-market bubble from 1995 to 2000. Money-supply changes and other Fed policies, such as changes in margin requirements on stock purchases, discussed below, matter, even though the Fed concentrates on targeting interest rates.

The Fed targets the interest rate on loans between banks, which frequently have a duration as short as overnight. There was an enormous discrepancy between the Fed's target interest rate and the rates of interest enjoyed by giddy stock-market investors and their cheerleaders on Wall Street. When the stock market began its crash in March 2000, those giddy dreams of stock-market profits turned to nightmares.

TO RAISE OR NOT TO RAISE MARGIN REQUIREMENTS, THAT IS THE QUESTION

Greenspan recognized in 1996 that there was a "bubble" in stock prices. At the FOMC meeting on September 24, 1996, he said: "I recognize that there is a stock market bubble problem at this point, and I agree with Governor Lindsey [Lawrence Lindsey, who in 2001 would become the chief economic adviser in the Bush administration for two years]."[19]

One policy Greenspan suggested at that meeting was to raise margin requirements—the percentage of the purchase price that can be borrowed to buy a stock—in order to reduce the speculative bubble in stock prices.[20] The effects of an increase in margin requirements are imprecise, for many reasons. Many financial assets that allow the purchase or sale of financial assets in the future are not covered by the margin regulations on stock purchases. They can be bought with very little cash. Nevertheless, raising margin requirements from the 50 percent level might have substantially reduced ballooning stock prices. The late Henry Reuss, a former chairman of the House Banking Committee, advocated just such a policy. Greenspan told the FOMC in 1996 that a rise in margin requirements would get rid of the stock-market bubble: "We do have the possibility of raising major concerns by increasing margin requirements. I guarantee that if you want to get rid of the bubble, whatever it is, that will do it. My concern is that I am not sure what else it will do."[21] Raising margin requirements was something Greenspan would discuss only behind closed doors; he spoke against it in public. Politically, it would have been difficult to raise margin requirements when much of the country was on the verge of reaping glorious returns from rising stock prices.

In 2002, Stephen Roach, chief economist for Morgan Stanley, read those transcripts and wrote that "Chairman Greenspan and his colleagues were not only very disturbed about the rapidly emerging bubble, they were also quite conversant in what it would take to pop it."[22] Roach related that in congressional testimony in 1999, Greenspan derided the very notion of raising margin requirements as an "anachronism."

Some raised the question of whether the start of a bubble could be identified. Nobel laureate Paul Samuelson said in 1997: "It's not a question anymore, the stock market is in a bubble."[23] He recounted asking Greenspan about margin requirements on one occasion:

> I heard Alan Greenspan say in a private dinner at the Boston Federal Reserve that the market crash [in 1987] was just to cool things off a little. So I asked with so many people worried, why the Fed didn't raise margin requirements? This would be a shot across the bow of the ultra-bulls. Greenspan responded, 'Paul, we don't know whether that'll end up doing good or otherwise.' He added that how things worked out in the aftermath of the 1987 crash may itself have added 3000 points to the present value of the Dow Jones Industrial Average, because a lot of people learned a lesson that cowardly people who sold after Black Monday [October 19, 1987] ended up with big losses.[24]

By 1998, the middle of the stock-market bubble, Greenspan changed from his view of attacking the stock market. He told the FOMC that he did not know if there was a stock-market bubble and that the "the notion of merely hitting the market itself [with tighter monetary policy] is an illusion."[25]

> But I ask myself, do I really know significantly more than the money managers who effectively determine the prices of these individual stocks? I must say that I, too, feel a degree of humility about my present ability to make such a forecast.
> The more interesting question is whether, even if we were to decide we had a bubble and we wanted to let the air out of it, we would be able to do it. I am not sure of the answer. We have observed, in fact, that letting the air out of the bubble, if it exists, could well be counterproductive.[26]

Alan Abelson, who had been very perceptive in judging the existence of the bubble, summarized Greenspan's stance: "Inaction was bad enough. But a passive transgression was compounded by a deliberate policy of public deceit. . . . Thus in March '97, in testimony before Congress, recounts Steve [Roach], Mr. Greenspan derided the very notion of raising margins as an 'anachronism.' In January 2000, he declared flat-out that 'the level of stock prices [has] nothing to do with margin requirements.'" Abelson then presented Stephen Roach's warning: "'From tulips to Nasdaq, the record of history is littered with the rubble of post-bubble economies. It takes both wisdom and courage to avoid such tragic outcomes. Sadly, as the full story now comes out, we find that America's Federal Reserve had neither.'"[27]

THE TECHNOLOGY BOOM, LOWER INFLATION, AND EXCESS SUPPLY

No matter how much praise the Fed chairman received for the prosperity of the 1990s, the Fed was not the cause of the information revolution, which resulted from decades of development. The Greenspan Fed fought technological change by throwing sand in the gears of digital check-clearing processes in the 1990s (see Chapter 7). It was finally forced to adapt to reality in 2003. It may continue to subsidize paper-check clearing and to try to thwart private firms that are more adept and innovative in developing and using digital technology.

What about the low rate of inflation during the booming 1990s? A number of external events helped hold down domestic prices. New technologies allowed more goods and services to be produced per worker. More important were the severe recessions and economic crises triggered around the world by a nosedive in the value of Asian currencies in the summer of 1997. This currency crisis was followed in 1998 by the Russian government's failure to make interest payments on its debt. These price-reducing events occurred during the Asian production "miracle" that vastly increased the supply of many imported commodities, including those associated with the production of computers.

The investment boom in the manufacture of digital communication and storage equipment created a huge increase in the supply of many products. This supply may well have outstripped demand, causing a downward pressure on prices.

An economic stimulus like the investment boom of the 1990s could cause prices to fall, a deflation, if it were to stimulate the supply of goods and services more than the demand for them. In 1976, I developed a mathematical model demonstrating the falsity of a widely held belief, namely, that an economic stimulus at full employment always causes rising prices, i.e., inflation.[28] I used classic economic tools: a Keynesian model (named for a famous economist, John Maynard Keynes) and a commonly used formula for production, both widely used in college textbooks. My mathematical finding turned the usual interpretation of this model on its head. Unfortunately, as of 2007, the usual interpretation has lived on in college textbooks throughout the world, causing support for misdirected economic policies.

RECESSION AND A LONG JOBLESS RECOVERY

Seven months before the beginning of the rapid collapse of stock prices, the Greenspan Fed announced that stock markets were "functioning more normally" and that it would raise interest rates to "diminish the risk of rising inflation going forward." This was a striking misreading of economic conditions:

Federal Reserve Press Release
Release Date: August 24, 1999
For immediate release
The Federal Open Market Committee today voted to raise its target for the federal funds rate by 25 basis points to 5 and ¼ percent. . . . *With financial markets functioning more normally,* and with persistent strength in domestic demand, foreign economies firming and labor markets remaining very tight, the degree of monetary ease required to address the global financial market turmoil of last fall is no longer consistent with sustained, noninflationary, economic expansion. Today's increase in the federal funds rate, together with the policy action in June and the *firming of conditions more generally in U.S. financial markets over recent months,* should markedly diminish the risk of rising inflation going forward.[29] (emphasis added)

Seven months after this announcement, in March 2000, the stock market began its crash, followed in mid-2000 by a dramatic fall in economic growth. The Greenspan Fed kept raising short-term interest rates, which reached 6.5 percent in May 2000. It was buying insurance against inflation with a "tighter" policy. It had missed the huge economic consequences of the stock-market collapse that was underway.

The Fed acknowledged the decline in economic activity when it issued a statement noting "stress in some segments of the financial markets" at the end of 2000: "The drag on demand and profits from rising energy costs, as well as eroding consumer confidence, reports of substantial shortfalls in sales and earnings, and stress in some segments of the financial markets suggest that economic growth may be slowing further."[30] Despite the "drag on demand and profits," the Fed "decided to maintain the existing stance of monetary policy, keeping its target for the federal funds rate at 6½ percent." The economy fell into a recession for eight months, beginning in March 2001.[31]

Where was the Greenspan Fed during all of this? A former Fed governor came to Greenspan's rescue in 2005 with a laudatory editorial that claimed Greenspan's special knowledge and acumen gave him the ability to foresee a slowing economy. Former Fed governor Lawrence Lindsey, in an editorial titled "Life after Greenspan," praised the chairman for his contrarian insight in foreseeing the decline in economic activity. Lindsey claimed that Greenspan cut the Fed's interest-rate target on January 3, 2001, when "available official statistics showed an economy growing robustly with growth averaging 4.25 percent during the first three quarters of 2000."[32] Lindsey attributes this decision to Greenspan's "access to, and understanding of, anecdotal information [combined with] his accumulated knowledge of market signals."

This claim of Greenspan having had unique knowledge is difficult to defend, since average growth rates for all of 2000 did not indicate what had happened. When the official statistics for the second quarter of that year were revised dramatically downward, press reports in October 2000 indicated that the economy was shifting into a lower gear.[33] The same press report said that presidential candidate George W. Bush cautioned that the good times might not last and suggested a tax cut as insurance. By December 22, 2000, the press reported that a new official estimate of third-quarter economic growth was revised down to 2.2 percent. The press also reported that this indicated, as a *Wall Street Journal* headline put it, that the "Economy Grew at Its Slowest Pace in Four Years" and that "the latest snapshot of the employment picture served as a reminder that a fourth-quarter rebound looks unlikely."[34] The dramatic slowdown in economic growth and the bursting of the stock-market bubble—which punctured the bubble of wealth of many investors—were known before January 3, 2001, when the Fed lowered the interest-rate target.

The Fed waited until January 2001 to "loosen monetary policy" to stimulate the economy, slowly lowering its interest rate until it reached 1 percent two and a half years later, on June 25, 2003. During the long recovery period of slower economic growth, which led to 8.7 million people being unemployed in December 2002,[35] the Fed announced—its customary opaqueness draped with a double negative—that there was a "current soft spot": "The limited number of incoming economic indicators since the November meeting, taken together, are not inconsistent with the economy working its way through its current *soft spot*" (emphasis added).[36]

"Out, damned spot! out, I say!" This garblement illustrates the need for full, accurate, and coherent Fed statements of policy objectives. The contributions of each of the Fed's decision makers to the nation's monetary policy should be revealed in timely publications of the transcripts of FOMC meetings. Guess which public officials might be against this kind of timely accountability.

A MONETARY POLICY OF FLEXIBLE RISK MANAGEMENT

So what was the Greenspan Fed's policy? A Fed official explained in 2003 that its monetary-policy decisions had no precise target for price stability or any specific method of operation.[37] The Fed's policy was described as a "flexible" one that, according to Greenspan, included a "risk management approach." These are extremely imprecise, flabby descriptions that are not tied to specific targets of policy, such as interest rates, inflation, or economic activity.[38]

These low-content descriptions impair the very important task of providing usable operating procedures for Fed policy makers who are currently in office or for those who follow. The inability of Fed officials to identify specific procedures for what they have done, the five-year delay in releasing edited and redacted transcripts of their secret policy discussions, and the shredding of unedited transcripts produce a substantial cost to the economy regarding future policy development.

In January 2003, Fed governor Donald Kohn, who spent a long career on the Fed staffs at the Kansas City Fed Bank and then at the Board, where he closely assisted Greenspan, repeated the Fed's legislated target: a "'dual mandate' of price stability and maximum employment."[39] He also said that the Greenspan Fed had neither had an explicit or implicit inflation-rate target. He described a "flexible" policy that included long-run price stability and at "few junctures in the past five years, the Federal Reserve exercised a more flexible monetary policy than inflation probably would have suggested or allowed."

The first such action occurred in response to the "'seizing up' of financial markets that followed the Russian default in the late summer of 1998."[40] Kohn said that "circumstances" would "arise in which the central bank" would be "faced with short-term choices between inflation stability and economic or financial stability." Thus, Kohn added another target: "financial stability," which means fairly stable financial-market prices and definitely precludes speculative bubbles.

The Burns Fed had added balance-of-payments considerations as a target in 1974, although Burns had a difficult time defining it. He said it was an ultimate target of "reasonable balance with foreign countries." His explanation of "reasonable" was buried in a dark hole of imprecision.[41] The four targets, together with the emphasis on flexibility, have little exact meaning.[42]

THE "SEIZING UP" POLICY'S DENSE FOG: A HUGE BAILOUT ORGANIZED BY THE FED WITH NO DETAILS TO CONGRESS

One part of the Fed's policy for dealing with potentially "seized-up" financial markets can be compared to the backdoor deals of business barons of an earlier age. The Russian default crisis caused a large U.S. hedge fund, Long-Term Capital Management (LTCM), to collapse in 1998. Hedge funds earn revenue from changes in the value of financial assets purchased with large amounts of borrowed funds. When LTCM failed—it lost $4.6 billion in four months—the Greenspan Fed considered the collapse potentially so harmful to financial markets as to require Fed intervention.

Working from the offices of the New York Fed Bank, the Fed orchestrated a bailout of LTCM by private-sector banks. LTCM had earlier rejected a bailout offer from Goldman Sachs, AIG, and Berkshire Hathaway.[43] Greenspan could not or would not tell Congress the details of the bailout, apparently because the nation's central bank produced no detailed public records of its actions. Hundreds of lawyers and many large financial firms were evidently involved in this operation. These actions put the Greenspan Fed in the same league as the tycoons of an earlier age, such as John Pierpont Morgan (1837–1913), whose enormous financial deals, which had widespread economic effects, were made out of sight of the public or its elected representatives.

The London edition of the *Financial Times* reported: "For more than three hours, members of the House Banking Committee lined up to condemn last week's bailout of Long-Term Capital Management. From both sides of the political debate, members attacked the operation as—at best—an indictment of the central bank's poor scrutiny of the US financial system, and—at worst—a piece of crony capitalism in which Mr. Greenspan and his senior colleagues were protecting the well fed princes of American banking."[44] The public's agents who run the central bank had conducted a major bailout involving leading private-sector firms but had left no public paper trail. Neither the public nor its representatives could determine if the Fed had acted properly, in the public interest, or without showing favoritism.

THE MICE CLICKED AWAY AT THE SIMPLE ASSOCIATION BETWEEN MONEY GROWTH AND INFLATION

There is a simple story about the Fed's monetary policy. The Fed can rapidly pump billions of dollars into or out of the economy. A burst of money growth can spur the economy and employment; it can also drive up inflation rates, sometimes for as long as several years. Rapidly contracting the money supply can pull the rug out from under an economy, causing a slowdown in economic activity and even a recession.

That simple story of the effects of the Fed's monetary policy (controlling money and targeting an interest rate) seemed straightforward to many observers before the early 1980s, as shown in Figure 11-2.[45]

The apparently simple relationship was in fact not so simple.[46] Although prices before the early 1980s appeared to have some simple, rough relationship with prior money growth (two years previously), as shown in Figure 11-2, this simple relationship subsequently fell apart. The Greenspan Fed's primary target was not to change the money supply, but to target interest rates by adjusting bank reserves and the amount of cash in circulation. The change in the broader money supply, including deposits at banks, was a by-product. The Fed might mention the money supply as a piece of information, although, like most central banks, it would sidestep any responsibility for what happened to it. Of course, this belies the uncomfortable fact that only the Fed can increase the amount of cash and bank reserves in circulation. As the Fed placed the growth rate of the money supply on a roller-coaster ride during the 1990s, the price level lost its simple relationship with prior money growth. What happened?

There was a huge change in the Fed's ammunition, making it much more difficult to aim its shotgun. First, a law that took effect in 1984 allowed U.S. banks to pay customers interest on their checking accounts.[47] That had been illegal since the 1930s, although banks provided their depositors with little gifts and amenities, such as free coffee in a sitting room. After 1984, customers learned that checking-account money had

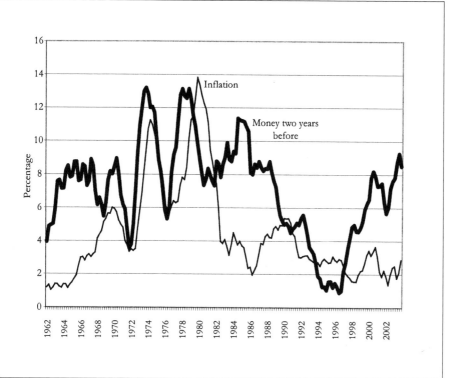

FIGURE 11-2. Current inflation and money growth two years before, 1962–2004. The simple relationship between these two measures (both are six-quarter moving averages) appears generally close from 1970 to the early 1980s, when it disappeared. The approximately two years it took for money growth to affect the prices of goods and services indicates one-way causation from prior money growth to inflation. The absence of this relationship after the early 1980s relates to the payment of interest on checking accounts (beginning in 1984) and the rise of digital technology and the Internet, which made transfers in and out of checking accounts as well as to and from other assets as easy and costless as a mouse click. Figure 11-1 shows the much more rapid interactions between money growth and stock prices in the 1990s.

characteristics similar to other things they could buy that were safe from default and paid interest.[48] Money lost some of its uniqueness.

This same law brought all U.S. banks under the reserve requirements of the Fed, although the banks found detours around reserve requirements.[49] They could keep more of their money out of the Fed with a neat accounting gimmick. They did this by doing a little "sweeping" from their deposit records. In a sweep account, money is taken out of a depositor's account just before the bank closes each day. Since the money is not in the account at closing time, it is not included in the official account data sent to the Fed and therefore is not used to compute reserve requirements. The money is redeposited into the account the next morning. Banks offered these accounts to many businesses and paid the lucky depositors near-market rates of interest. Part of the checking-account money disappeared and was reported in a different form.

Bank employees did not physically withdraw the deposits before closing and put them back into the accounts in the morning. The "zero balance" account story is just a cover for legally putting the money in an account that pays higher interest than a regular checking account. There are other methods for avoiding reserve requirements, such as putting the deposits in a foreign branch of a domestic bank, perhaps in London or the Cayman Islands.[50]

Then came the digital revolution. It became nearly cost free, with the click of a mouse, to switch money between interest-paying checking accounts and many other kinds of financial assets—stocks and bonds—that were more profitable.[51] The uniqueness of money as a reserve source of liquidity—for making payments on goods, services, and debts—was radically diminished.

The changes in the characteristics of money were profound. No longer was it primarily an "abode of purchasing power"—to cite a well-worn phrase from money and banking textbooks—a commodity used to store wealth in the most liquid form. People could now digitally move money at virtually zero cost into many types of assets.[52]

Banks could end up being bypassed. Banks providing checking services would change or disappear in their present form unless governmental restrictions prevented nonbank payment systems, although such restrictions would become a losing defense against the instant digital transmission of payment information. Buyers and sellers might choose to keep account balances with each other or with a third party that was not a chartered bank. Such "nonbanks" might pay higher interest to attract these balances. The balances might be considered fairly safe, since they could be accessed with the click of a mouse.[53]

Also, much U.S. currency, perhaps somewhere near the questionable Fed estimate of two-thirds, is circulating outside the United States, where its use is not directly related to domestic prices. Unknown changes in the amount of U.S. currency overseas makes it more difficult to determine how much of the money supply is being used domestically, where it affects prices and economic activity in the United States. These reasons mean that it has become more difficult to estimate how much money people would hold or spend. And when the Fed increases or decreases bank reserves or cash, or changes its own targeted interest rate, the effects on inflation, economic activity, and employment are more uncertain.

It is true that rates of inflation never reached the 1970s and 1980 heights of over 10 percent during the time of the Greenspan Fed. However, the association between money growth and the prices of goods and services in the United States largely disappeared after 1984 with the introduction of digital technology.[54]

MONEY STILL MATTERS

The increase in money growth during the last half of the 1990s did appear to have a very significant effect on stock prices, as shown in Figure 11-1. Large sustained expansions or contractions of the money supply can also affect the prices of goods and services. Currency, coin, and bank reserves—the monetary base—which can only be issued by the government, are valuable assets that underlie what we currently call the "money supply." Rapid and sustained contractions in money growth can cause severe recessions with mass unemployment. There is abundant evidence from different countries and over long time intervals that money growth plays a significant role when a government floods the economy with money, debasing its value.[55] This is the virulent disease of rapid inflation, which can wipe out the purchasing power of much of the population. Rapid inflation produces economic uncertainty that can then cause investment and economic activity to collapse. The cure is painful: stop the galloping inflation by reining in money-supply growth, a policy that drives the country into a recession.

CHAPTER 12

BRING THE FED INTO
THE DEMOCRACY

TURN OFF THE SHREDDERS AND BEGIN
TIMELY ACCOUNTABILITY

Stop destroying the unedited transcripts of the policy-making committee of the nation's central bank, the Federal Open Market Committee. Stop developing the nation's monetary policies, foreign loan policies, and all other FOMC deliberations, including discussions of how to play the public and Congress, off the record. Anything the twelve decision makers have to say about Fed policies, including strategies on how to play Congress and the public, should be in the transcripts. All deliberations of this twelve-person committee—five of whom are internally appointed—should be recorded, and the unedited transcripts should, ideally, be available within one month to the chairmen and ranking members of the Senate and House Banking Committees, provided that they have security clearances.

FOMC transcripts should be edited by a committee that includes professional archivists from the National Archives and Records Administration. The committee would decide on redactions according to specific legislated rules.[1] The edited FOMC transcripts must be published within sixty days. Accountability cannot wait five years. The issuance of incomplete "minutes" without attributions should be ended. Only a clearly worded directive should be published immediately after a policy change. The meetings of the boards of directors of the Fed Banks and their branches should follow the same policy. The minutes discussed in Chapter 2, which include "Murder at the Richmond Fed" and vacuumed minutes, vividly demonstrate the need for complete transcripts.

Unelected Fed decision makers should not be given carte blanche to decide what the public should know about how they are running the central bank. The full record of what they are doing must be preserved. Financial markets work best when they receive full information—not rumors, leaks, and opaque, coded garblements—from the nation's central bank.

NO MORE SUBSERVIENT FOMC MEMBERS: ONLY CONSTITUTIONAL OFFICERS SHOULD SERVE

The Fed Bank presidents are internally appointed and are subservient to the members of the Board of Governors. Their salaries and their retention are in the hands of the Board, which means the chairman. As a result of their yearly review by the Board, they can fall behind other Fed Bank presidents in salary or even be told to leave. This means that there are FOMC members who are under pressure to support and vote with the chairman. Many Fed presidents would not admit this pressure exists: they knew the score when they were appointed, and they may have accommodated themselves and their views to the reality of their position.

No one should be given the immense powers bestowed on the Board of Governors and the FOMC without having his or her credentials publicly examined. All Fed officials voting on the FOMC should be constitutional officers, which means that they should be appointed by the president and confirmed by the Senate. FOMC members should serve eight- or ten-year terms instead of the current fourteen-year terms. This would still be a long enough tenure to allow them to carry out short-term monetary policy without the pressure of short-term job insecurity, although the record of their FOMC deliberations should provide full public accountability for their actions.[2] Ten years has been the term of the comptroller general of the GAO, a period that has provided enough job security to attract competent, principled people.

The appointment and term of the chairman and vice chairman of the Board of Governors should be simultaneous with the four-year term of a presidential administration. Fed chairman Burns killed this change in the 1970s because he thought it would make the appointments too political. A continuation of the present procedure can lead to serious, disruptive political problems if an administration does not like the Fed chairman it inherits. An example was discussed in which a gang of four reportedly rebellious FOMC members appointed by the Reagan administration managed to assist in showing Fed chairman Volcker the door. Such interference can sidetrack monetary policy and lead to unnecessary fights with the administration. The administration should have to take full responsibility for the long-range monetary targets set by the Fed and not be able to blame them on a chairman from a previous administration.

There should be a targeted range for inflation and precise policy changes to be made if economic activity slows and unemployment rises. The targets should not be immovable. A simple rule with weighted precise objectives will not fit all environments. The first key to credibility and the reduction in leaks, rumors, and false information is full, accurate, public disclosure of the Fed's targets. The second key is publication of the complete record of individual decision makers' skill in developing policies to achieve these targets, as shown in the transcripts of its meetings.

CHANGE FED FACILITIES THAT REFLECT THE POPULATION IN 1913

The Fed is an out-of-date, inefficient governmental bureaucracy with a bloated hierarchy. The obsolescence of much of its workforce was plainly evident from the body blows it began receiving from modern digital information technology (discussed in Chapter 7). In 2007 it still had twelve district banks, which had been placed according to political influence and the distribution of private banks in 1913, when the Fed was created. Because of the distribution of population and private-sector banks in 1913, the western United States was given only one district. Today that district, the twelfth, with the San Francisco Fed Bank as its headquarters, advertises the poor allocation of Fed districts when it notes that it is "home to approximately 20 percent of the nation's population."[3]

Interested citizens of Missouri may not wish to highlight this subject, since Missouri received two of the twelve Fed Banks, one in St. Louis and one in Kansas City, Missouri. Citizens of Washington, D.C., may praise the highlighting of the location of the Fed's facilities, since the nation's capital has been without any Federal Reserve facilities. Richmond, Virginia, has a Fed facility, and this is where D.C. banks must send an officer to obtain Fed loans. The primary sponsor of the Federal Reserve Act of 1913, the act that created the Fed, was Senator Carter Glass, a Democrat from Virginia. Baltimore, Maryland, has a Fed facility for clearing paper checks and for withdrawing and depositing U.S. currency and coin for D.C. banks. This continued lack of Fed facilities in the nation's capital has a single cause. The District of Columbia does not have a voting member in Congress.

On May 2, 2000, the Fed held a groundbreaking ceremony for a cash-operations facility in Phoenix, Arizona. The Fed's new Phoenix facility was needed because it was inefficient to transport currency and coin to the LA branch bank 400 miles away. This new facility was a step in recognizing the change in the distribution of the population since 1913. Hopefully, this process can continue under a reorganized Fed that is primarily constructed for cash facilities and emergency backups for the electronic payment system.

Most officials and legislators from the twelve cities with Fed Banks consider a Fed Bank an important sign of status. One state did not want a Fed facility: Hawaii.[4]

END THE FED'S SEVERE CONFLICTS OF INTEREST AND PLACE BANK REGULATION IN A SEPARATE ENTITY

The Fed should concentrate on monetary policy and end the extreme conflicts of interest generated by sharing its operations with the financial institutions it regulates. The regulation of financial institutions should be under a separate federal regulator. The Federal Reserve should concentrate on monetary policy without all the surrounding hodgepodge. That muddle includes boards of directors, two-thirds of whose members are elected by the bankers in the twelve supposedly private—but really governmental—Fed banks, and the Board of Governors. This change to an entity concentrating on monetary policy was made at the Bank of England under Prime Minister Tony Blair's government.

Bank regulation and functions such as currency and coin services should be centralized in a separate entity that combines all federal bank regulation and supervision under one authority. This would reduce the nightmare for bankers, who are inspected by numerous federal regulators, each enforcing different regulations. The present regulatory maze increases the costs of banking services. It may be politically impossible to put the whole tangled web of federal bank regulation under one regulator. For many bankers—but not one of the leading trillion-dollar conglomerates with ample resources—the number of regulators marching into their office can drive them up the wall. The Federal Reserve regulates financial holding companies, corporations that own one or more banks. National banks are regulated by the Comptroller of the Currency. The Federal Deposit Insurance Corporation (FDIC) regulates all banks with federal deposit insurance. These three federal regulators should be combined into one entity—but not the Fed.[5]

The hodgepodge of bank regulation was made less efficient by the 1999 Financial Services Modernization Act (the Gramm-Leach-Bliley Act). It stipulated that the part of a bank responsible for selling insurance should be, under normal operating conditions (that is, when the bank is not failing), regulated by state insurance regulators. It added the Securities and Exchange Commission (SEC) as a bank regulator.[6] The SEC was needed for the part of the financial holding companies that operates brokerages and underwrites new stock offerings.

Small independent bankers are at a substantial disadvantage. They cannot afford the services of teams of accountants and lawyers specialized in banking regulation.

At the beginning of the Clinton administration, in 1993, officials from the Treasury lobbied Congress to pass a rational bank regulatory system by consolidating the bank regulators into one agency.[7] A large audience of House Banking personnel, both Republican and Democratic staffers, including me, gathered in the House Banking chambers to hear the undersecretary of the treasury pitch the proposed regulatory-consolidation bill. When the undersecretary finished, I suggested this proposed legislation would never get past the Federal Reserve bureaucracy, which had tremendous political muscle and little taste for giving up power. The Treasury official dismissed this concern because the Clinton administration's plan was based on a rational improvement. Of course, the Greenspan Fed would not support the plan, which then went nowhere, and the Treasury official soon took a high-paying job with a large commercial bank.

It was no surprise to Chairman Henry Gonzalez that Greenspan went on the attack: "In his effort to thwart this reform, Federal Reserve Chairman Alan Greenspan uncharacteristically wrote an editorial for *The Wall Street Journal* attacking the Administration's plan. He talked about the need for 'hands-on supervision,' though Chairman Greenspan failed to tell us where the Fed really has its hands when it comes to supervising banking competition. . . . The only hands that should be on Federal bank regulation are those of neutral bank regulators."[8]

In defense of the present system of regulation, the argument is made that the different bank regulators are competing to do the best job. The argument evokes a pretty picture of competition, but it is out of focus for multiheaded federal enforcers. One of the problems with the present system has been the lack of coordination between the many examiners. Governmental entities guard their turfs. Bureaucrats do not want their bureaucracy to be downsized or embarrassed because other bureaucracies are seen as being more effective. Thus, if a regulator were to find some juicy infraction, the least desirable choice could be to tell regulators from another turf to intercede.

This was the problem in the 1970s in a "rent a bank" scheme at a bank in Texas. An investigation by the House Banking Committee showed that the scheme operated by inducing a bank manager to lend most of the small bank's deposits to some crooks, who would then use the money to buy the bank. Once the bank was bought, all the deposits could be emptied into loans to the crooks and the bank could declare bankruptcy. Since most of the depositors would be insured by the FDIC, they would not be hurt and complaints would be minimal. The crooks would be long gone with the money. The scheme failed, and the crooks met justice. The problem was discovered by the FDIC, which allegedly investigated it without promptly telling the other regulators what it found.

To prevent turf guarding by the withholding of information and to provide uniform principles and report forms, a coordinating entity was established in 1979. Despite its austere, longish name, the Federal Financial Institutions Examination Council (FFIEC) will have a hard time, given its limited resources, accumulating all useful information from the tangled regulatory web and promptly notifying all appropriate parties.[9] The FFIEC does not have jurisdiction over state insurance-regulatory functions that examine the insurance operations in banks. It does not replace consolidation into one efficient bank regulator, an action the Federal Reserve would be unlikely to support unless it were to become the entity that swallowed the other regulators. The FFIEC is likely to have as much effect on the Fed bureaucracy as hitting it with a wet noodle.[10]

STOP ISSUING GARBLEMENTS

The Fed should not issue information about Fed policy that is muddled and nearly meaningless. Fed officials are public servants, not wizards behind a curtain issuing puzzling grunts and sighs for others to try to interpret. Consider part of the Fed press release issued one day before the start of the Iraq War:

In light of the unusually large uncertainties clouding the geopolitical situation in the short run and their apparent effects on economic decision making, the Committee does not believe it can usefully characterize the current balance of risks with respect to the prospects for its long-run goals of price stability and sustainable economic growth. Rather, the Committee decided to refrain from making that determination until some of those uncertainties abate. In the current circumstances, heightened surveillance is particularly informative.[11]

The attempt to convey zero information with its peculiar, empty, fortune-cookie advice—"heightened surveillance is particularly informative"—may have been successful in the short run, since it did not appear to move the financial markets. This press release probably conveyed the impression that the central bank, not knowing what to do, was powerless. Alan Beattie had another suggestion: "Anxious corporate executives wracked by uncertainty on the eve of a war with Iraq might derive wry comfort from the fact the Federal Reserve does not know what is going on either."[12]

Hiding behind convoluted language may diminish the credibility of the nation's central bank, although a case can be made that undecipherable noises embellished the reputation for wizardry of the nation's former guru, Chairman Greenspan, and promoted him as being the only one who could fully understand his peculiar utterances. It would be better for the long-run credibility of the Fed to simply state, for example, that there is no change in Fed policy and to publish the edited FOMC transcript within a month. This procedure would provide useful information on each FOMC member's views in developing the nation's monetary policy. They would be held individually accountable for the policies they prepared, instead of being able to hide behind a buffet of phrases and an empty, fortune-cookie closing. Those who have little knowledge of what they are doing and emit muddled comments would be more likely to be exposed. Presentations at FOMC meetings would likely be better prepared, and the debate on policy more informative.

REMOVE THE RESTRICTIONS ON GAO AUDITS OF THE FED OPERATIONS

Examination of the Fed's accounting practices and operations is essential. Congressional oversight and audits by the Government Accountability

Office (GAO), part of the legislative branch of the federal government, must examine all the Fed's operations. At present, GAO audits are severely limited by law, thanks to the Fed's lobbying for broad exemptions. The GAO group assigned to Fed audits must be reconstituted with personnel who are experts in central-bank operations. That way it can provide knowledgeable and complete reports on any waste, security problems, deceptive or corrupt practices, and unneeded personnel.

THE FED SHOULD NOT BE ALLOWED TO ORGANIZE OR SUPPORT LOBBYING BY THOSE IT REGULATES

According to House Banking chairman Henry Reuss: "The compelling evidence of extensive lobbying on the part of the Fed raises very serious questions. Attempts by regulatory agencies to orchestrate lobbying campaigns against bills affecting their agencies are illegal when money appropriated by the Congress is used. [The relevant law is *U.S. Code* 18, § 1913.] The Fed is technically exempt from this statute because its funds are not appropriated by Congress. But the spirit which prompted the ban on organizing lobbying by officials of other agencies should certainly be observed in practice by the Federal Reserve as well."[13] That was said thirty years ago, and little may have changed in the interim.

END THE FARCE OF AN INSPECTOR GENERAL WHO IS AT THE MERCY OF THOSE INVESTIGATED

Inspectors general and their staffs at governmental bureaucracies should be important vehicles for investigating and suggesting remedies for problems. Central-bank employees and members of Congress who believe they have found a problem should be able to trust that their inquiries will be properly evaluated and investigated by the Fed IG.

The Fed IG is at the mercy of the leaders of the bureaucracy he or she investigates. The Board set up the IG office in 1987, with the provision that the "Chairman can prohibit the Inspector General from carrying out or completing an audit or investigation, or from issuing a subpoena, if the Chairman determines 'that sensitive information is involved.'"[14] Furthermore, the Fed's Office of the Inspector General must receive its financing from the Board, as declared in the Fed's *Annual Report: Budget Review,* as a procedure that conforms to the independence of the IG.[15] The writers and the officials who wrote and approved the report must think independence and dependence are synonyms. At present, the IG can issue nicely bound, thin reports and tenderly suggest a few improvements, which can easily be ignored.

The Fed IG should be nominated by the president and confirmed by the Senate. The IG should be given a budget defined by statute and given jurisdiction to examine all Fed operations. He or she should limit but not withhold the exposure of problems of national security to the president, constitutional officers at the Fed, and the chairmen and ranking members of the Banking Committees (those that have security clearances). Fed officials who handle this information should also have the security clearance given other governmental officials by the FBI or the Secret Service.

ELIMINATE FED STOCK AND THE ENTICING STASH OF MEANINGLESS CASH

All national banks are members of the Fed. State-chartered banks can join the Fed if they wish. Each Fed member bank is given stock that can be held only by private-sector member banks. The stock is not like any stock sold in a traditional stock market. Fed stock cannot be sold and must be returned to the Fed if the bank leaves its membership status in the Fed. Owning Fed stock entitles member banks to vote for directors of their district Fed Bank. The stock does not entitle holders to any profits except for the 6 percent interest earned on the stock. This default-free rate of interest looks great when market interest rates are substantially below 6 percent. When market interest rates are substantially above 6 percent, it loses its charm. Fed member banks must pay 3 percent of their paid-in surplus (essentially their profits) to the Fed. This money is kept in a special Fed account that excites periodic congressional interest. It is tempting to say: "Since it's just sitting there, and is even called the 'surplus' account, let's grab the money and use it to finance my proposed legislation. It won't cost anything." This suggestion was made in 2003 in a bill to pay interest on reserves. A newly appointed Fed governor, Donald Kohn, and I both testified on March 5, 2003, before a subcommittee of the House Committee on Financial Services on that subject. We apparently agreed on one point: congressional use of the "surplus account" cash at the Fed would not relieve taxpayers from footing the bill.[16]

One-half the "surplus" funds were used to "finance" the original deposit-insurance system in 1933, as stipulated in the Banking Act of that year. Using the surplus funds to finance governmental expenditures is not costless to taxpayers. The accounting transfer of surplus funds from the Fed to the Treasury represents no additional sources of funds for the federal government taken as a whole. The actual transfer of funds to the government occurs when private-sector member banks send the money to the Fed each year. These funds either reduce a deficit or increase a surplus on the federal government's books if the transfer is properly recorded to include both the Fed and Treasury. Transferring money between governmental accounts does not produce governmental revenue. End this meaningless stash of cash (the surplus account) by ending the issuance of Fed stock. This action would also eliminate ridiculous rumors about the owners of stock that have no relationship to the reality that Fed stock can be held only by member banks and it cannot be sold.

THE INDEPENDENCE EXPLANATION BYPASSES LORD ACTON'S WARNING

The academic literature on what may be called the "independence explanation" is fairly extensive. This explanation alleges that the greater a central bank's independence from politics, the lower the rate of inflation in the country. The intuitive reason is that once freed from politics, central bankers will have the courage to slow down money growth even when politicians argue for faster money growth to stimulate the economy.

Some of the statistical evidence of independence is based on the length of service or turnover of central-bank officials. If they disappear rapidly, that is taken as an indication that the central bankers have little power and that the politicians are really running things. There are reasonable intuitive rationales that, along with some statistical results, support the independence explanation. There have been serious errors, such as assuming that the low inflation policy of the Bank of Japan was related to its independence, when in fact it has been a dependent bank under the control of the minister of finance.[17] The average tenure of governors in the U.S. central bank has been falling. It is probably not a sign of decreased independence. Rather, it is likely due to wage-enhancing job opportunities.

The most important problem with the independence theory and the goal of independence from political constraints is that it disregards the possibility that central bankers may abuse the power they have been given and act against the public interest. As described in this book, these deleterious actions go beyond monetary policy. There are many reasons for such actions, including the desire to preserve the power and prestige of the central-bank bureaucracy. The independence explanation bypasses Lord Acton's often-quoted aphorism: "Power tends to corrupt and absolute power corrupts absolutely."[18] Applied to the Fed, it warns about the effects of independent power. A democracy cannot afford its government to be detached from politics.

This book contains a record for a central bank that most economic studies hold to be independent. Arthur Burns and G. William Miller ran this model, independent central bank during a period of rapid inflation. The Burns and Miller Feds played a major role in contributing to rapid inflation. These records are not innocuous outliers for the United States, which suffered severe depressions in the 1980s before the inflation was tamed by Volcker. The abusive and deceitful practices of the Burns and Greenspan Feds described in this book had many deleterious effects that may not show up in tests of the independence explanation.

The second major problem concerns initial causes of central-bank policies. Germany had a noninflationary monetary policy before it adopted the euro. Its central bank was used as an example of an independent central bank. The underlying reasons for its central-bank policies were two devastating periods of hyperinflation that Germany had suffered. The population would not tolerate a policy producing another rapid inflation, whether or not its bank was independent as measured in tests of this theory. This means that in a well-functioning democracy, politics in the best sense—the will of the people—can have a primary effect on the country's monetary policy. If Fed decision makers were confirmed constitutional officers who served for ten years, as suggested, they would have enough job security to allow them to guard short-term monetary policy from changes they deemed inappropriate. Of course, there is no real guarantee against someone not being swayed by short-term political winds, except perhaps a perfectly motivated, brilliant dictator who could disregard the public will—an ethereal concept of absolute power.

LIMITING THE POWER OF GOVERNMENTAL OFFICIALS IN A DEMOCRACY

After reading the record presented in this book, one might readily conclude that some Fed officials would strongly reject most of the suggested remedies. This is an understatement. The Fed's reactions might include the brush-it-under-the-rug approach: a cordial acknowledgment to an inquiring legislator of different opinions, as occurred when corrupted records were found in the operation of its airplane fleet. As Greenspan testified: "In hindsight are there some decisions that should have been made differently? Almost surely."[19]

The Fed might issue an opaque reply that draws on the talents of some of its 500-plus economists, who can assist in constructing erudite convolutions that lead nowhere. Its PhD economists should not be used to "pile higher and denser" the Fed's efforts to camouflage its operations and policies. It might issue false and deceptive statements, as it did in connection with hiding its source records for seventeen years and then misleading Congress in 1993, a practice revealed by the plans that were recorded before its officials testified. It might simply continue to feed its source records to the shredders. Real changes that Henry B. Gonzalez sought—and partially achieved—are required to protect our great democracy from the consequences of Lord Acton's warning, which belongs on the Fed's front door in a slightly changed form: "Independent power corrupts absolutely."

APPENDIX
Excerpts from Waste and Abuse in the
Federal Reserve's Payment System

Note: Formatting differs from that used in the original report, and any emphasis has
been added. Footnotes from the original report are identified as such.

INTERDISTRICT TRANSPORTATION SYSTEM
CLEARING PAPER CHECKS

The Federal Reserve's Interdistrict Transportation System (ITS) office at the Federal
Reserve Bank of Boston contracts a fleet of 47 airplanes and auxiliary ground services
that transport an average of $10 billion in canceled paper checks across the country
each night, Monday through Thursday. The ITS handles checks cleared between Federal Reserve Banks, both those initially cleared and those that have been returned
for insufficient funds. ITS planes make approximately 200 flights nightly, Monday
through Thursday, with some additional weekend flights. The ITS also contracts with
freight forwarders which are companies that transport checks for ITS on Tuesday
through Friday mornings using commercial airlines. The freight forwarders transport
the checks via private air freight carriers. In 1994, the Federal Reserve spent $35 million
on its ITS operations.

POSSIBLE VIOLATION OF THE MONETARY CONTROL ACT
[FROM PART I OF THE REPORT]

The Federal Reserve may have violated the Monetary Control Act of 1980. This law
requires the Federal Reserve to charge competitive prices by matching its costs and
revenues for its priced services, thus permitting private enterprise to compete with
commercial operations of the Federal Reserve. Although the Fed reported near 100
percent cost/revenue matching, the ITS staff stated its revenues accounted for only 80
percent of ITS costs for the past four years, or 75.5 percent if the FRBB had not col-

lected extra revenue by overcharging the Treasury. ITS staff said they were ordered to manipulate the data to project higher cost/revenue ratios.

IMPROPER CONTRACTING PRACTICES [FROM PART 3]

The FRBB officers supervising ITS paid millions of dollars to private companies without any competitive bidding even though it has used competitive bidding for these contracts in the past. The Fed circumvented the competitive bidding process in some cases by making prior arrangements to pay favored, low bidders additional funds after the contracts were awarded. The ITS staff told the Committee it may have been supplied with a "bogus" bid to make it appear there had been competitive bidding for an ITS freight forwarding contract.

"GIFTS" TO NONPERFORMING CONTRACTORS [FROM PART 4]

In mid-1995 the FRBB officers supervising ITS extended the contracts of three private carriers without competitive bidding. These extensions included payments for nonexistent spare planes that were unavailable to ITS despite a contractual obligation. All of these contracts were extended at substantially higher rates (5 to 11 percent higher than previous amounts), according to Federal Reserve officials.

FEDERAL RESERVE OVERCHARGING THE U.S. TREASURY [FROM PART 5]

The FRBB has been improperly charging the U.S. Treasury 67 percent more than it charges private sector companies for transporting canceled Treasury checks, costing taxpayers millions of dollars. The Committee has discovered that this discrepancy between the rate the Fed charges the Treasury and what it charges private companies, was not known to Treasury officials.

WASTE AND DECEPTION, AND INSUFFICIENT CONTROLS [FROM PART 6]

The ITS engaged in budget dumping by making lump-sum payments to contractors toward the end of the year for future services. (This practice allows the ITS to falsely justify its funding in subsequent budgets.) In one case $700,000 was paid to a private company that failed before it performed approximately $420,000 in services. FRBB officials made no attempt to recoup this loss from the company during bankruptcy proceedings.

COMPLAINTS OF INTIMIDATION [FROM PART I]

Fed staff who sent numerous signed statements about ITS management in response to the Committee's inquiries, with copies to the FRBB Executive Vice President and General Counsel William N. McDonough, complained that they were intimidated for what they believe to be truthful replies.

AVERSION TO FULL PUBLIC ACCOUNTABILITY FOR ITS OPERATIONS [FROM PART I]

The Committee inquiry into the Federal Reserve's payment system entered an area which one Federal Reserve official thought should not receive close public scrutiny. On April 26, 1994 Senior Vice President of Check Services of the Federal Reserve Bank of Philadelphia, Blake Prichard, told a conference of the First Vice Presidents of the Federal Reserve Banks ". . . the ITS operates under more public scrutiny than is fair or reasonable. This scrutiny is primarily from US CHECK, the only surviving private overnight check air courier of any significance. Concerns over our management of ITS have to date stymied any consideration of pricing options that might legitimately promote expanded use of ITS by large volume check shippers."[1]

HIDING BEHIND THE AEGIS OF THE FEDERAL RESERVE BANKS' QUASI-PUBLIC CORPORATE STRUCTURE [FROM PART I]

The Federal Reserve often resorts to special protection from normal oversight given to government agencies by citing the quasi-public corporate organization of its 12 Federal Reserve Banks that do not use congressionally authorized funds. Vice President Prichard of the Philadelphia Federal Reserve Bank told the conference of First Vice Presidents, "The ITS is at long last recognized for what it really is—a private transportation utility run for the exclusive use of important overnight deliveries between Federal Reserve offices."[2]

However, the fact that the 12 Federal Reserve Banks are organized as quasi-public corporations does not spare the taxpayers from paying for Federal Reserve expenses. All funds received by the Federal Reserve that are not used for expenses or added to its surplus are returned to the U.S. Treasury and reduce the federal government's deficit. In addition, ITS is clearly part of the central bank of the United States and it is involved in interstate commerce. The FRBB and the ITS office at the FRBB are subject to supervision from the Board of Governors which is the Federal Reserve's ruling body and is an independent entity in the executive branch of the federal government.[3]

$1.5 MILLION FOR A MISSING BACKUP AIRCRAFT
[FROM PART 4]

Payments for the warm standby aircraft continued even though the ITS personnel told the Committee that they knew at that time that [an airplane contractor] had not been providing a warm standby backup as specified in a April 23, 1991 letter of agreement.

THE MISSING WARM STANDBY AIRCRAFT AT TETERBORO
[FROM PART 4]

The [an airplane contractor] (also called "EJ") warm standby jet required in the agreement was missing from Teterboro Airport nearly all the time in 1992 before the Fed authorized a doubling of annual payments for this aircraft, from more than $624,000 to $1.248 million (plus tax).

The ITS staff recorded information from the ITS' operational notes on the availability of the warm standby spare for 1992 through September 1995. They could find only one entry, April 16/17, 1992 before May 7/8, 1992 in which a spare was recorded as being at Teterboro Airport. From January 1992 to September 1995 the spare was recorded as present 58.1 percent of the time. *Federal Reserve officials defend the payment for the missing plane by arguing that a plane in maintenance could be considered the "warm standby Lear 35 jet to be based at Teterboro Airport during the week."* Federal Reserve officials argued that even if the spare plane were not at Teterboro at the beginning of the evening, even if Santa Express' central control facility recorded, "EJ no spare," the spare was present. In fact, they argued that it was always present.

A September 22, 1993 ITS on-site staff report stated: "[Vendor] was short two aircraft, and the other was the phantom spare that no one has seen in Teterboro in '93."

GROUNDING OF NORTH COAST AVIATION BY THE FAA
[FROM PART 4]

On July 17, 1990, the Federal Aviation Administration (FAA) revoked the FAA Part 135 certificate of North Coast Aviation, Inc. (NCA) for alleged safety violations including "knowingly and intentionally" falsifying aircraft identification numbers to avoid mandatory maintenance. The FAA Part 135 Air Carrier Operating Certificate is required by the ITS for their contracted private air carriers. This FAA order was sent to the Federal Reserve and stamped "received." The charges that NCA officials fraudulently entered identification numbers should have raised concerns about the company. The FRBB officers supervising ITS authorized double payments for services contracted to NCA when NCA was grounded. On each route both NCA and a substitute air carrier were paid. After the final revocation order, ITS paid NCA for services clearly not rendered.

SPURIOUS INVOICES

Four invoices were paid by ITS for four weeks' service by NCA following this final revocation order when no service could have been performed. It is clear from the dates of alleged NCA services after September 24, 1990 on these invoices that no service was provided by NCA on these dates. It was certainly improper to pay for these invoices and ITS personnel knew this.[4]

"SUBSTANTIAL SAVINGS TO THE TAXPAYERS BY SHIPPING CANCELED U.S. TREASURY CHECKS OUTSIDE OF ITS"

Canceled U.S. Treasury checks returned to the Federal Reserve are transported to a processing office in each Federal Reserve District.[5] . . . Since they are not time sensitive, canceled U.S. Treasury checks could be transported outside ITS for substantially less than the nearly $5 per pound being charged by ITS.[6]

NOTES

CHAPTER 1

1. Michelle Mittelstadt, "Gonzalez Remembered for Many Accomplishments," Associated Press, September 4, 1997. Gonzalez was a member of the Banking Committee for thirty-seven years.

2. This story is from one of Gonzalez's Friday-evening meetings with me. I, as well as some of the staff and a number of reporters, will always remember the Friday evenings we sat in Henry B.'s congressional office. He loved to talk for hours one-on-one. Since I was an economist and taught statistics, he would even talk about his interest in calculus, drawing on his days as an engineering student at the University of Texas. He spoke several foreign languages in addition to Spanish and read German newspapers. He had a law degree from St. Mary's College.

3. The timeline for Henry B. Gonzalez's accomplishments can be found on the Web site of the Center for American History, at the University of Texas at Austin: http://www.cah.utexas.edu/feature/0611/bio.php.

4. Review of Stephen K. Beckner, *Back from the Brink: The Greenspan Years* (1996), *Financial Times* (London), March 20, 1997, 30.

5. A new governor who is fulfilling the unexpired term of a governor who has resigned would have a shorter tenure. Governors cannot serve consecutive terms. A few governors have flouted this rule by waiting a day—or, conceivably, given the logic, five minutes—after the expiration of their first term, and then being appointed for another fourteen years. These governors were then conveniently considered to have served nonconsecutive terms.

6. There are few legislative actions that a legislator can use to censure officials of the federal government; see Jack Maskell and Richard S. Beth, "'No Confidence' Votes and Other Forms of Congressional Censure of Public Officials," Congressional Research Service, June 11, 2007, order code RL34037 (available at http://www.opencrs.com/rpts/RL34037_20070611.pdf). Congressman Ronald M. Mottl (D-OH) offered

a concurrent resolution (HCR 247, January 1, 1982) expressing the sense of Congress that Fed chairman Paul Volcker should resign. Four years before he became House Banking chairman, Gonzalez offered a resolution (HR 101, March 12, 1985) asking for the impeachment of Fed chairman Volcker and the other Fed governors. These symbolic attempts to reprimand Fed officials drew very little support. They were not a substitute for congressional oversight or the kinds of hearings that Gonzalez led as chairman.

7. The twelve district Fed Banks are in Atlanta, Boston, Chicago, Cleveland, Dallas, Kansas City, Minneapolis, New York, Philadelphia, Richmond, San Francisco, and St. Louis.

8. The twelve Fed Banks were designed to look something like private-sector banks. The Fed's Board of Governors in Washington, D.C., was designed to be part of the executive branch of the federal government. The organizational muddle grew out of an attempt in 1913 to satisfy opposing views regarding central control. There were strongly held critical beliefs about money, loans, and banks. There was also the justifiable fear of the immense power a governmental bank would acquire. A central bank is needed if the government wishes to directly manage the amount of money in circulation. A primary original purpose of the Fed was to be the lender of last resort, lending money to banks especially to deter or end bank runs. During bank runs in the early 1930s, private-sector banks were besieged by large groups of depositors trying to convert their deposits to cash. Most of the deposits were invested in loans and other income-earning assets. Many banks did not have enough cash on hand to immediately meet the withdrawal demands of large groups of depositors. Where was the lender of last resort? It was run by a large headless committee that failed to come to the aid of private-sector banks. Approximately one-third of the banks failed or were merged with other banks, and the U.S. money supply (which included checking accounts at banks) fell by one-third. This collapse in the money supply severely deepened the Great Depression. From one-fourth to one-third of the U.S. labor force was unemployed, and the output of goods and services fell by approximately half. This perilous economic condition was due in large part to the failure of the Fed to carry out the functions for which it had been explicitly established in 1913. Bank runs gradually declined after Congress instituted federal deposit insurance in 1933. Congress reorganized the Fed in 1935, putting it into its present form. It transferred much of the authority for running the nation's central bank to the Fed's Washington, D.C., headquarters, the Board of Governors. The head of a district bank was to be called "president," and his or her election, by the board of directors of a Fed Bank, was subject to approval by the Board of Governors. The board was to be an "independent" center of power and control for the operation of the Federal Reserve.

9. The Treasury agreed to give that power entirely to the Fed under an agreement called the Treasury–Federal Reserve Accord.

10. Henry Reuss, "What the Secret Minutes of Federal Reserve Banks Meetings Disclose," 95th Cong., 1st sess., *Congressional Record* 123 (May 24, 1977): H 16235–16240.

11. *USA Today,* "Evidence Is In," February 23, 1995, editorial page.

12. The Fed has many remarkable employees, including well-qualified economists. Many have been and are dedicated scholars. One example is Bray Hammond (1886–1968), who was employed at the Fed for twenty years, serving as assistant secretary to the Board of Governors from 1944 to 1950. His writings include the Pulitzer Prize-winning *Banks and Politics in America,* a classic book on banking in the United States before the Civil War. It remains a primary reference for the early history of banking in the United States.

13. See Robert Auerbach, "Institutional Preservation at the Federal Reserve," *Contemporary Policy Issues* 9 (July 1991): 46–58.

14. *From Max Weber: Essays in Sociology,* 228–229.

15. Ibid., 233.

16. House Committee on Banking, Finance and Urban Affairs, *H.R. 28, the Federal Reserve Accountability Act of 1993,* "Statement by Representative James A. Leach before the Committee on Banking, Finance and Urban Affairs on Reforming the Federal Reserve System, October 1993," 103rd Cong., 1st sess., 1993, 51.

17. Federal Reserve System, Federal Open Market Committee (FOMC), conference-call transcript, October 15, 1993, 1; available online at http://www.federalreserve.gov/FOMC/transcripts/transcripts_1993.htm.

18. House Banking Committee, *Federal Reserve Accountability Act,* 77.

19. FOMC conference-call transcript, October 15, 1993, 2.

20. Remarks delivered by U.S. Representative Henry B. Gonzalez at the John F. Kennedy Library and Museum, September 11, 1994 (available at http://www.jfklibrary.org/Education+and+Public+Programs/Profile+in+Courage+Award/Award+Recipients/Henry+Gonzalez/Acceptance+Speech+by+Henry+Gonzalez.htm).

CHAPTER 2

1. During his time as a professor, Burns also served as director of the National Bureau of Economic Research (1948–1953, 1956–1961), a distinguished private research group, and chairman of the president's Council of Economic Advisers (1953–1956).

2. Mitchell deserves much of the credit for their early theory of the business cycle.

3. "The Politicization of Research at the Fed," July 16, 1979, 115.

4. Ibid., 106.

5. Jake Lewis, who was Patman's close staff adviser, recalled this joke.

6. House Concurrent Resolution 133 (1975) advised the Fed to formally report to the House and Senate Banking Committees four times a year, alternating between the two. The Fed was asked to give target ranges for the money growth it hoped to achieve over the next twelve months. The quarterly reports ended in 1978 with passage of the Humphrey-Hawkins Act (the Full Employment and Balanced Growth Act of 1978, Public Law 95-523, Title 1), which called for more detailed reporting and required the Fed to present its reports twice a year (in January and July) to both Banking Commit-

tees. These reports later faced an uncertain future before being saved: "The statutory requirements for semi-annual monetary policy reporting, the board's annual report and several other reports would have been discontinued by provisions of the 1995 Federal Reports Elimination and Sunset Act (P.L. 104-66). Provisions contained in P.L. 106-569, [Title X,] enacted on December 27, 2000, reinstated these requirements" (Pauline Smale, "Structure and Functions of the Federal Reserve System," Congressional Research Service, RS20826, June 15, 2005; available at http://www.fas.org/sgp/crs/misc/RS20826.pdf).

7. Hobart Rowen, "New Restraints Set on Money Growth; Burns Acts to Restrict Money Supply Growth; Burns Defends Interest Rate Actions," *Washington Post*, November 10, 1977. The law requiring Fed reports excluded any predictions of future interest-rate policies, but it did not exclude an evaluation of past Fed policies and the outlook for the economy. One comedy of confusion and error came during Burns's magisterial oration on various technical definitions of money. The nation's economic guru drove most of the legislators away from inquiries about the Fed's money policies—or out of the chamber—when he said he preferred a concept known as M_5, which he then incorrectly described. My staff colleague Robert Weintraub and I reported to House Banking chairman Reuss that on February 3, 1977, Burns testified that publishing estimates of M_1, M_2, or M_3 probably confused the public and that he paid more attention to M_5, which was not published. M_5 was in fact published in the monthly *Federal Reserve Bulletin* and differed from M_3 only by large negotiable bank certificates of deposit (CDs).

8. Asking the Fed chairman about technical aspects of Fed policy was an arduous and infrequent part of proper Fed oversight hearings. Sometimes Burns would reply to these questions with answers that needed to be cleaned up when the transcript was sent to the Fed for correction before being published. Everyone is expected to make some mistakes in the heat of these heavily covered events. Burns maintained his magisterial demeanor even when he apparently was not sure of particular numbers, which, he announced, could later be corrected. Generally, these changes would be allowed if they did not change the complete meaning of a reply. I was often assigned to the task of reviewing changes in the transcript sent to House Banking by the Fed.

9. Rebecca Strand Johnson, "Arthur F. Burns," in Schweikart, *Encyclopedia of American Business History and Biography: Banking and Finance, 1913–1989*, 39–40.

10. During World War II and until passage of the Treasury–Federal Reserve Accord, in 1951, the two governmental entities cooperated to keep the prices of the large bond holdings of the nation's banks from falling. The war had been partly financed by the purchase of these bonds. Low interest rates, which are equivalent to higher bond prices, were needed to protect the value of their holdings. Interest rates on three-month Treasury securities had risen slightly, to 1.4 percent, by March 1951. Keeping the interest rate at this level meant that there would be no discretionary policy to control the money supply and short-term interest rates. The accord gave that discretionary policy solely to the Fed.

11. Burns had supported tax reductions, advocating tax breaks for those in higher

income brackets as a way to spur investment. He also opposed increased governmental spending.

12. FOMC paraphrased transcripts for August 15, 1972, and October 17, 1972; House Banking Committee collection.

13. These comments appear in the FOMC paraphrased transcripts for September 1971, 914; August 15, 1972, 83; and October 17, 1972, 969.

14. Without knowing the date, someone would find it virtually impossible to look at a graph of the consumer price index and pick the date when price controls began. See Robert D. Auerbach, *Money, Banking, and Financial Markets*, 525.

15. This 7.05 percent pay increase applied to civil service employees (Rowen, "New Restraints Set on Money Growth," *Washington Post*, November 10, 1977).

16. Burton A. Abrams, "How Richard Nixon Pressured Arthur Burns: Evidence from the Nixon Tapes," Working Paper no. 2005-04, Department of Economics, University of Delaware (available at http://www.lerner.udel.edu/Economics/WorkingPapers/2006/UDWP2006-04.pdf).

17. A little over a month before the election, on September 19, 1972, Burns indicated to the FOMC that "he definitely did not want to press eagerly toward higher funds rates [which would have slowed down money expansion] regardless of circumstances" ("Minutes of Actions," FOMC meeting, 927, also labeled 83). The very rapid predicted growth at annual rates of 10.5 percent [for the narrow definition of money (M1)] and 10 percent [for the broader definition of money (M2)] for the third quarter of 1972 were in Attachment B, page 935 of these FOMC minutes. (Explanatory definitions added.) Monthly money growth surpassed these high estimates from June 1972 to January 1973, and then collapsed to less than 2 percent in March 1973. They did not return to these high levels until 1975.

18. Two governors dissented from the vague directive for monetary policy that was adopted by the FOMC on September 19, 1972. Bruce K. MacLaury dissented because "the Committee's current operating procedures did not assure that money market conditions would be permitted to tighten sufficiently to slow this excessive monetary growth in the near future" ("Minutes of Actions," FOMC meeting, 931, also labeled 87). J. L. Robertson dissented because the "rate at which reserves were being fed in to the banking system by [the Fed] . . . might result in a new groundswell of inflation later on" (ibid.).

19. There was an "external shock" to the economy, similar to an increase in taxes collected by foreign oil producers. Petroleum prices began rising in 1972; in 1973, the Arab members of OPEC stopped exporting petroleum to the United States (as well as to Western Europe and Japan). Higher gasoline prices added to the fairly rapid inflation that pushed up interest rates.

20. The real losers were pensioners on fixed incomes, poor people receiving governmental aid, and anyone who suffered from a huge rise in interest rates.

21. From 1970 to 1980, the average annual inflation rates were, in order, 5.88, 4.22, 3.27, 6.25, 11.01, 9.14, 5.77, 6.50, 7.63, 11.25, and 13.55 percent. The rate dropped to 10.33 percent in 1981.

22. Rowen, "New Restraints Set on Money Growth," *Washington Post,* November 10, 1977.

23. The salaries of the twelve Fed Bank presidents are made public.

24. Burns to Patman, June 25, 1974; author's collection.

25. Jake Lewis, who served on the House Banking Committee under chairmen Wright Patman, Henry Reuss, Fernand St. Germain, and Henry Gonzalez, played a major role in preparing this report.

26. House Committee on Banking, Finance and Urban Affairs, *Federal Reserve Directors: A Study of Corporate and Banking Influence,* 94th Cong., 2nd. sess., August 1976, v.

27. House Banking Committee, *Federal Reserve Directors,* 5, 120.

28. Burns to Reuss, September 15, 1976; author's collection.

29. Reuss to Burns, September 23, 1976; author's collection.

30. Burns to Reuss, November 16, 1976; author's collection. "A" is Arthur Burns's signature. By issuing a press release specifying what the Fed had agreed to, Reuss prevented its officials from claiming ambiguity or forgetfulness as reasons for not abiding by the terms of the agreement.

31. FOMC transcript, November 16, 1976, 17. Roos, president of the St. Louis Fed from March 1976 to 1983, was newly appointed at the time.

32. Burns to Reuss, December 20, 1976; collection of the Gerald R. Ford Presidential Library (hereafter, Ford Library). The letter continues: "You can appreciate that the public disclosure of such matters may offer the potential for misunderstandings and conjecture, and could significantly compromise a given board's relations with the Board of Governors or its own officers and employees, as well as injure the Reserve Bank's relations with the financial institutions it regulates and with sundry business and personal interests within its district."

33. The minutes were made available to reporters. One reporter, Eric Planin, noted: "An economist for the House Banking committee [the author], who read the minutes of all 12 regional banks, last week said that he turned up nothing unusual in the minutes of the Minneapolis Federal Reserve Bank" ("Documents Hint Abuse of Power at Fed," *Minneapolis Tribune,* June 26, 1977).

34. Reuss, floor speech, 95th Cong., 1st sess., *Congressional Record* 123 (May 24, 1977): H 16239, quoting Board of Directors Minutes, Federal Reserve Bank of Richmond, March 9, 1972, 19 (in the Board of Directors Minutes for 1972, 1974, and 1975, as delivered to the House Banking Committee).

35. This material is taken from Auerbach, "Institutional Preservation at the Federal Reserve," 54–55.

36. Proxmire to Burns, June 19, 1972.

37. Burns to Proxmire, June 19, 1972; author's collection.

38. The seven hundred-dollar bills allegedly paid by a contributor in Texas and laundered through Mexico and a Miami bank were investigated by the House Banking Committee.

39. House Banking Committee, *Federal Reserve Accountability Act,* 2–3.

40. "FBI Release," February 9, 1972; Ford Library.

41. House Banking Committee, *Federal Reserve Accountability Act*, 2–3.

42. They were unsuccessful in an entry attempt on May 25, 1972. The second entry, on May 27, 1972, was not successfully completed. On May 28, 1972, they wiretapped two phones, including one used by the late Lawrence O'Brien, the national chairman of the Democratic Party. Wiretap logs were kept under the code name Gemstone. On January 24, 2007, in the *New York Times*, Tim Weiner reported in the obituary of E. Howard Hunt, the leader of the Watergate burglars, that "Mr. Hunt led a break-in at the offices of the Democratic National Committee at the Watergate complex to bug the telephone lines. The job was botched and the team went in again [June 17, 1972, when they were arrested] to remove the taps." The information can be found in "FBI Watergate Investigation: OPE Analysis," July 5, 1974 (declassified on July 17, 1980), including the "Summary of the October 1975 Report of Watergate Special Prosecutor Force," both reproduced, with redactions, at http://www.watergate.info/background, under the heading "Burglary."

43. The average quarterly growth of the money supply (currency, coins, checking accounts, and money market funds) exceeded 10 percent in every quarter from the second quarter of 1975 to the second quarter of 1977.

44. Rowen, "New Restraints Set on Money Growth," *Washington Post*, November 10, 1977.

45. Burns testified before the Senate Banking Committee on November 9, 1977, that the FOMC had a money target of 4 to 6.5 percent for money (defined as M2). Hobart Rowen reported that he said a "crucial consideration" in lowering those targets for money growth through September 1978 was "to reaffirm [the committee's] intent of gradually bringing down the growth of the monetary aggregates to rates compatible with reasonable price stability" ("New Restraints Set on Money Growth," *Washington Post*, November 10, 1977).

46. Hearing before the House Banking Committee, April 10, 1978, 142–143. See also Robert D. Auerbach, "G. William Miller," in Schweikart, *Encyclopedia of American Business History and Biography: Banking and Finance, 1913–1989*, 302–305. My biography omitted one position that Miller (1925–2006) held for several years. When I accepted my present position at the LBJ School of Public Affairs, in 1998, I saw a plaque on the wall near the entrance of the building, indicating that Miller had briefly held a faculty chair at the school after leaving his position as secretary of the treasury under Carter.

47. Art Pine and John Berry, "Fed Chairman, Carter Adviser Named; Carter Named Fed Chief, Senior Aide," *Washington Post*, July 26, 1979.

48. Volcker's tenure at the Fed began in a period of high inflation, which climbed to over 13 percent in 1980. In 1979 he led the Fed in a determined and unprecedented fight against inflation by slowing down the growth of the money supply, which had already slowed during Miller's leadership of the Fed. On Saturday, October 6, 1979, the Fed raised the rate at which banks could borrow from the Fed (the discount rate) to 12 percent. The Fed then increased the amount of cash reserves that private banks had to

hold on many of their deposits and short-term loans. Volcker also helped finalize the important Fed legislation that his predecessor Miller was developing, working with Congress and various interest groups. The Carter administration failed to cooperate with Congress or lend its support to the passage of this legislation, even though both chairmen were Carter appointees. The Monetary Control Act is the first part of a larger bill called the Depository Institutions Deregulation and Monetary Control Act of 1980.

49. C. Frederic Wiegold, "Fed Hikes Discount Rate 12%; Imposes New Reserves; Halts Fund Rate Emphasis," *American Banker,* October 8, 1979.

50. Ibid.

51. The first dip into recession was from January 1980 to July 1980, and the second was from July 1981 to November 1982. The unemployment rate was 10.8 percent in December 1982.

52. Bob Woodward, *Maestro: Greenspan's Fed and the American Boom,* 16.

53. Ibid., 24. The quotation appears to be at least secondhand; it does summarize the desire to dump Volcker.

54. Robert D. Hershey, Jr., "Out after 8 Years As Federal Reserve Chief; Reagan Chooses Greenspan," *New York Times,* June 3, 1987.

CHAPTER 3

1. An extensive biography of Greenspan's early life is found in Jerome Tuccille, *Alan Shrugged: The Life and Times of Alan Greenspan, the World's Most Powerful Banker;* see especially part I, "All That Jazz," 3-43.

2. Ibid., 30.

3. Neely Tucker, "Careful, That Dish Is Hot; At the Gridiron Dinner, Hams Glazed With Condi," *Washington Post,* March 13, 2005: "The Gridiron Club—whose active membership of 65 comprises senior print journalists, bureau chiefs, columnists and the like—puts on a show each spring that hosts the president, Cabinet secretaries, military brass and other elites . . . then in came Alan Greenspan." Available online: http://www.washingtonpost.com/wp-dyn/articles/A30807-2005Mar13.html.

4. Woodward, *Maestro,* 22. Attaching probabilities to statements can be an attempt at precision if they are carefully derived and combined with past occurrences either through formal methods (such as Bayesian analysis) or through less formal intuitive insights. Some successful traders in the financial markets have this intuitive ability, while others use formal models with algorithms to calculate probable outcomes.

5. "As Greenspan knew, for somebody with mathematical capability, econometrics [the name given to statistics used by economists] was like a drug. He would have been sucked in himself, but such study was not available when he was a student at New York University and Columbia in the 1940s and 1950s" (Woodward, *Maestro,* 167).

6. Tuccille, *Alan Shrugged,* 43.

7. Justin Martin, *Greenspan: The Man behind Money*, 55.

8. In *Encyclopedia of American Business History and Biography: Banking and Finance, 1913–1989*, see Rebecca Strand Johnson, "Arthur Burns," 38–42, and Douglas K. Pearce, "Alan Greenspan," 175–182. The quotation is from 177.

9. Tuccille, *Alan Shrugged*, 265.

10. As of 2004, the recession was the longest—sixteen months, from November 1973 to March 1975—of the ten recessions in the post–World War II period. Real economic growth in the country (real gross domestic product) turned negative (-1.6 percent annual rate) in the third quarter of 1973 and economic growth was negative in three of the four quarters of 1974.

11. Inflation was 8.7 percent in 1973 and 11.5 percent in 1974. The combination of inflation and high unemployment was called "stagflation."

12. An external tax can reduce the demand for goods and services, even causing a recession. Fighting an external tax imposed from a rise in the price of imported oil requires a different short-run policy than fighting inflation caused by consumers' increased demand for goods and services. Policies to reduce demand, such as cutting back the money-supply growth or raising interest rates managed by the Fed, can intensify the effects that the external tax has on economic activity. The inflation fought by the Burns Fed was mainly caused by the external tax. The rapid money-supply growth it had managed declined during the recession in 1973 and 1974, intensifying the effects of the external tax.

13. Jerald F. Terhorst, "Ford Losing Confidence in Econ Aides," *Detroit Daily News*, December 16, 1974. Senator Tom Harkin (D-IA) repeated Terhorst's statements on June 20, 1996, when Greenspan was successfully confirmed for another four-year term as Fed chairman: "To be blunt about it, the President has lost confidence in the ability of his economic advisers to predict the economic future. This fall, when he fashioned the anti-inflationary package he presented Congress following the series of economic summit meetings, Ford relied heavily on the forecasts of his consultants, including Economic Council Chairman Alan Greenspan. They assured him that rising prices and production costs were the prime enemy of a healthy America. He was advised that while a recession lurked distantly on the horizon, it was not an imminent prospect that would confront him immediately" (*Congressional Record* 142 [June 20, 1996]: S 6572).

14. See a similar view in Michael Shanahan and Miles Benson, "Getting an Earful on Economy; 200 Plan to Attend Clinton-Gore Town Meeting This Week," *Cleveland Plain Dealer*, December 13, 1992. House Banking chairman Wright Patman attended the WIN conference at the White House.

15. Under special circumstances, previously written scholarly work is substituted for a PhD dissertation. For example, Harry Johnson (1923-1977), who later held joint appointments on the faculties of the University of Chicago and the London School of Economics, came to Harvard University with a number of terminal masters degrees, but a PhD was required for a faculty appointment. He submitted one of his brilliant

earlier articles, and received a Harvard PhD in 1958. Normally, an unpublished dissertation must be defended before a faculty committee; at the University of Chicago Economics Department, one negative vote could kill it.

16. Justin Martin, *Greenspan*, 139.

17. A record in *Dissertation Abstracts* indicates a submission of the work, dated 1977, for the PhD at the New York University Graduate School of Business Administration.

18. I did not request it from Greenspan. The publication of a scholarly addition to existing knowledge is the obligation of the university and the PhD candidate.

19. Bruce Bartlett—who helped draft the Kemp-Roth tax bill, which formed the basis for Ronald Reagan's tax cuts in 1981, when he was the deputy director of the Joint Economic Committee of Congress—said that "pillars of the GOP establishment like Alan Greenspan and Herb Stein [member (1969-1971) and chairman (1972-1974) of the Council of Economic Advisers under Presidents Nixon and Ford] supported the Reagan tax cuts in 1981" (Bruce Bartlett, "Tax Cuts, the Right Way," *National Review Online*, July 26, 2004; http://www.nationalreview.com/nrof_bartlett/bartlett200407261019.asp).

20. The Economic Recovery Tax Act of 1981 (ERTA) lowered these marginal rates and reduced corporate tax rates. ERTA also authorized indexation of personal exemptions to changes in inflation (measured by the consumer price index).

21. Greenspan continued to advise Reagan in 1981 after his election: "The third member of the new administration's economic triumvirate, the chairman of the Council of Economic Advisors, has not been appointed. His place on the economic policy planning group, which will be headed by [David] Stockman until the inauguration and by Mr. [Donald] Regan thereafter, is being taken by Alan Greenspan, a New York economist and consultant who was President Ford's chairman of the council" (Steven Rattner, "Reagan Advisers Ask for Fast Action on Budget Plan," *New York Times*, January 12, 1981).

22. The members of the Greenspan Commission, as it was called, were Alan Greenspan, chairman; business representatives: Robert A. Beck, Mary Falvey Fuller, Alexander B. Trowbridge, and Joe D. Waggonner, Jr.; labor representative: Lane Kirkland; Senators William Armstrong, Robert Dole, John Heinz, and Daniel Patrick Moynihan; Congressmen William Archer, Barber Conable, Claude Pepper; Robert M. Ball, former commissioner of Social Security, 1962-1973; and former congresswoman Martha E. Keys. Source: www.socialsecurity.gov.

23. David Shribman, "Senate Approves Plan on Solvency of Social Security," *New York Times*, March 24, 1983.

24. The combination lowered taxes on higher incomes and raised payroll taxes on lower incomes. There were some offsetting parts of the compromise, such as a temporary tax credit for those paying payroll taxes.

25. Since there are a chain of effects on many different parts of the economy from a given tax change, it is very difficult to measure all the distribution effects for a measure

such as eliminating the income tax on dividends. Nevertheless, these effects should not be ignored. Milton and Rose Friedman advocated the elimination of the double taxation of dividends by eliminating the corporate tax (*Free to Choose*, 306). Stockholders would pay income tax on the entire profits of the corporations they own, including retained earnings.

26. The Garn–St. Germain Depository Institutions Act of 1982 gave regulatory agencies the authority to increase savings and loans' assets with "Net Work Certificates" in amounts up to 70 percent of their losses. For a more detailed account of these certificates and the savings and loan crisis, see Robert D. Auerbach, *Money, Banking, and Financial Markets*, Chapter 6.

27. The remainder of the Keating Five were Donald W. Riegle (D-MI), John McCain, (R-AZ), and Dennis W. DeConcini (D-AZ). Allegations against them were brought before the Senate Ethics Committee. In August 1991, the committee found that Cranston, DeConcini, and Riegle had substantially interfered with the FHLBB's enforcement efforts regarding Keating. It recommended censure for Cranston, and it criticized the other four for "questionable conduct." Information about these events can be found in William K. Black, *The Best Way to Rob a Bank Is to Own One: How Corporate Executives and Politicians Looted the S&L Industry*.

28. Greenspan to Thomas Sharkey, principal supervisory agent, Federal Home Loan Bank, San Francisco, February 13, 1985. The letter is included as an exhibit in Senate Select Committee on Ethics, *Preliminary Inquiry into Allegations regarding Senators Cranston, DeConcini, Glenn, McCain, and Riegle, and Lincoln Savings and Loan: Open Session Hearings before the Select Committee on Ethics*, 101st Cong., 2nd sess., November 15, 1990–January 16, 1991, Exhibit 203, 1105.

29. Woodward, *Maestro*, 66. The quote is from Greenspan's "unusual on-the-record" interviews with the *Washington Post* and the *New York Times*.

30. William Black is an associate professor of economics and law at the University of Missouri–Kansas City School of Law and the executive director of the Institute for Fraud Prevention. He is a lawyer with a PhD in criminology, law, and society.

31. Black to author, July 22, 2005.

32. "The total cost of protecting insured depositors from loss as a consequence of the collapse of the savings and loan industry is currently estimated to be approximately $150–170 billion on a present value basis—about 2.5–3 percent of current gross domestic product" (National Commission on Financial Institution Reform, Recovery and Enforcement, *Origins and Causes of the S&L Debacle: A Blueprint for Reform; A Report to the President and Congress of the United States*, 4). The GDP needs some adjustments to be equal to total value of goods and service produced in a year.

33. The interview was broadcast Sunday, June 7, 1987, as reported by the Associated Press, "Greenspan predicts '89 recession," June 8, 1987. In July 1987, Townsend-Greenspan was closed.

34. He warned about the deficit, the national debt, the saving rate, and the amount of investment: "Greenspan said he was 'uncomfortable' with the growth of debt and

warned that if nothing is done about it the federal deficit, now estimated at about $140 billion for fiscal 1987, 'will probably get worse. . . . At some point, some economic accident would likely happen . . . and we could be in the worst economic straits for any period since the 1930. . . . If America does not increase its capital investment rates, which means increase its basic savings, we are going to fade from the scene as a huge superpower eventually'" (ibid.).

35. See House Committee on Banking, Finance and Urban Affairs, *The Federal Reserve's 17-Year Secret*, 37, 39.

36. Inflation rates increased from 4.4 percent in 1988 to 6.17 percent in 1990. Then, as the recession hit, the rate of inflation fell to 3.08 percent in 1991.

37. Review of Beckner, *Back from the Brink*, *Financial Times*, March 20, 1997, 30.

38. Woodward, *Maestro*, 229.

39. Alan Greenspan, "The Challenge of Central Banking in a Democratic Society" (remarks at the Annual Dinner and Francis Boyer Lecture of the American Enterprise Institute for Public Policy Research, December 5, 1996), 4; available at http://www .federalreserve.gov/BoardDocs/speeches/1996/19961205.htm. Representative Barney Frank corrected Greenspan at a hearing in 1998. He asked the chairman if it was not Henry Gonzalez who should be congratulated for bringing some transparency to the Fed. I heard a nearly inaudible yes from Greenspan. Frank, the ranking member of House Banking in 2003, said, "It was his [Gonzalez's] pressure that led them to start being open about what they were doing" (Michelle Mittelstadt, "Gonzalez Remembered for Many Accomplishments," Associated Press, September 4, 1997).

40. The term "job loss recovery" was used by Bob Hebert, "Despair of the Jobless," *New York Times*, August 8, 2003.

41. Tim Ahmann, "Bush Taking Time to Renominate Fed Chief Greenspan," Reuters, May 12, 2004; David Wessel, "Bush Renominates Greenspan to Lead U.S. Federal Reserve," *Wall Street Journal*, May 19, 2004.

42. James Kuhnhenn, "Harry Reid, a Soft Spoken Lawmaker with a Punch," Knight Ridder newspapers, March 3, 2005. The article used this quote from Judy Woodruff's CNN program *Inside Politics*.

43. Nell Henderson, "Fed Chief Urges Cut in Social Security Future Benefits; Must be Curtailed, Greenspan Warns," *Washington Post*, February 26, 2004.

44. FOMC conference-call transcript, October 5, 1993, 10; available online at http:// www.federalreserve.gov/FOMC/transcripts/1993/931005ConfCall.pdf.

45. Ibid.

46. The text of the press release is available online at http://www.federalreserve .gov/boarddocs/press/monetary/2003/20030506/default.htm. The phrase "unwelcome substantial fall in inflation" in this Fed announcement was interpreted to be an important signal. Slowing inflation too rapidly could cause a deflation.

47. Laurence H. Meyer, *A Term at the Fed*, 160.

48. Greenspan, quoted in Woodward, *Maestro*, 227.

49. Meyer, who was governor at the time, explains at some length the meaning of policy hints that were contained in the code words, and on balance thinks some of the

language adopted after May 1999, such as referring to the "foreseeable future (rather than to the intermeeting period) was, in my view, a step in the right direction" (Meyer, *A Term at the Fed*, 161).

50. FOMC minutes, July 2–3, 1996, 95. The minutes are available online at http://www.federalreserve.gov/FOMC/minutes/19960702.htm. Part of the paragraph is found in Meyer, *A Term at the Fed*, 49.

51. Meyer, *A Term at the Fed*, 49.

52. Ibid., 75.

53. Ibid., 76.

54. Ibid., 51.

55. Larry Kahaner, *The Quotations of Chairman Greenspan: Words from the Man Who Can Shake the World*, 228–229. The average federal funds rate, the rate of interest on short-term loans between banks, fell after June 1995.

56. Federal Reserve, press release, October 25, 2006. The text of the press release is available online at http://www.federalreserve.gov/boarddocs/press/monetary/2006/20061025/default.htm.

CHAPTER 4

1. Greenspan to Gonzalez, December 5, 1996, 2; author's collection.

2. Henry B. Gonzalez, press release, March 20, 1997. The press release also contained a committee phone number for parties interested in receiving a copy of "Chairman Greenspan's Letter Detailing Thefts at Fed."

3. PR Newswire Association, Inc., "Former Federal Reserve Bank Employee Sentenced for Embezzling $70,000 in Cash from the Federal Reserve Bank of Boston, U.S. Attorney Announces," January 11, 1995.

4. "A former employee of the Atlanta Federal Reserve in New Orleans was sentenced Wednesday to a year and day in prison for embezzling money" ("Ex-Bank Worker Gets Year in Jail," *New Orleans Times-Picayune*, March 9, 1995). The former employee "pleaded guilty to taking $267,000 over two years. She was sentenced and ordered to pay $117,634 in restitution," and she "must undergo five years of supervision after her release."

5. Greenspan to Gonzalez, December 5, 1996, attachment 1, titled "Summary of Prosecutions for Currency Thefts From Federal Reserve Banks For the past 10 year period—1987 through 1996."

6. Gonzalez, press release, July 15, 1996, 1, "Attached: June 3, 1996 Banking Committee News Release and Letters Requesting GAO Investigation of the L.A. Fed."

7. U.S. Congress, General Accounting Office, *Federal Reserve Banks: Inaccurate Reporting of Currency at the Los Angeles Branch*, GAO/AIMD-96-146, September 30, 1996. The report is headed *Report to the Ranking Minority Member [the Honorable Henry B. Gonzalez], Committee on Banking and Financial Services, House of Representatives.* Available at http://www.gao.gov/archive/1996/ai96146.pdf.

8. Ibid., 4–6. The GAO team gave examples of mistakes. A bank had brought a

deposit of $432,000 to the Fed, and Fed employees mistakenly entered the transaction as $8,640,000. When Fed employees in the cash department counted the deposit and discovered an $8,208,000 mistake, "they overrode the system control in the cash inventory system and forwarded the money for further processing. Although this error was corrected when the problem was detected at the end of the day, this resulted in an erroneous entry being made in the L.A. Bank's ledger for $8,640,000 that increased the cash in the vault amount and the depository institution's account. L.A. Bank officials had no explanation for why this occurred." The GAO also found many other problems:

> We attempted to perform a comprehensive review of the L.A. Bank's internal controls and accounting practices over the money flowing through the Bank. Our efforts to perform a comprehensive review were substantially limited by the Bank's inability to provide the information needed for such a review.... we requested that the Bank provide us with ... a general ledger history of all of the activity in its general ledger cash accounts for October through December 1995. [The bank did not provide the] general ledger of cash transactions because Bank officials stated that it would take them 3 weeks.

9. An external accounting firm, Coopers and Lybrand, conducted an audit of the LA Branch Bank cash department in 1995. The Fed said, "The external auditors informed the Board that they had identified no factors that would indicate the potential for inaccuracies or misstatement of the Branch's cash position as reported in the general ledger or in the balance sheet." Read that quotation again to admire its obscurity.

10. I took my MBA students on this tour several times in the 1980s. I do not recall the exact amount on the check that was found, although it was large, far in excess of $10.

11. Of course, the Fed Board of Governors took "exception to the two major conclusions in the draft GAO report.... First the draft report concludes that errors ... may be indicative of more serious problems with the financial integrity of its financial accounting records, and perhaps those of other Reserve Banks.... Second, the draft report expresses concern that the Board does not require the same level of precision in the informational cash reports than it does in the Reserve Banks' financial statements. In particular, the draft report recommends that the Board re-examine its policy that allows a $3 million tolerance in the reported level of month-end vault holdings" (GAO, *Federal Reserve Banks: Inaccurate Reporting of Currency at the Los Angeles Branch*, Fed replies).

12. Ibid., 40.

13. Rich Miller, Reuters, July 27, 1996. These statements also appear in Alan Greenspan, "Recent Reports on Federal Reserve Operations," testimony before the Senate Committee on Banking, Housing and Urban Affairs, July 26, 1996,

104 Cong., 2nd sess., 5; available at http://www.federalreserve.gov/Boarddocs/Testimony/1996/19960726.htm.

14. Henry B. Gonzalez, "Federal Reserve Is Run by the Bankers," speech on the House floor, March 7, 1994, 103rd Cong., 2nd sess., *Congressional Record* 140: H 1062.

15. Corrigan to Gonzalez, May 18, 1993; author's collection.

16. Ibid.

17. Gonzalez to Corrigan, May 24, 1993; author's collection.

18. *Federal Reserve Bank of New York Uniform Code of Conduct,* sent to Gonzalez under a cover letter from William J. McDonough, May 27, 1994; author's collection. See 6–7 for the quoted material.

19. Ibid., 10.

20. The Fed examines banks in bank holding companies, financial holding companies (created by the 1999 modernization law), foreign banks operating in the United States, foreign-bank activities of U.S. banks, and state-chartered banks that are Fed member banks; the Fed also examines banks for compliance with the Community Reinvestment Act (which broadly requires banks to serve people in underserved areas in the locality of the bank) and other consumer-protection laws. The foreign-bank regulatory responsibilities are emphasized because they are an important regulatory obligation of this governmental bureaucracy.

21. Gonzalez, press release, April 30, 1993, 1.

22. Ibid.; Greenspan to Gonzalez, April 5, 1993, 2–4.

23. Greenspan to Gonzalez, April 5, 1993, 2–3.

24. The phrase "mass distribution of resumes" is in J. Virgil Mattingly, Jr., general counsel, Board of Governors, "To the General Counsels of the Federal Reserve Banks," October 3, 1990. Mattingly says that the Office of Government Ethics guidelines for the mass distribution of resumes does not require disqualification of the governmental employee from matters pertaining to those entities to which resumes are sent" (1). Other quotes are from Greenspan to Gonzalez, April 5, 1993, 3–4. The federal law is *U.S. Code* 18, § 208(a). It is not clear if the federal law applies to the muddled public-private Fed Banks, although as shown for the Civil Rights Act of 1964, from which the Greenspan Fed claimed to be exempt, judges may hold differently. As discussed later, the Fed Banks presumably adopted a code of conduct in 1997 that prohibits employees "from participating in any Bank matter that will affect the financial interest of any organization or person with which you are seeking employment or have an arrangement for future employment" (*Code,* § 6). It is not clear how this will or has affected examiners sending resumes to banks being examined. Careful oversight and inspection are needed.

25. On December 8, 2005, the Board of Governors, Division of Banking Supervision and Regulation, issued the following explanation of a provision of the special "Post-Employment Restriction Set Forth in the Intelligence Reform and Terrorism Prevention Act of 2004 (SR 05-26): SUBJECT Special Post-Employment Restriction

Set Forth in the Intelligence Reform and Terrorism Prevention Act of 2004," with the following in a table: "If, during two or more months of the last twelve months of service, the examiner serves as the 'senior examiner' for a [state member bank, bank holding company, or foreign bank] . . . Then, for one year after leaving the Reserve Bank, the 'senior examiner' may not knowingly accept compensation as an employee, officer, director, or consultant from [roughly, these same banks and companies]"; available at http://www.federalreserve.gov/boarddocs/srletters/2005/SR0526.htm.

26. Marcy Gordon, "Banker Imprisoned in BNL Case Tells Story to House Committee," Associated Press, November 9, 1993.

27. U.S. Department of Justice, Public Affairs Office, "Former Executive of Atlanta Agency of Italian-Owned Bank Pleads Guilty to Conspiracy," June 2, 1992; released on U.S. Newswire.

28. Peter Mantius, "Drogoul Given 37 Months; Judge in BNL Case Also Blasts Actions of U.S. Prosecutors," *Atlanta Journal-Constitution*, December 10, 1993.

29. Henry B. Gonzalez, "Reduction in Regulatory Control of Federal Reserve Board Is Subject to Proposed Legislation," statement on the floor of the House, March 9, 1994, 103 Cong., 2nd sess., *Congressional Record* 140: H 1140.

30. Many governmental regulatory agencies examine banks. They include the Fed; the Federal Deposit Insurance Corporation (FDIC), for all insured banks; and the Office of the Comptroller of the Currency (OCC), for all national banks; in addition, state bank regulators examine state-chartered banks. Bank managers and owners must face the nightmare of examiners from different agencies, sometimes with different regulations, and overlapping jurisdictions. Bank regulators were required to examine each bank at least once every eighteen months. They generally gave the bank a composite rating from 1 (best) to 5 (worst). The acronym for this rating was called the bank's CAMEL rating because operations were judged on the basis of capital protection (C), asset quality (A), management competence (M), earning strength (E), and liquidity risk (L).

31. FOMC meeting transcript, November 1, 1988, 22. Transcript available at http://www.federalreserve.gov/FOMC/transcripts/1988/881101Meeting.pdf.

32. FOMC meeting transcript, March 22, 1994, 4-5. Later in the meeting, Greenspan said he agreed with President Broaddus but that he recognized other issues: "I'm afraid my views are more like those of Presidents [Jerry] Jordan and Broaddus than anything else, but I do recognize that there are other issues involved" (12-13). Transcript available at http://www.federalreserve.gov/FOMC/transcripts/1994/940322Meeting.pdf.

33. The Exchange Stabilization Fund of the U.S. Treasury has its own limited finances. It was established in 1934 with an initial $2 billion for trading activities in foreign currencies and gold. Its assets rose in value primarily in the 1960s through its holdings of foreign currencies and securities. Congress gave control of the fund to the Treasury, removing it from budget authorizations and scrutiny. Since 1979, the administrative expenses of the ESF have been subject to the budget process. Although its initial purpose was to intervene in foreign-exchange markets and support the U.S.

dollar, the ESF is also a piggy bank that the Treasury can and has used to pay salaries of personnel without obtaining congressional authorization. See William P. Osterberg and James B. Thomson, "The Exchange Stabilization Fund: How It Works"; Anna J. Schwartz, "From Obscurity to Notoriety: A Biography of the Exchange Stabilization Fund." Warehousing occurs because of limitations placed on the ESF for financing interventions in foreign-exchange markets. When it is out of U.S. dollars, it must use "an off-balance-sheet financing arrangement with the Fed, referred to as warehousing." Osterberg and Thomson report that the size of the warehouse arrangement was increased to $20 billion in 1995 for the "Mexican financial assistance package" ("Exchange Stabilization Fund," 2).

34. FOMC meeting transcript, March 27, 1990, 75–76. Transcript available at http:// www.federalreserve.gov/FOMC/transcripts/1990/900327Meeting.pdf. The inserted "[legally]" is bracketed in the published transcript, indicating a later insertion; the other bracketed additions were made by the author.

35. Ibid., 76.

36. Osterberg and Thomson, "Exchange Stabilization Fund," 3.

37. Ibid.

38. FOMC meeting transcript, February 4–5, 1997, 7–8. Available at http://www .federalreserve.gov/FOMC/transcripts/1997/19970205Meeting.pdf. Because of some confusion about the vote on warehousing and another matter, there was a second perfunctory vote of approval on the same warehousing authority recorded on this transcript.

39. Some of the material in this section, including the quote by Secretary Dillon, is discussed in Robert Auerbach, "A Budgetary Bias for United States Intervention in Foreign Exchange Markets."

40. The Bank of England official was quoted in *Business Week*, March 14, 1964, 134. In 1961 there was an intensified concern about the stability of the exchange rate of U.S. dollars with other currencies and the maintenance of the price of gold. There was another increase in the price of gold after a stock market decline, and a few months later, in April, the United States support of an unsuccessful invasion of Cuba at the Bay of Pigs increased world tensions. These tensions could have driven up the price of gold and caused a run on dollars. The Kennedy administration took the lack of a run on the dollar as a successful defense of the dollar. A gold pool was established by the U.S. (which supplied 50 percent of the funds) and European central banks to keep the price of gold within a narrow range.

41. FOMC Memorandum of Discussion (MOD), February 13, 1962, 62; copy sent to House Banking in 1976. Charles A. Coombs was the vice president in charge of the Foreign Department of the New York Fed Bank and special manager of the System Open Market Account.

42. Also at this meeting, FOMC members were told of the intention to discuss the Fed's future foreign-exchange operations with the Treasury, although the Treasury would not be allowed to veto Fed actions. Robertson voted against amending a regulation to authorize the Fed to conduct the planned exchange operations; the

amendment passed 6–1. He did not oppose the vote the next day on the authorization of foreign-exchange operations.

43. FOMC MOD, February 13, 1962, 71.

44. Ibid., 79.

45. U.S. Congress, Joint Economic Committee, *January 1962 Economic Report of the President: Hearings before the Joint Economic Committee*, 87th Cong., 2nd sess., January 30, 1962.

46. Ibid., 2.

47. Ibid., 182.

48. House Banking Committee, hearing, February 28, 1962, Henry Reuss speaking; reported in Gonzalez to Greenspan, August 25, 1944. Congressman Brent Spence, then chairman of House Banking, said the statements were not germane to the bill being discussed, and ended discussion about the Fed's authority. In 1976, I assisted Chairman Reuss in preparing an objection. At a minimum, the chairmen and ranking members of the congressional Banking Committees who have security clearance should be kept fully informed.

49. Greenspan to Gonzalez, May 9, 1994, in response to a number of questions Gonzalez had raised.

50. Ibid., 1.

51. One form of a swap can simply be explained as lending U.S. dollars (at today's "spot" prices) to a foreign central bank with the agreement (a "forward" agreement) to repay the loans on a specific date. The U.S. dollars can be used by a foreign central bank to buy a foreign currency to affect the international price of its country's currency. Greenspan said these "are not loans." This protects the Fed from admitting it is making loans to foreign countries. Regardless of this semantic diversion, swaps are loans secured by collateral when foreign currency is held by the Fed and when there is an agreement with a foreign central bank to repay the U.S. dollars. The recipient as well as the Fed may lose or gain depending on the international value of dollars at the time of repayment. Swap lines, officially called "reciprocal currency arrangements," are credit lines between governments or central banks. They "allow either country to borrow the other's currency" (Osterberg and Thomson, "Exchange Stabilization Fund," 3).

52. Greenspan to Gonzalez, May 9, 1994, 2.

53. Ibid., 5.

54. Greenspan said the authorization for the "exchange operations" comes from the Federal Reserve Act, which, among other seemingly unrelated provisions, allows the Fed to "maintain accounts in foreign countries." He also cited a 1961 "memorandum to the FOMC from its General Counsel, a copy [of which] was twice provided to Congress, and a copy is enclosed with this letter." He went on to say that the conclusions of the memorandum were endorsed contemporaneously by the general counsel of the Treasury and the attorney general of the United States in 1961 (ibid., 2).

55. Greenspan also said that Congress in 1980 allowed the Fed to invest its foreign currencies in foreign-government securities.

CHAPTER 5

1. "Bond" is used as a generic term for debt instrument. The security is a contract to buy three-month Eurodollar time-deposit futures at near today's prices at a specific date when the Fed moves. In September 1998, when Gonzalez left Congress, a $1 million contract, called the "trading unit," could be purchased for $470.

2. The Fed determines the interest rate at which it will lend money to financial institutions. It lends this money through a window located in the lobby of each Fed Bank. The loan facility is called the Discount Window because of the original practice of lending money against part of the value of the loan document, a discounted value, that the commercial banks submitted as collateral. Today the loans extended through the Discount Window are straight advances of money, with government securities used as collateral. Originally, each Fed Bank set its own loan rate or discount rate. That practice changed with the 1935 reorganization of the Fed.

3. FOMC meeting transcript, December 19, 1989, morning session, 54. Available at http://www.federalreserve.gov/FOMC/transcripts/1989/891219Meeting.pdf.

4. Ibid.; newspaper affiliations added.

5. Ibid.

6. Ibid.; bracketed are words on the transcript.

7. See the testimony of three witnesses, Robert Craven, Anna Schwartz, and James Meigs, in *H.R. 28, the Federal Reserve Accountability Act of 1993: Hearing before the Committee on Banking, Finance and Urban Affairs*, October 19, 1993.

8. *Wall Street Journal*, October 19, 1993, based on Michael T. Belongia and Kevin Kliesen, "Effects on Interest Rates of Immediately Releasing FOMC Directives," *Contemporary Economic Policy* 12 (October 1994): 79–91.

9. David Skidmore, "Greenspan Defends Secrecy Surrounding Key Central Bank Committee," Associated Press, October 19, 1993. In 2006, Skidmore was assistant to and chief spokesman for the Board in the Office of Board Members, which conducts public relations and lobbies Congress.

10. David Wessel and Anita Raghavan, "A Glowing Glasnost at the Fed Is Dispelling a Lot of Its Mystique," *Wall Street Journal*, March 24, 1994.

11. Henry Gonzalez, press release, May 19, 1994.

12. *H.R. 28, the Federal Reserve Accountability Act of 1933*, 12.

13. Bill Montague, "Fed under Fire; Critics Say Public Is Being Shortchanged," *USA Today*, September 24, 1996.

14. Greenspan to Gonzalez, April 25, 1997.

15. Ibid., 2.

16. Meyer, *A Term at the Fed*, 99.

17. Ibid.

18. Ibid., 100.

19. Gonzalez to Greenspan, August 11, 1994, 2.

20. Greenspan to Gonzalez, July 5, 1994, 5.

21. Gonzalez suggested this solution in a press release dated August 11, 1994.

22. Greenspan, speech at the Securities Industry Association annual meeting, Boca Raton, Florida, November 6, 2003.

23. David Leonhardt, *New York Times,* November 9, 2003.

24. Michael E. Kanell, "Jobless Claims Nosedive; Economy Ratchets Up," *Atlanta Journal-Constitution,* November 7, 2003.

25. Warren Vieth, "Fed Chairman Predicts Upturn Soon in Hiring; Greenspan Also Warns of Danger from Budget Deficits," *Los Angeles Times,* Business sec., November 7, 2003.

26. John M. Berry, "Greenspan Buoyant on Jobs Outlook," *Washington Post,* Financial sec., November 7, 2003.

27. U.S. Department of Labor, Bureau of Labor Statistics, "Employment Situation Summary," November 7, 2003, 1: "Nonfarm payroll employment rose by 126,000 in October [2003], following a similar increase (as revised) in September."

28. Greenspan first mentioned the labor market in his speech by saying: "There have been some signs in recent weeks that the labor market may be stabilizing." That is difficult to interpret, since it could be "stabilizing" at a low number. Later in the speech, Greenspan turned to a more optimistic description of the labor market: "The odds, however, do increasingly favor a revival in job creation."

29. Alan B. Krueger, "Economic Scene: In Numbers We Trust, Provided They're Safe from Political Meddling," *New York Times,* May 30, 2002. The Fed sometimes signals future monetary policy changes to an administration. John Berry reported how Greenspan passed information to the Clinton administration about raising the Fed's interest-rate target in 1994 ("Fed Kept White House Informed on Rate Increase," *Washington Post,* Financial sec., February 12, 1994).

30. The Confidential Information Protection and Statistical Efficiency Act of 2002 (CIPSEA) "authorized the limited sharing of business data among the Bureau of the Census, the Bureau of Economic Analysis (BEA), and the Bureau of Labor Statistics (BLS) for statistical purposes. Allowing the agencies to share certain businesses data has improved the accuracy and reliability of economic statistics" (Randall S. Kroszner, "Innovative Statistics for a Dynamic Economy," remarks at the National Association for Business Economics Professional Development Seminar for Journalists, Washington, D.C., May 24, 2006; available at http://www.federalreserve.gov/Boarddocs/speeches/2006/20060524/default.htm). Fed governor Kroszner "helped lead the effort to urge passage of the CIPSEA." The act was in part intended to limit the duplication of estimates of the same variables by different governmental agencies. There is no direct evidence available that Greenspan used inside information or knew that the information from the Labor Department may have been sent to the Fed.

31. The Associated Press reported on Greenspan's statements:

"How do we know when irrational exuberance has unduly escalated asset values," Greenspan, renowned for intentionally leaving his comments open to interpretation, said in a speech at the American Enterprise Institute. Greenspan also said that a drop in stock prices might not necessarily be bad for the economy. The markets took Greenspan's comments as a sign that the Federal Reserve might be willing to raise interest rates to squeeze out any speculation in the market. "We as central bankers need not be concerned if a collapsing financial asset bubble does not threaten to impair the real economy, its production, jobs, and price stability. Indeed, the sharp stock market break of 1987 had few negative consequences for the economy," he said.

"Greenspan Warns of 'Irrational Exuberance' in Stock Market," Associated Press, December 6, 1996.

32. Meyer, *A Term at the Fed,* 98.

33. As in the press rooms in the House and Senate, attendees at the Fed chairman's secret (from the public) off-the-record press conferences should be in the hands of the press where press credentials are verified.

34. Jake Lewis and I organized a symposium held at the National Press Club on January 7, 2002, entitled "The Federal Reserve: Reality vs. Myth." It was sponsored by Ralph Nader and televised by c-span. I participated in a number of sessions.

35. Nicholas von Hoffman left the *Washington Post* and became a columnist at the *New York Observer.* His books include *Capitalist Fools: Tales of American Business, from Carnegie to Forbes to the Milken Gang* (1992) and *Citizen Cohn* (1988), a biography of Roy Cohn. He also wrote the libretto for the opera *Nicholas and Alexandra* by Deborah Drattell. See his biographical note at http://www.lamama.org/archives/2001_2002/Geneva.htm.

CHAPTER 6

Part of this chapter was presented at the Western Economic Association International Meetings, July 1, 2000. I thank Anna Schwartz (the discussant for my paper) and Walker Todd for their comments.

1. Fed Bank presidents, who serve five-year terms, can be terminated. Governors can be removed from office only by impeachment.

2. Beginning in 1922, abbreviated minutes of Open Market Committee meetings were maintained but restricted to internal use.

3. Patman (1893–1976; chairman, 1963–1975) and Reuss (1912–2002; chairman, 1975–1980) were both considered "liberals. Reuss had an image as a dignified intellectual and modern while Patman seemed a throwback to an earlier age" (Robert D. Auerbach, "Henry Reuss," *Encyclopedia of American Business History and Biography: Banking and Finance,* 371). Reuss's penchant for thorough intellectual discussions and his staff hiring practices did not fit under the rubric "liberal." Patman and Reuss both developed important legislation and initiated useful oversight of the Fed.

4. Milton Friedman and Anna Schwartz, "A Tale of Fed Transcripts," *Wall Street*

Journal, December 20, 1993. They place much of the blame for the "financial catastrophe in the United States from 1929 to 1933," that is, the beginning of the Great Depression, on the policies of Fed officials (Milton Friedman and Anna Schwartz, *A Monetary History of the United States,* 419).

5. The Directive is also called the Record of Policy Actions, which was published in the Fed's annual report before 1967. Beginning in 1967, it was published with a ninety-day delay. In 1975 the delay was reduced to forty-five days. From May 1976 until February 1994 it was released a few days after the following FOMC meeting. Beginning in February 1994, it was released at approximately two thirty in the afternoon on the day of the policy change.

6. This was the description used by Governor J. L. Robertson in questioning the beginning of the swap-loan facility described in Chapter 4; see FOMC MOD, February 13, 1962, 62.

7. *Government in the Sunshine Act,* Public Law 94-409, *U.S. Statutes at Large* 90.stat 1241 (1976); codified at *U.S. Code* 5 (1994), § 552b; section title: Open Meetings. The quoted material is from § 552b(f)(2).

8. Memorandum to Chairman Burns from Arthur L. Broida, secretary to the FOMC, April 16, 1976, 1 (document located in the Ford Library). On April 19, 1976, Burns sent a "Strictly Confidential" memorandum to FOMC members on his decision to end the MODS: "My conclusion reflects our experience in connection with the recent Court order that we make 'segregable facts' from the memorandum available to a plaintiff" (Burns's memorandum to FOMC members, April 19, 1976, 1).

9. Burns to Patman, April 18, 1974.

10. House Committee on Banking, Finance and Urban Affairs, *Maintaining and Making Public Minutes of Federal Reserve Meetings: Hearings before the Subcommittee on Domestic Monetary Policy . . . October 27, 28, November 17, 1977,* 95th Cong., 1st sess., 1977, 57; testimony of Arthur Burns.

11. FOMC MOD, May 18, 1976; tape 2, executive session, 2.

12. The replies were tabulated and studied by Erica Ellis, a student in my 2006 central banking class at the Lyndon B. Johnson School of Public Affairs. The replies are in House Banking Committee, *Maintaining and Making Public Minutes of Federal Reserve Meetings,* Appendix III, Compilation of Opinions Received from Prominent Business Leaders and Economic Professors on H.R. 9465 and H.R. 9589, 187–312. Had they become law, those two bills would have required the Board of Governors to keep "detailed minutes" and the Boards of Directors of the Fed Banks to keep "verbatim transcripts."

13. House Banking Committee, *Maintaining and Making Public Minutes of Federal Reserve Meetings,* 57; testimony of Arthur Burns.

14. Original in the Ford Library, lightly edited by the National Archives and Records Administration.

15. FOMC meeting transcript, May 18, 1976, 7; transcripts in the Ford Library.

16. Ibid.

17. FOMC meeting transcript, September 29, 1998, 14; bracketed information added. Transcript available at http://www.federalreserve.gov/FOMC/transcripts/1998/980929meeting.pdf.

18. From HR 28, Federal Reserve System Accountability Act of 1993:

(1) TRANSCRIPTION AND VIDEOTAPE OF EACH MEETING—A written copy of the minutes of each meeting of the Federal Open Market Committee and a transcription and a videotape of the discussion at each such meeting shall be made available to the public before the end of the 60-day period beginning on the date of the meeting and shall be treated as a Government publication for purposes of making such material available to depository libraries . . .

(2) PROMPT DISCLOSURE OF POLICY ACTIONS—An explicit, written description of any determination, decision, directive, or other conclusion made by the Federal Open Market Committee at any meeting of the committee, including any directive or instruction sent to any Federal reserve bank or Federal reserve agent in connection with any open market operation shall be made available to the public by the end of the 1-week period beginning on the date of the meeting.

(3) MEETING INCLUDES EXECUTIVE SESSION—For purposes of this subsection, the term "meeting" includes any executive session of the Federal Open Market Committee or any informal meeting or other occasion at which a quorum of the members of the committee are present.

19. FOMC meeting transcript, November 17, 1992, 49–64, and conference-call transcript, December 14, 1992, 1–5. The November transcript is available at http://www.federalreserve.gov/FOMC/transcripts/1992/novmeet.pdf; the December transcript is at http://www.federalreserve.gov/FOMC/transcripts/1992/decconf.pdf.

20. FOMC conference-call transcript, December 14, 1992, 1.

21. Statement by President Clinton, October 4, 1993: "I therefore call upon all Federal Departments and agencies to renew their commitment to the Freedom of Information Act, to its underlying principles of government openness, and to its sound administration."

22. FOMC conference-call transcript, October 15, 1993, 3; bracketed words are in the record.

23. Galbraith to Neal, September 27, 1976. The letter is included in House Banking Committee, *Maintaining and Making Public Minutes of Federal Reserve Meetings*, 203.

24. Directive, May 18, 1976.

25. Seventeen of the nineteen presidents of the Fed Banks and the members of the Board of Governors were witnesses at the House Banking hearing. They faced Chairman Gonzalez and, initially, seventeen of the fifty Banking Committee members.

26. House Committee on Banking, Finance and Urban Affairs, *H.R. 28, the Federal Reserve Accountability Act of 1993*, October 19, 1993, 26; statement of Robert D.

McTeer. McTeer resigned in 2004 to become chancellor of Texas A&M University for several years.

27. Ibid., 82–83; statement of Alan Greenspan.

28. Ibid., 32.

29. Ibid., 39; bracketed phrase added.

30. Jim McTague, "Greenspan Has Himself to Blame for Fervid Interest in Transcripts," *American Banker,* December 1, 1993, 24.

31. Dave Skidmore, "Greenspan Defends Secrecy Surrounding Key Central Bank Committee," Associated Press, October 19, 1993.

32. Dave Skidmore, "Lawmaker Criticizes Federal Reserve for 'Code of Silence,'" Associated Press, October 26, 1993.

33. David Wessel, "Federal Reserve to Release Transcripts of Past Sessions After Five-Year Delay," *Wall Street Journal,* November 18, 1993.

34. Greenspan to Gonzalez, October 26, 1993.

35. House Committee on Banking, Finance and Urban Affairs, *The Federal Reserve's 17-Year Secret,* 42.

36. John M. Berry, "What the Fed Hadn't Said; Gonzalez Sees Red over Undisclosed FOMC Tape Transcripts," *Washington Post,* October 27, 1993.

37. Security material, individual personnel evaluations, and foreign countries' private Fed accounts have been (and should be) redacted from the public copy.

38. Paul Starobin, *National Journal,* December 18, 1993.

39. Gonzalez, press release, October 26, 1993. Gonzalez cited examples: J. Alfred Broaddus, Jr., president of the Richmond Fed Bank: "I would oppose the preparation of a detailed record currently" (letter, January 13, 1993); Edward G. Boehne, president of the Philadelphia Fed Bank: "Verbatim transcripts and videotapes of FOMC meeting . . . would substantially undermine the deliberative process" (letter, January 13, 1993); Silas Keehn, president of the Chicago Fed Bank, advised against "a more detailed written record or a tape of the proceedings of the FOMC meeting," declaring that "any change to the minutes and record keeping process currently used by the FOMC will be ill advised" (letter, January 13, 1993).

40. *The Federal Reserve's 17-Year Secret,* 16.

41. Greenspan to Gonzalez, January 7, 1994:

Even though a reading of that testimony should have put this matter to rest, the FOMC has decided to allow review of the conference call tape for one reason: because we cannot allow an allegation of misconduct, no matter how unfounded, to linger. . . . We recognize that the contents of the conference call although not involving current or future monetary policy settings, are nonetheless the sort of deliberative material explicitly privileged and protected from disclosure under federal law and therefore we take this step with great reluctance. . . . Because of the sensitive nature of these discussions and their privileged status, we will be making them available for in camera review to your staff [the majority Democratic staff], the staff of the ranking [Republican] minority member of the Banking Committee, and the staff of the Chairmen of the Economic Growth and Credit Formation and Financial Institutions Subcommittees. We trust that you and your staff will respect the privileged status of these materials.

Greenspan's allegation of "one reason" pointedly did not reflect that Congress had obtained information that Greenspan had orchestrated an FOMC conference call to plot the actions to be taken at the hearing on October 19, 1993. The transcript of the FOMC conference call on October 15, 1993, was placed on the Fed's Web site after the customary five-year (plus) delay, where it remains at this time.

42. Participants generally identified themselves in the conference call. The FOMC conference call was at four thirty on October 15, 1993. According to the attachment to Greenspan's letter of November 2, 1993, eleven presidents and four governors participated in this conference call. Also, twenty-three staff members were in attendance. It was not known at the time that Gonzalez's pressure would cause the transcript of this meeting and others to be made public on the Board's Web site five years later. The transcript lists only four staff members who spoke. This subsequent publication illustrates a seriously incomplete record of who is privy to exploitable, secret interest-rate policy.

43. FOMC conference-call transcript, October 15, 1993, 20.

44. Ibid., 26.

45. Ibid., 7.

46. Ibid., 21.

47. Ibid., 21–22.

48. Greenspan: "No, I disagree with that . . . The facts are that the existence of the tapes and transcripts was never considered to be a particularly important issue by the staff that was doing it. They were merely employing them as a means to get appropriate minutes done. . . . The presumption that there is something that was disclosed to Board members and [not] to Presidents is factually false. Most of the Board members didn't know about it" (ibid., 22).

49. Ibid., 8.

50. *H.R. 28, the Federal Reserve Accountability Act of 1993*, October 27, 1993, 14. McDonough said he was aware of the green light and "thought that the purpose of the light was to say that the sound is in operation" (*The Federal Reserve's 17-Year Secret*, 24–25). After the hearing "on October 29, 1993, a Banking Committee staff member telephoned Vice Chairman McDonough and asked how many FOMC meetings he had attended before he was an FOMC member. He replied, 'Twelve' . . . Greenspan [informed the Committee] that the tape-recording of FOMC meetings was 'common knowledge'" (*The Federal Reserve's 17-Year Secret*, 25).

51. *H.R. 28, the Federal Reserve Accountability Act of 1993*, October 27, 1993, 30.

52. FOMC meeting transcript, January 31–February 1, 1995, 22. Transcript available at http://www.federalreserve.gov/FOMC/transcripts/1995/950201Meeting.pdf.

53. Ibid., 27:

> MS. PHILLIPS. I was thinking about legislative matters such as what is happening on the Hill, those kinds of discussions?
> MR. PARRY. That is not done during the meeting.
> MR. KOHN. It is done when the meeting is over.
> CHAIRMAN GREENSPAN. We usually do that at lunch because it is not part of the FOMC deliberations.
> MR. KOHN. And the tape is not on.

54. Ibid., 24.
55. Ibid., 27.
56. Ibid., 29.
57. Evidence from FOMC telephone conferences indicates that the tape recorder has been turned off more than once. The following example came during a period when the Fed was moving short-term interest rates up to near 10 percent. FOMC conference-call transcript, June 5, 1989:

> CHAIRMAN GREENSPAN. Good afternoon, everyone. I believe we are all accounted for with the exception of Governor Heller who is away. Sam Cross, could you bring us up to date on anything pending?
> MR. CROSS. Yes sir. Mr. Chairman. [Statement—not transcribed.]
> CHAIRMAN GREENSPAN. Thank you. Mr. Cross. Any questions for Mr. Cross? Peter Sternlight, would you update us?
> MR. STERNLIGHT. Certainly. Mr. Chairman. [Statement—not transcribed.]
> CHAIRMAN GREENSPAN. Joyce Zickler. Could you bring us up to date on your appraisal of the Friday [employment] report?
> MS. ZICKLER. [Statement—not transcribed.]
> CHAIRMAN GREENSPAN. Any questions for Ms. Zickler?

Another example came when a "Mexican agreement" was to be discussed. FOMC conference-call transcript, July 26, 1989:

> CHAIRMAN GREENSPAN. Good afternoon, everyone. There are two issues I'd like to discuss this afternoon. One is monetary policy and the other is the Mexican agreement. . . .
> [Secretary's note: The reports of Vice Chairman Corrigan and Mr. Truman on the Mexican negotiations were not transcribed.] END OF SESSION

The recorder should not be turned off even if there are separate written reports that are read (in part or in full) into the record, since important remarks and interactive material may be missed, as is evident from congressional testimony.

58. Donald Kohn to Auerbach, November 1, 2001, 2.

59. Greenspan to Congress, February 21, 1995. The letter was sent to two members of the Senate Banking Committee, Chairman Alfonse D'Amato and Paul Sarbanes, and to four members of the House Banking Committee: Chairman Jim Leach, Henry Gonzalez, Michael Castle, and Floyd Flake.

60. Ibid., 1.

61. Greenspan, "Challenge of Central Banking in a Democratic Society," 4.

CHAPTER 7

1. *American Banker,* December 6, 2002, 9.

2. Federal Reserve Bank of Boston, Financial Services Policy Committee, "Federal Reserve Banks Announce Changes to Increase Efficiency in Check Services as Check Volumes Decline Nationwide," press release, February 6, 2003, 1; available at http://www.bos.frb.org/news/press/2003/fspc020603.pdf.

3. The profit-maximizing price could be lower or higher. If the Fed raised its prices and its revenue fell sharply, it might lose money at higher prices. Whatever the case, a governmental service provider should not operate with a subsidy. If the subsidy ends and the Fed cannot cover its costs, then that is an additional argument for leaving the check-clearing business to more-efficient private-sector competitors.

4. I assisted Banking chairman Henry Reuss in the development of this 1980 legislation.

5. In 2001, Fedwire was used by more than 9,000 depository institutions and handled an average daily volume of transfers of funds of $1.6 trillion. Fedwire also transfers funds for some other firms, such as brokerages. It also transferred an average daily volume of $849 billion in securities for banks. The brokerages must initiate these security transfers on Fedwire through a bank. The Fed seeks to guarantee the transfers made on Fedwire, but there is the risk that some party will not cover its payment or, in the language of the Fed, "exceed its daylight overdraft capacity level." This is especially true on the immediate settlement of a payment as opposed to longer settlement periods—overnight—for funds transferred. A large default could initiate a domino effect in the payments system. The receiving party may then find its transfers are not covered.

6. The federal government began processing Social Security checks through the automatic clearinghouses (ACHs) in 1975. The Fed's ACH uses electronic transactions for payroll payments. ACH transactions are electronic, but they are not immediately settled (credited to a payee's account). They may be initiated a number of days before they are settled. ACH transactions are also conducted by private-sector clearinghouses such as VISANet (Visa), the American Clearing House Association (American), and the New York Automated Clearing House (NYACH).

7. Michael Higgins, "The Check Isn't in the Mail," *Wall Street Journal,* May 1, 2002. Praising the increased use of debit cards, the article ends with a debit-card advocate saying, "I'm still nervous about letting someone charge my account directly."

8. Many people still use paper checks for paying bills they do not settle with

currency and coin. American consumers and businesses wrote 40 billion paper checks (183 per capita) in 2002; the U.S. Census Bureau's noninstitutionalized civilian population of sixteen years and older is used for the per capita calculation (Federal Reserve, Financial Services Policy Committee, "Federal Reserve Banks Announce Changes to Increase Efficiency In Check Services as Check Volumes Decline Nationwide," press release, February 6, 2003). The 40 billion-check estimate, rounded to the nearest billion, may be very inexact. James McAndrews and William Roberds reported that 66 billion checks were used in 1997, or 250 per capita ("The Economics of Check Float," *Economic Review* [Federal Reserve Bank of Atlanta] 85, no. 4 (2000): 17; available at http://www.frbatlanta.org/publica/eco-rev/rev_abs/00er/q4/roberds.pdf). This substantial decline hopefully indicates a change to more digital transfer of third-party payment information. It can also be partly caused by increases in transactions using currency to avoid records.

9. Report from the Fed, under a cover letter from E. Gerald Corrigan, president of the Minneapolis Fed Bank, April 26, 1984; Garn's question is at the top of 14; author's collection.

10. Ibid. For larger returned checks (over $2,500) a "wire advice" (wire or telephone) of return was sometimes used, though the Fed warned: "It is not possible to provide statistical information on the benefits of wire transactions because it has not been extensively used. The institutions in the collection chain often do not provide wire notification" (20).

11. The Monetary Control Act of 1980 required this float to be priced at the federal funds rate. Float also increases the supply of money in the country. The Fed may choose to offset the increases in the money supply by selling securities. The interest on these securities is also a cost to the taxpayers. Unexpected changes in the float make it difficult for the Fed to control either the money supply or to hit an interest-rate target. Mistakes can cause instability and uncertainty that disrupt financial markets.

12. This is required under the Expedited Funds Availability Act of 1987. Congress expanded the Federal Reserve's powers by giving it the authority to regulate check payments that were not processed by the Fed. Since 1994, under Regulation cc, the same-day-settlement rule, collecting banks have the right to receive funds from paying banks on the same day that checks are presented as long as that occurs by eight in the morning, local time of the paying bank. This regulation caused more checks to be cleared outside the Fed with direct presentment between the collecting and paying banks.

13. The its had five hub cities and airports: New York, Teterboro Airport in New Jersey; Cleveland, Burke-Lakefront; Atlanta, Hartsfield; Chicago, Midway; and Dallas, Love Field. The Fed facility at the Teterboro Airport was shut down after a congressional investigation revealed the "phantom airplane" that was supposedly there. The Fed moved its facility to the Philadelphia International Airport. There were forty-three spoke cities in the its operations.

14. McAndrews and Roberds, "Economics of Check Float," 24.

15. AirNet: http://www.airnet.com/Operations/operationsFrame.htm.

16. Federal Reserve Bank of St. Louis, "Contingency Plans Tested Sept. 11: Did the Fed Pass?" *Central Banker,* Winter 2001; available at http://stlouisfed.org/publications/cb/2001/d/pages/p1-article1.html. The computer problems expected to result from Y2K, such as changing the year to 2000 on software programs, turned out to be minimal.

17. Ibid.

18. Jeffrey M. Lacker, "Payment System Disruptions and the Federal Reserve following September 11, 2001," *Journal of Monetary Economics* 51, no. 5: 936; available at http://www.carnegie-rochester.rochester.edu/Nov03-pdfs/lacker.pdf. Lacker became president of the Richmond Fed Bank in 2004.

19. Information was taken from Paul Jack's research paper on the check-payment system. He was a student in my class at the LBJ School of Public Affairs. The statistics for Canada were accessed from a data source other than the one used for the remainder of the data, which are from Bank for International Settlements, *Statistics on Payment Systems in the Group of Ten Countries: Figures for 1999,* online: http://www.bis.org/publ/cpss44.pdf.

20. One Federal Reserve article states: "In Europe and other industrialized parts of the world, electronic payments mechanisms have largely replaced checks. But in the U.S., paper checks are still very common, accounting for more than 60% of retail payments" (Gautam Gowrisankaran, "Why Do Americans Still Write Checks?" FRBSF *[Federal Reserve Bank of San Francisco] Economic Letter* 2002-27 [September 20, 2002]; available at http://www.frbsf.org/publications/economics/letter/2002/el2002-27.html). Historically in Europe, many payments were made through the postal service and its nationwide branch offices. Private banks developed their own payment network and did not rely on the central bank for clearing payments.

21. See Committee on Banking and Financial Services, Democratic Staff, *Waste and Abuse in the Federal Reserve's Payment System,* 104th Cong., 2nd sess., January 5, 1996; note: "This report has not been officially adopted by the Committee on Banking and Financial Services and may not, therefore, necessarily reflect the views of its members." Impaired bidding practices were also found by the General Accounting Office in many other parts of the Fed (GAO, *Federal Reserve System: Current and Future Challenges Require Systemwide Attention,* June 1996; see especially 131–134; available at http://www.gao.gov/archive/1996/gg96128.pdf).

22. Office of Inspector General, Board of Governors of the Federal Reserve System, *Semiannual Report to Congress, April 1, 1994–September 30, 1994* (October 1994), 31.

23. Jerry Knight, "Gonzalez Urges Probe of Fed's Check-Flying; Congressman Sees Waste in System," *Washington Post,* January 17, 1996.

24. *Waste and Abuse in the Federal Reserve's Payment System,* sec. 3A.

25. Justin Fox, "Fed Check Transport Hit by Democrats as Anticompetitive, Costly," *American Banker,* January 10, 1996, 2.

26. Senate Banking Committee, confirmation hearings for Alan Greenspan, July 26, 1996; statement of Greenspan, 14–15.

27. Federal Reserve Board Staff, response to Congressman Gonzalez's May 6, 1996, letter on ITS, 2; author's collection.

28. Gonzalez to Greenspan, July 26, 1996, 5; author's collection.

29. Greenspan to Maloney, September 15, 1997, 5; author's collection.

30. Greenspan adds a statement that would be reiterated in a different form the next day at the hearing: "The purpose of our internal records is to help us run ITS not to show an accounting profit" (Greenspan to Maloney, September 15, 1997, 2). This is not a justification for corrupted Fed records that lead to subsidized prices for Fed services.

31. Also, saying that ITS covers "marginal costs" is the use of a concept that sounds good but was not relevant. Marginal cost is the change in all the costs when output is increased. The Monetary Control Act refers to covering total costs, including fixed costs that do not change.

32. Maloney to Rivlin, December 11, 1997, 2; author's collection. See also Robert Auerbach, "Pensions, Planes and Priced Services," 8. The percentage of the Fed's priced services operating expenses was estimated by the Financial Markets Center to be: 1998, 13.3 percent; 1997, 9.3 percent; 1996, 6.8 percent; 1995, 5.4 percent; and 1994, 2.9 percent.

33. "In 1987 the Fed began using plan surpluses to take advantage of Financial Accounting Standard No. 87. Introduced years earlier by the Financial Accounting Standards Board, Rule 87 was designed to let companies with underfunded retirement plans count their pension obligations as a cost against their operating income. But corporations and public agencies with overfunded plans soon exploited FAS 87 to book their surpluses as operating income—a so called pension cost credit" (Financial Markets Center, "Uncivil Service: Pension Rebellion Stirs the Fed," *FOMC Alert* 4, no. 5 [August 22, 2000], 5, 6); available at http://www.fmcenter.org/atf/cf/%7BDFBB2772-F5C5-4DFE-B310-D82A61944339%7D/Aug00_FOMCAlert.pdf.

34. The Gramm-Leach-Bliley Act of 1999.

35. Patrick K. Barron, "National Strategies for Electronic Check Presentment," speech at the BAI National Electronic Check Collection Service, Tucson, Arizona, October 1, 2001; available at http://www.atl.frb.org/invoke.cfm?objectid=AB173 F9D-C173-11D5-898500508BB89A83&method=display.

36. Committee on the Federal Reserve in the Payments Mechanism, *The Federal Reserve in the Payments Mechanism*, January 1998, 15, 16; available at http://www.federalreserve.gov/BOARDDOCS/PRESS/general/1998/19980105/19980105.pdf.

37. John Wilke, "Showing Its Age, Fed's Huge Empire, Set Up Years Ago, Is Costly and Inefficient," *Wall Street Journal*, September 16, 1996, 1.

38. Board of Governors, "Federal Reserve System 2005 Check Restructuring Fact Sheet," 1; available at http://www.federalreserve.gov/BOARDDOCS/PRESS/Other/2004/20040802/attachment2.pdf.

39. McAndrews and Roberds, "Economics of Check Float," 18. The estimate is based on an interpolation from 1993 data.

40. David C. Wheelock and Paul W. Wilson, "Trends in the Efficiency of Federal

Reserve Check Processing Operations," *Review* [Federal Reserve Bank of St. Louis] 86, no. 5 (September–October 2004): 7; available at http://research.stlouisfed.org/publications/review/04/09/Wheelock.pdf.

41. Federal Reserve, Financial Services Policy Committee, press release, August 2, 2004, 2; and "Federal Reserve System 2005 Check Restructuring Fact Sheet," 1.

42. Dow Jones newswires, September 28, 2006.

43. United States Action, "Electromagnetic Pulse Risks and Terrorism," available at http://www.unitedstatesaction.com/emp-terror.htm. This material is quoted from a Northwestern University Physics Department site (http://www.physics.northwestern.edu/classes/2001Fall/Phyx135-2/19/emp.htm.) that has been taken down.

44. Ibid.

CHAPTER 8

1. Greenspan to Gonzalez, October 29, 1996, 3; author's collection.

2. Gonzalez and Jackson, press release and letter to Greenspan, March 6, 1997; the quotation is from the letter, 2; both in author's collection.

3. Greenspan to Gonzalez, April 14, 1997, Attachment II; author's collection.

4. The quote is from the Federal Trade Commission Web site: http://www.ftc.gov/bcp/conline/pubs/credit/ecoa.shtm.

5. Three of the nine directors—the Class C directors—at each of the twelve Fed Banks are appointed by the Board of Governors. The other six directors are elected by the member banks (private commercial banks) in the district. The Federal Reserve Act stipulated that these six directors were to be elected in two groups: three Class A directors were selected from banks, and three Class B directors were selected from industry. The composition of the boards mirrored the composition of leaders in the banking industry, white males.

6. House Committee on Banking, Currency and Housing, *Federal Reserve Directors*, 5.

7. Reuss, press release, June 10, 1976. A note from the Fed's congressional liaison, Don Winn, showing the dissemination of this press release to the Fed's governors is in the Burns Collection at the Ford Library. It may have annoyed them to find that they had been urged to "live up to the [Federal Home Loan Bank Board's] FHLBB's example," as Don Winn reported in his attached memo.

8. Reuss to Burns, August 30, 1976, 1.

9. For information on Jean Andrus Crockett, see "Jean Andrus Crockett, Professor: Led Philly Federal Reserve," *Wharton Alumni Magazine,* Spring 2007; available at http://www.wharton.upenn.edu/alum_mag/issues/125anniversaryissue/crockett.html. For information on Generose Gervais, see Jeff Hansel, "Sister Generose: Hands and Heart for God," *Rochester (MN) Post-Bulletin,* May 28, 2007; available at http://search.live.com/results.aspx?FORM=DNSAS&q=news.postbulletin.com%2fnewsmanager%2ftemplates%2flocalnews_story.asp%3fa%3d295641%26z%3d2.

10. House Committee on Banking, Finance and Urban Affairs, *Status of Equal*

Employment Opportunity at the Federal Reserve: Diversity Still Lacking, Part 1 (1,100 pages) and Part 2 (1,001 pages); and *A Racial, Gender, and Background Profile of the Directors of the Federal Reserve Banks and Branches* (60 pages). A wider view of federal banking agencies is reported in House Committee on Banking, Finance and Urban Affairs, *Problems with Equal Employment Opportunity and Minority and Women Contracting at the Federal Banking Agencies: Hearing before the Committee on Banking, Finance and Urban Affairs* (1,163 pages).

11. *Racial, Gender, and Background Profile,* viii.

12. Quoted in a press release by Gonzalez, October 30, 1992; author's collection. Gonzalez noted: "One of the minutes I received [from a Fed Bank board of directors meeting] stated that a Federal Reserve president told his directors on September 14, 1990, that the Banking Committee's August 1990 staff report entitled *A Racial, Gender, and Background Profile of the Directors of the Federal Reserve Banks and Branches* 'appears to be biased and not representative.'"

13. Quoted in ibid.

14. Ibid.

15. Press release, "Rep. Henry B. Gonzalez Finds Only Slight Progress in Diversity in Hiring at the Federal Reserve," August 21, 1996, 1; author's collection.

16. Karen Gallo, "Fed Doubles the Number of Staff Making Over $125,000 A Year," Associated Press, September 11, 1996. The headline for this story in the *Washington Times* (front page, September 12, 1996) read: "Where a Janitor Earns $163,800, Federal Reserve Defends Big Salaries."

17. Ibid.

18. Henry B. Gonzalez of Texas, "Reduction in Regulatory Control of Federal Reserve Board Is Subject to Proposed Legislation," statement on the floor of the House, March 9, 1994, 103rd Cong., 2nd sess., *Congressional Record* 140: H 1140. Gonzalez asked the Fed's Inspector General "to insure that no retaliatory actions are taken against examiners who have reported unethical behavior." Given the IG's reticence to look into Fed Bank matters when asked to do so by Gonzalez, this request was probably futile.

19. Gonzalez and Jackson to Greenspan, March 6, 1997, 1; author's collection.

20. Bureau of National Affairs, "Race/Retaliation; Black Woman Denied Job at Federal Reserve Awarded $150,000, Promotion for Race Bias," *Employment Discrimination Report* 3, no. 17 (November 2, 1994), 3.

21. Ibid.

22. Ibid.

23. *Bennett v. Greenspan,* Dt. D.C., C.A. No. 93-1813-RMU; filed April 20, 1993; decided October 17, 1994.

24. Jesse Jackson, Jr., "Federal Reserve Board Civil Rights Compliance Act of 1999 Introduced" (press release), July 1, 1999; available at http://www.jessejacksonjr.org/query/creadpr.cgi?id=579.

25. Greenspan to Gonzalez, April 14, 1997, Attachment 1, 2; author's collection.

26. "Discrimination at the Fed," *Nader Letter,* January 18, 1998, 9.

27. All money the Fed does not "need" is sent back to the U.S. Treasury.

28. Jesse Jackson, Jr., press release, July 1, 1999.

29. "Discrimination at the Fed," *Nader Letter*, January 18, 1998, 9. Ralph Nader was assisted by Jake Lewis, who served on the House Banking staff for twenty-seven years and before that was a reporter in Texas.

30. Ibid.

31. Federal Reserve, Board of Governors, press release, December 23, 1996; available at http://www.federalreserve.gov/boarddocs/press/boardacts/1996/199612233/.

32. The conference included a speech by President Clinton.

CHAPTER 9

1. These are targets for the federal funds rate, a lending rate for loans between banks. The Fed's monetary policy attempts to keep this interest rate near a target figure.

2. I thought that I should present my true views and not obfuscate. The institutional routines that are based on preserving the proper forms and rituals can be depicted as a metaphoric opera. The ritual survey did not really matter, since the Fed Bank president voted with the Fed chairman. This filing of a survey report was just part of the first act. In the second act, the Fed's chorus of 500-plus economists breaks into a discordant refrain on a platform at the back of the stage, which then sinks out of sight. The Fed chairman comes forward, surrounded by eleven whispering people, who nod their heads in unison as the chairman sings the final aria, the one for public consumption. In the third act, the members of the media fill the stage, all running in different directions as they inharmoniously emit their views about the aria's deep meaning.

When I left the Fed Bank to take a position in Washington, D.C., I left on the best of terms. During my two years of employment, I had published a number of articles, some with a coauthor, in the Fed literature and in academic journals.

3. Meyer, *A Term at the Fed*, 53

4. Meyer, *A Term at the Fed*, 39.

5. Darryl R. Francis was president of the St. Louis Fed Bank from 1966 to 1976. He steadfastly argued for slower money growth to fight inflation. As William Poole, currently president of the same Fed Bank (and who, as a distinguished faculty member at Brown University, assisted in editing one of my textbooks), relates, "In plain terms, he said that the organization he [Darryl Francis] worked for was responsible for creating and maintaining inflation. That was not a popular position at the Fed's Board of Governors in Washington, and I know that a lot of pressure was applied to get Darryl to be quiet" (William Poole, "Eulogy for Darryl R. Francis, 1912–2002," Federal Reserve Bank of St. Louis *Review*, March–April 2002, 1). Darryl Francis and his staff of economists, who derived a mathematical model that included the economic effects of changes in the money supply, received praise from Milton Friedman.

6. Melody Petersen, "William McChesney Martin, 91, Dies, Defined Fed's

Role," *New York Times,* July 29, 1998. Martin was not as clueless as this quote implies. His father, a St. Louis banker, had helped President Woodrow Wilson draft the 1913 Federal Reserve Act. His father became president of the St. Louis Fed Bank, and McChesney would follow a similar path. He became an examiner after graduating from Yale with an undergraduate degree in Latin and English. At thirty-one he became president of the New York Stock Exchange. He was also chairman of the Export-Import Bank and assistant secretary of the treasury. Martin was knowledgeable in some areas of finance and banking areas. On Martin's death, Fed chairman Greenspan said that he had set a "masterful example."

7. Friedman to Auerbach, February 26, 1993.

8. In addition, Burns became a strong advocate for wage and price controls, even on stock dividends; it is difficult to imagine Martin having taken such a position. Of course, it is even more difficult to understand why Burns or President Nixon would have advocated such policies, given their otherwise conservative beliefs.

9. At the beginning of 2003, the money supply—defined to include currency, coin, checkable deposits, and consumer money-market funds—was $5.8 trillion, an enormous amount, enough to buy 55 percent of the goods and services produced the previous year in the United States.

10. This table is from an attachment to a Greenspan letter to Gonzalez (September 15, 1993). The note on the table reads: "This table covers all formal positions involved in economic research/management activities. For Reserve Bank only filled positions are counted, but vacancies are included in the Board count."

11. Number of economists at some federal entities in 2000: Agriculture Department, 525 (the Fed may well have more than 525 if all those in the bureaucracy who have economic training are counted); Army, 198; Commerce Department, 400; Energy Department, 112; Environmental Protection Agency, 151; Health and Human Services, 111; Labor Department, 1,076; State Department, 138; Treasury Department, 400. These estimates were supplied by Terry Schau, an economist at the Bureau of Labor Statistics (e-mail to the author, May 6, 2002). I was not able to obtain the number for the CIA.

12. The contract total was $2,919,281, an average of $13,967.85 for each consultant.

13. This information was given to the press. See Stephen A. Davies, "Fed May Be Stifling Criticism by Hiring Outside Academics, according to Critics," *Bond Buyer,* November 4, 1994, 1.

14. Ibid., 8.

15. Friedman to Auerbach, February 26, 1993.

16. Reuters, July 7, 1993; the quotations are attributed to Friedman.

17. The Fed acts as the agent of the U.S. Treasury. When the Treasury needs funds, it notifies the Fed to hold an auction in the Fed Banks. This is done nearly every week. Those seeking to buy Treasury securities can go to the nearest Fed Bank or branch and make a written bid. When the time limit for the auction closes—say, Tuesday at two, Eastern Standard Time—the bids are opened and the desired amount is sold to the highest bidders. The cost of the securities is not a fixed amount, since people are

bidding on them and only bids at or above the auction price are accepted. Buyers can specify "noncompetitive" bids by indicating they will accept whatever price is determined in the auction. Buyers need not go all the way to Fed Banks or branches to buy these securities. Local banks provide that service for a small fee. The big news was that Treasury bills had a face value (the final payment) that was much smaller than in the past. Normally, the Treasury bills had been sold with a minimum face value of $10,000. The mistake announced on the morning news show was that anyone could now go to a bank or the Fed and buy a Treasury bill at a cost of $1,000.

18. Davies, "Fed May Be Stifling Criticism," 1. The House Banking Committee received a copy of the "Nondisclosure Clause" of the vendor's agreement in 1994, with the note that this "nondisclosure clause is signed by all Board contractors as a condition of their contracts.

19. Ibid., 9.

20. Federal Reserve Bank of New York, *Research Update*, 2006, no. 1; available at http://www.newyorkfed.org/research/research_update/ru04_06.pdf.

21. Henry B. Gonzalez, statement on the floor of the House, February 9, 1994, 103rd Cong., 2nd sess., *Congressional Record* 140: H 400. Gonzalez added: "That kind of camaraderie and benevolence from the Federal Reserve Bank of Atlanta will produce many friends among experts in financial derivatives—the very area that the Banking Committee is considering legislation."

22. Robert P. Forrestal, president of the Atlanta Fed Bank, to Auerbach, December 16, 1993. He said he interviewed the staff member I contacted, who "said she never made any statement to anyone of the kind you described to me." He continued: "Such statements would not only have been untrue, but would have had the effect of trivializing an important conference." He then said his staff "would welcome an apology from you or some clarification of the source of this information."

1. Grassley later became a senator and chairman of the Senate Committee on Finance. This section, including the colloquy between Grassley (R-IA) and Miller and some of the other sections on the political history of the Fed, are taken from Auerbach, *Money, Banking, and Financial Markets*, 710–721.

2. House Banking Committee, *Quarterly Hearings on the Conduct of Monetary Policy*, 95th Cong., 2nd sess., April 10, 1978, 142–143. Also see Auerbach, "G. William Miller," 347.

3. Examples of the interaction between politics and monetary policy: President Truman assigned Fed chairman Martin to take monetary policy authority away from the Treasury, which had pegged interest rates at a low level, keeping the market price of Treasury securities high in order to protect and reward banks during and after the World War II period. The banks had helped finance the war by heavily investing in Treasury securities. By September 1953, Martin had announced that this practice was over: President Eisenhower wanted slower money growth, and the Martin Fed obliged

by instituting a growth rate of 1.73 percent. This analysis was done by the late Robert Weintraub, a former professor, staff member of the House Banking Committee, and a noted monetarist. A description is reported in Auerbach, *Money, Banking, and Financial Markets*, 714. Under President Nixon, Fed chairman Burns rejected a restrictive monetary policy. This changed when Gerald Ford became president. The Burns Fed provided slower money growth (4.7 percent), in line with the president's desire to control inflation. After the second quarter of 1975 and continuing until Jimmy Carter was elected president, the Burns Fed accelerated money-supply growth, presumably to help Ford get elected. The Fed then began to raise interest rates to slow money growth. Carter appointed G. William Miller to be the Fed chairman. Money growth reached an annual rate of 8.5 percent. The inflation rate went into double digits, reaching an annual rate of nearly 14 percent in June 1978. This loss of purchasing power for U.S. dollars affected all those whose incomes rose at a slower rate. To indicate a change in his priorities, Carter moved Miller to the Treasury and appointed Paul Volcker to chair the Fed. Inflation raged on, reaching an annual rate of 16 percent in May 1979 and nearly 20 percent in March 1980. The inflation drove up interest rates. The advertised prime rate rose to nearly 20 percent in May 1980, and many businesses with prime-plus loans became saddled with failure-producing debt loads. Volcker's tight-money policies halted inflation, but at the cost of double-dip recessions in 1980 and 1981. The harsh, tragic results of the recessions were part of the costs of reining in inflation.

4. I assisted him with testimony on Fed policy.

5. I was one of the staff advisers at the Treasury writing these papers.

6. "The President also said that the recent jump in the money supply, to an annual rate of growth far above the Federal Reserve's targets, 'sends, I think, the wrong signal to the money markets'" (Jonathan Fuerbringer, "Reagan Criticizes Fed's Move," *New York Times*, January 20, 1982). The money supply grew rapidly, at annual rates of 11.37 percent, 10.04 percent, 14.02 percent, and 10.82 percent from October 1981 through January 1982, and then in February it dropped to 3.02 percent.

7. William Jones, "Regan, Volcker Fail to Budge On Fed Policy," *Washington Post*, October 8, 1981.

8. The Kemp-Roth tax-cut legislation (the Economic Recovery Tax Act of 1981) reduced the top marginal income tax rate from 70 percent to 28, and all marginal tax rates by 25 percent on average.

9. Fuerbringer, "Reagan Criticizes Fed's Move."

10. Council of Economic Advisers, *Economic Report of the President: Annual Report*, 99th Cong., 2nd sess., February 1986, 359.

11. Fuerbringer, "Reagan Criticizes Fed's Move."

12. This quotation and much of this discussion is found in Auerbach, *Money, Banking, and Financial Markets*, 718.

13. "Greenspan predicts '89 recession," Associated Press, June 8, 1987: "Meanwhile, Treasury Secretary James A. Baker III confirmed for the first time Sunday that President Reagan did not ask Volcker to remain for a third term as Fed chairman. Baker's

statement contradicts that of White House spokesman Marlin Fitzwater, who told reporters last week that Reagan had asked Volcker to remain."

14. Robert D. Hershey, Jr., "Volcker Out after 8 Years as Federal Reserve Chief; Reagan Chooses Greenspan," *New York Times*, June 3, 1987.

15. Hobart Rowen, "After Angell: A New Face May Help Open Up the Fed," *Washington Post*, January 23, 1994, Financial sec.

16. Erich Heinemann, "Volcker Is Victim of White House Cabal as US Economy Heads toward Reflation," *American Banker*, March 24, 1986, 4. Volcker was reported to be "likely to resign his post—rumor has it to register as a Democrat and run for the United States Senate against Republican Alfonse M. D'Amato of New York." Volcker served until 1987 and did not enter politics. He continued a distinguished career that included service on public commissions.

17. Hershey, "Out After 8 Years."

18. The bracketed "[correctly]" is in the transcript, indicating Fed editing.

19. FOMC conference-call transcript, December 14, 1992, 1–2.

20. FOMC meeting transcript, July 2–3, 1991, 34; transcript available at http://www .federalreserve.gov/FOMC/transcripts/1991/910703Meeting.pdf.

21. Henry Reuss, "What the Secret Minutes of Federal Reserve Banks Meetings Disclose," speech in the House of Representatives, May 24, 1977, 95th. Cong., 1st sess., *Congressional Record* 123: H 16235–16240. Reuss's speech also noted the following: "Lobbying efforts by the Fed System are not confined to the U.S. Congress. The Fed also organizes lobbying against bills it opposes in State legislatures. The minutes of the Philadelphia Fed for May 4 and May 18, 1972, describe a lobbying effort in New Jersey which involved enlisting private commercial banks and the New Jersey Bankers Association against a bill which might have attracted independent banks away from the Fed.

Pages 57–58, Federal Reserve Bank of Philadelphia board minutes—1972, 1974, and 1975, as delivered to the House Banking Committee: "President Eastburn said there was a Bill in the New Jersey Assembly to permit nonmembers to keep up to 50 percent of their reserves in government securities. He indicated that this Bank had been in touch with New Jersey bankers, the New Jersey Bankers Association and key legislators to express the feeling that the bill would be divisive, inequitable, and disruptive, and would have an adverse effect on membership. He reported that the Bill had recently been sent back to Committee. ——— (name omitted) said he would meet with the governor to discuss the Bill."

And then 2 weeks later, the Philadelphia minutes contain a followup report- in the same place, page 62: "——— (name omitted) reported that the proposed New Jersey Legislation, which would permit banks to invest part of their reserves, had been sent back to committee. He said he had talked with the Governor who will look into the situation."

The pattern of lobbying with the U.S. Congress against the GAO audit bill and the Sunshine Act appears to be carried through by the regional banks for State legislation. The bank, as the Philadelphia minutes show, mobilizes the State bankers association and local bankers in its legislative campaigns. (16237)

22. The designation "emphasis added" appears in the *Congressional Record*.

23. Reuss, "Secret Minutes," 16237.

24. The exclusions cover foreign transactions with governments, central banks, or nonprivate financing organizations; deliberations and decisions on monetary policy and open-market operations; transactions made under the direction of the FOMC; and parts of the discussion or communication among or between Board members and officers and Fed employees related to any of the previous three categories.

25. Stephen A. Rhoades, "Bank Mergers and Banking Structure in the United States, 1980–1998," Staff Study 174, Board of Governors of the Federal Reserve System, August 2000, 31; available at http://www.federalreserve.gov/pubs/staffstudies/2000-present/ss174.pdf. The number of bank branches and automatic teller machines (ATMs) has continued to grow. In many countries, such as Canada, there are relatively few banks, though each has many branches. In Germany there are many banks owned by cities and states, and the number of branches per person is greater than in the United States. According to reported figures, U.S. banks in 2002 had 77,752 bank branches, or 282 per million people; Germany had 42,351 branches, or 515 branches per million people. See Mark Landler, "Commerzbank Reflects Germany's Many Banking Ills," *New York Times*, November 9, 2002. Data are from Schroder Smith Barney. Obviously, bank branches of the same bank are not a substitute for different banks, which compete for business.

26. Liz Laderman, "Trends in the Concentration of Bank Deposits: The Northwest," *FRBSF Economic Letter* 2002-21, July 26, 2002, 1; available at http://www.frbsf.org/publications/economics/letter/2002/el2002-21.html.

27. The official name of the law is the Riegle-Neal Interstate Banking and Branching Efficiency Act of 1994 (HR 3841); its sponsors were Senate Banking chairman Donald W. Riegle, Jr. (D-MI) and Congressman Stephen L. Neal (D-NC), the next-highest ranking Democrat to Gonzalez on House Banking. Riegle-Neal changes Section 3(d) of the Bank Holding Company Act of 1956 (*U.S. Code* 12 (2004, as amended), § 1842(d)), and the Fed has regulatory authority over bank holding companies. The interpretation of this law is summarized from M. Maureen Murphy, *The Riegle-Neal Interstate Banking and Branching Efficiency Act of 1994*, CRS [Congressional Research Service] Report 94-744 A, September 26, 1994. In addition, the law requires banks to demonstrate that they are complying with the Community Reinvestment Act; such compliance is documented by a satisfactory report from the Fed.

28. Riegle-Neal, Section (2): Interstate banking, Concentration limits: "(A) Nationwide Concentration Limits. The Board may not approve an application pursuant to paragraph (1)(A) if the applicant (including all insured depository institutions which are affiliates of the applicant) controls, or upon consummation of the acquisition for which such application is filed would control, more than 10 percent of

the total amount of deposits of insured depository institutions in the United States." The initial reported estimate of 9.8 percent of nationwide deposits for the proposed merged operation had not been verified by the Fed, which is instructed in Riegle-Neal to use the definition of deposits in Section 3(l) of the Federal Deposit Insurance Act. The proposed enlarged Bank of America entity was estimated to have 33 million customers, 5,669 brick-and-mortar banking offices, and 16,551 ATMs. See Patrick Mc-Geehan, "Banking Giant: The Strategy, Buy Leaves Bank Short of Wall St. Dreams," *New York Times,* October 28, 2003.

29. Valerie Bauerlein and Damian Paletta, "Bank of America Quietly Targets Barrier to Growth; Law Capping Deposits Favors Foreign Rivals, Big U.S. Lender Says," *Wall Street Journal,* January 16, 2007; available at http://online.wsj.com/article_email/ sb116891898174977348-lmyQjAXMDE3NjE4Njkxkx MTY4Wj.html.

30. Jathon Sapsford, Laurie P. Cohen, Monica Langley, and Joseph T. Hallinan, "J.P. Morgan to Buy Bank One," *Wall Street Journal,* January 15, 2004.

31. Krysten Crawford, "Bank of America Inks $35B Card Deal; No. 3 Bank to buy MBNA, Creating the Nation's Largest Card Issuer; 6000 jobs to be cut," *CNNMoney. com,* June 30 2005, http://money.cnn.com/2005/06/30/news/fortune500/boa/.

32. Proponents of larger banks can point to England and Canada, where a few large domestic banks dominate.

33. According to one account:

"It's only a matter of time before . . . the cap has to be lifted, but in the short run it would be a mistake to willy-nilly raise the cap without examining its competitive implications," said a lobbyist at a large banking company, who did not want to be named. What about Bank of America? A Bank of America spokeswoman insisted that it has no intention of lobbying Congress to alter the 10% limit. That's an understandable stance for a company that just absorbed FleetBoston Financial Corp. and angered some influential New England lawmakers in the process. Still, most observers expect the ever-ambitious company to gun for the cap sooner or later. In fact, some say all the big banking companies will eventually do so.

Michele Heller, "Deposit Cap Is One Fight B of A Peers May Sit Out," *American Banker,* September 13, 2004, Washington in Focus sec., 1.

34. Bauerlein and Paletta, "Bank of America Quietly Targets Barrier to Growth."

35. The standard analysis indicates that given no changes in efficiency, a move from more to fewer firms results in higher prices for fewer services. The value of the services not captured by the large firms is called a deadweight loss, which entails a reduction in consumer welfare.

36. "Most say raising the cap [in the near future] would be a tough sell on Capitol Hill. For example, when B of A [Bank of America] laid off hundreds of employees in New England last week and announced plans to move its small-business and Latin American banking divisions out of Massachusetts, Rep. Barney Frank of Massachu-

setts, the ranking Democrat on House Financial Services, said the rules regulators use to judge merger and acquisition deals should be toughened" (Heller, "Deposit Cap," 1).

37. This allegation was made in "The Wall Street Fix," a segment on the PBS television program *Frontline*, with correspondent Hedrick Smith, May 8, 2003.

38. From "The Wall Street Fix," *Frontline*, May 8, 2003 (http://www.pbs.org/wgbh/pages/frontline/shows/wallstreet/weill/):

> Hedrick Smith [moderator]: What was Chairman Alan Greenspan's role in this? What was his thinking? Was he for this? Was he an advocate? What did he do? Professor Alan Blinder [former vice chairman of the Fed]: He was certainly for it. The Federal Reserve Board, in fact, had been for repeal repeatedly through the 1990s. . . . I think [Greenspan] played a substantial role, in the sense that were he against it, it could not have happened. He could not have stopped the market from encroaching over boundaries — those were sort of natural market events. But he could've stopped — at least slowed down and, I think, probably stopped — the friendlier regulatory environment. . . .
>
> I don't think in any sense — at least from my knowledge — was he driving the political process that led eventually to repeal. But he was definitely an advocate. He was called to testify on this many times in front of the Congress over many years, and was always in favor of repealing Glass-Steagall.

The law was named for Senator Carter Glass (D-VA) and Rep. Henry Bascom Steagall (D-AL), who cosponsored several laws in the early 1930s to assist the troubled banking system. Their legislation from 1932 and 1933 has been called the Glass-Steagall Acts. The 1932 act liberalized the terms for member-bank borrowing from the Fed. The 1933 law, also called the Banking Act, separated commercial banking from underwriting and other activities of investment banks. The act established federal deposit insurance and formed the Federal Deposit Insurance Corporation (FDIC). It also placed ceilings on the interest that could be paid by banks on deposits; zero interest on consumer demand deposits (commercial-bank checking deposits) was in force until 1984, and zero interest was still in force for business demand deposits in 2002. The belief that competition was a cause of bank failures was the mistaken rationale that allowed this cartel pricing to deprive consumers of payments for money essentially loaned to banks. During the 1990s, the regulations of the 1933 act came increasingly under question by legislators who favored bank deregulation. In 1998, Citicorp and the Travelers Group, Inc. agreed to a merger valued at $70 billion in stock and predicated on lifting the restrictions, which were finally repealed in 1999.

39. "The initial concept of one-stop financial supermarket — pioneered by Citigroup in the 1990s" began to fade somewhat as Citibank began to sell off some its insurance units, including Travelers Life and Annuity in 2005 (Dennis Berman and Theo Francis, "MetLife to Buy Citigroup Unit," *Wall Street Journal* online, January 31, 2005).

40. The comptroller of the currency, Eugene Ludwig, issued exceptions to Glass-Steagall until his five-year term ended, in April 1998; two months later he became vice chairman of Bankers Trust. Ludwig left shortly thereafter, when Bankers Trust was sold to Deutsche Bank.

41. Before Gramm-Leach-Bliley, banks were prohibited from owning brokerages that offered investment advice or from owning other financial companies. The prohibited entities included insurance companies in localities of over 5,000 people.

42. Senate Banking, Housing and Urban Affairs Committee, *Hearings on HR 10: The Financial Services Act of 1998*, 105th Cong., 2nd sess., June 17, 1998. The hearing was chaired by Senator Alfonse D'Amato. There were disagreements between Greenspan and Rubin in 1998 over whether the new financial holding companies should organize as they determined to be best for them—the Rubin-administration position—or whether they should develop new activities in subsidiaries of the holding company—the Greenspan position, which sought to isolate the banking functions, which are covered by federal deposit insurance and include the right to borrow from the Fed.

43. "The Wall Street Fix," transcript.

44. Ibid.

45. Ibid., introduction; http://www.pbs.org/wgbh/pages/frontline/shows/wall street/etc/synopsis.html.

46. Ibid., transcript.

47. Arianna Huffington, "Wild on Washington: Free Food, Exotic Locales, Topless Lobbyists," January 22, 2003, http://ariannaonline.huffingtonpost.com/columns/column.php?id=34.

CHAPTER 11

1. On February 4, 1994, the Fed raised the federal funds target from 3 percent to 3.5 percent. This was the first of seven interest-rate increases that led to a doubling of the target rate, to 6 percent, on February 1, 1995. Ostensibly, the Fed was conducting a preemptive strike against inflation, even though the consumer price index rose by 2.69 percent in 1994 and Greenspan had contended it was as much as 1.5 percent overstated. Greenspan did testify (e.g., May 27, 1994, before Senate Banking) that he thought the average price of equities was too high. He did not indicate he would use monetary policy to fine-tune equity prices. The press reported that he was worried about a low real federal funds rate. Raising this theoretical point served to limit questions about monetary policy from most members of Congress who were not versed in economics.

2. The average yearly inflation rates for 1993 and 1994 were, respectively, 2.77 percent and 2.69 percent; the unemployment rates were 6.9 percent and 6.1 percent.

3. Staff and wire reports, "Banks Pushing Prime to 6.25%; Increased Mark 1st Concerted Effort to Hike Rate since '89," *Columbus (OH) Dispatch*, March 24, 1994.

4. "Jobs versus Inflation at the Fed," editorial, *New York Times*, August 30, 1994. The editorial notes that these views were not too distant from Greenspan's view that reducing inflation increases economic activity and reduces unemployment. However,

the difference was whether employment or inflation should be the immediate primary target.

5. Parts of this section appeared in Robert D. Auerbach, "Greenspan's Needle," *Barron's*, July 24, 2000, 17. FOMC meeting transcripts have provided a useful tool for analyzing monetary-policy formation. Monetary policy is difficult to unravel from the speeches of Fed officials or from the Fed chairman's statements in February and July before the House and Senate Banking Committees, which were required by the Humphrey-Hawkins Act (Full Employment and Balanced Growth Act of 1978, an amendment to the Federal Reserve Act).

6. FOMC conference-call transcript, February 28, 1994, 6; available at http://www .federalreserve.gov/FOMC/transcripts/1994/940228ConfCall.pdf; bracketed phrase added.

7. FOMC meeting transcript, March 22, 1994, 41.

8. FOMC conference-call transcript, April 18, 1994, 2; available at http://www .federalreserve.gov/FOMC/transcripts/1994/940418ConfCall.pdf.

9. FOMC meeting transcript, May 17, 1994, 32; available at http://www.federal reserve.gov/FOMC/transcripts/1994/940517Meeting.pdf.

10. FOMC meeting transcript, November 15, 1994, 39; available at http://www .federalreserve.gov/FOMC/transcripts/1994/941115Meeting.pdf.

11. Committee on Banking and Financial Services, *Conduct of Monetary Policy: Hearing before the Committee on Banking and Financial Services . . . July 25, 2000*, 21; response by Chairman Greenspan.

12. Ibid., 30.

13. The yearly average growth rates of the money supply (primarily currency, checking accounts, and money market funds) dropped from 5.8 percent in 1988 to 3.7 percent in 1990 and then to under 2 percent in 1992 and 1993. In 1996 it rose to 4.7 percent and in 1998 it reached 8.8 percent. The high rate of money growth was a product of the Fed's policy during 1998. A default on Russian bond payments in August 1998 and the collapse of the Long-Term Capital Management (LTCM) hedge fund began the following month. The Fed did not shift its interest-rate policy. It continued to lower its short-term target interest rate (the federal funds rate) as it had done since March 1997. It continued lowering the rate until August 1999, when it reversed course and began raising the target. The graph uses a six-quarter moving average of the quarterly rates of growth of money and the S&P 500 stock index.

14. The S&P 500 index more than tripled between January 1995 and January 2000.

15. A small additional adjustment could be made for dividends.

16. There was also some increase in the money supply because of the fear of computer problems at the turn of the century. However, the 7.3 percent growth rate during the last quarter of 1999 fell to 5.9 percent in the first quarter of 2000, so the moving-average growth rate shown in the graph is not significantly affected.

17. Milton Friedman, "A Natural Experiment in Monetary Policy Covering Three

Episodes of Growth and Decline in the Economy and the Stock Market," *Journal of Economic Perspectives* 19, no. 4, (Fall 2005): 145. Friedman continues: "The near identity of the three stock market series during the boom is truly remarkable. Yet even the minor deviations that exist reflect to some extent the differences in money growth" (149).

18. Robert D. Auerbach, "Money and Stock Prices," *Monthly Review* [Federal Reserve Bank of Kansas City], September–October 1976, 3–11; available at http://www.kc.frb.org/Publicat/econrev/EconRevArchive/1976/3q76-S-O.pdf. Previous average rates of change in stock prices were statistically related to rates of change in money (M2). There was a small significant correlation.

19. FOMC meeting transcript, September 24, 1996, 30–31; available at http://www.federalreserve.gov/FOMC/transcripts/1996/19960924Meeting.pdf. Greenspan continued: "We have a very great difficulty in monetary policy when we confront stock market bubbles. That is because, to the extent that we are successful in keeping product price inflation down, history tells us that the price-earnings ratios under those conditions go through the roof. What is really needed to keep stock market bubbles from occurring is a lot of product price inflation, which historically has tended to undercut stock markets almost everywhere. There is a clear tradeoff. If monetary policy succeeds in one it fails in another." This analysis does not accurately describe the situation that the Fed faced. The stock-market bubble grew during the 1990s and collapsed in 2000, but rapid product inflation was not associated with either event. The collapse of tech stocks occurred after the continual trumpeting of false information by Wall Street tipsters began to be uncovered. After WorldCom stock hit its peak in 1996, there began "a catastrophic ride, $2 trillion in losses on WorldCom and other telecom stocks," as noted in the last chapter. The signs of collapse should be given attention in substantial further research by experts not connected to the Fed. Did the Fed miss the genesis of this tech-stock collapse, which was seen by many others, especially those brokerage firms that were providing false information?

20. Ibid., 31.

21. Ibid.

22. Stephen Roach, quoted in Alan Abelson, "Irrational Adulation," *Barron's,* July 22, 2002.

23. Paul Samuelson, quoted in Robert Mundell and Paul Zak, eds., *Monetary Stability and Economic Growth: A Dialog between Leading Economists,* 27.

24. Ibid., 30–31.

25. FOMC meeting transcript, May 19, 1998, 86; transcript available at http://www.federalreserve.gov/FOMC/transcripts/1998/980519meeting.pdf; bracketed phrase added. A fuller quotation: "I have concluded that in the broader sense we have to stay with our fundamental central bank goal, namely, to stabilize product price levels. To the extent that the financial markets affect the factors that influence product price levels, I think monetary policy action is appropriate. But I believe the notion of merely hitting the market itself is an illusion" (85–86).

26. Ibid., 84–85.

27. Alan Abelson, "Irrational Adulation," *Barron's*, July 22, 2002, 3–5. Alan Abelson is the former editor of *Barron's* who now writes the magazine's lead column, "Up and Down Wall Street."

28. Robert D. Auerbach, "A Demand-Pull Theory of Deflation and Inflation."

29. The full text of the press release is available at http://www.federalreserve.gov/boardDocs/press/general/1999/19990824/default.htm.

30. Fed press release, December 19, 2000; available at http://www.federalreserve.gov/boarddocs/press/general/2000/20001219/.

31. In November 2001, economists of the Business Cycle Dating Committee at the National Bureau of Economic Research, a private group that currently makes such calls, declared that a recession had begun in March 2001; see http://www.nber.org/cycles/november2001/. The actual dates of the recession are an arbitrary judgment, not a precise statistical finding, of when the economy is sick enough to warrant such a diagnosis.

32. Lawrence B. Lindsey, "Life after Greenspan," *Wall Street Journal*, December 6, 2004.

33. Jeannine Aversa, "Economy Slows in Third Quarter," Associated Press, October 27, 2000.

34. Nicholas Kulish, "Economy Grew at Its Slowest Pace in Four Years," *Wall Street Journal*, December 22, 2000.

35. The civilian unemployment rate was 5.8 percent in 2002 and 6 percent in 2003.

36. Fed press release, December 10, 2002; available at http://www.federalreserve.gov/boarddocs/press/monetary/2002/20021210/.

37. See Greenspan's opening remarks at "Monetary Policy and Uncertainty: Adapting to a Changing Economy," a symposium sponsored by the Kansas City Fed Bank at Jackson Hole, Wyoming, August 28–30, 2003 (available at http://www.kc.frb.org/publicat/Sympos/2003/pdf/Greenspan2003.pdf); see also "Remarks by Governor Donald L. Kohn: Comments on Marvin Goodfriend's 'Inflation Targeting in the United States?'" which was delivered at the National Bureau of Economic Research Conference on Inflation Targeting, Bal Harbour, Florida, January 25, 2003 (available at http://www.federalreserve.gov/Boarddocs/speeches/2003/20030324/default.htm). Kohn was a longtime Greenspan staff adviser and a newly appointed Fed governor. Kohn's remarks were very similar to Greenspan's. Kohn said that "circumstances" would "arise in which the central bank" would be "faced with short-term choices between inflation stability and economic or financial stability."

38. There has been some new research showing that the Fed reacted to shocks in its goals of reducing unemployment and inflation by learning from past mistakes. The paper finds that actions taken by the Volcker Fed to end inflation were consistent with the evidence. See Thomas Sargent, Noah Williams, and Tao Zha, "Shocks and Government Beliefs: The Rise and Fall of American Inflation," Working Paper 2004-22,

Federal Reserve Bank of Atlanta, September 2004; available at http://www.frbatlanta
.org/filelegacydocs/wp0422.pdf.

39. Kohn, "Remarks by Governor Donald L. Kohn." This "dual mandate" is required for federal-government entities by the Employment Act of 1946, Public Law
79-304.

40. Ibid., 3.

41. Discussed in Auerbach, *Money, Banking, and Financial Markets*, 655–657. Burns
elaborated: "But I must say to you in all honesty that no two of us may agree as
to the precise definition of a disorderly market or the precise way to recognize one
when it exists" (Committee on Banking, Finance and Urban Affairs, *Conduct of Monetary Policy: Hearings before the Committee on Banking, Finance and Urban Affairs*, 95th
Cong., 1st sess., July 28–29, 1977, 28; testimony of Arthur Burns).

42. It may be more accurate to define the Fed's targets according to the individual
views of its policy makers. Many officials may agree with the chairman in order to
preserve the power and prestige of the Fed bureaucracy. The late Thomas Havrilesky
developed tests of Fed officials' biases using statistical tests of their recorded votes.
Since the chairman tries to obtain unanimity, then even if there is dissent that in-
fluences monetary policy, the votes provide very incomplete information on policy
formation; see Thomas Havrilesky and John Gildea, "The Biases of Federal Reserve
Bank Presidents."

43. William Lewis and Tracy Corrigan, "Buffett in Hedge Fund Run like LTCM's,"
Financial Times, October 15, 1998.

44. "Losing Moral Authority," *Financial Times*, October 3, 1998.

45. The chart shows a smoothed moving average of money growth (M2, which
includes currency, coin, checking accounts, and consumer money-market funds) and
inflation (using the consumer price index).

46. Modern statistical tests revealed some problems in previous tests. The relationship between money and other economic variables, such as inflation or economic
activity, sometimes produced what looked like a relationship because these variables
along with many other economic variables moved together over business cycles and
had common trends. Establishing cause and effect can be difficult. Groundbreaking
statistical analysis in economics introduced thirty years ago by recent Nobel laureate
Clive Granger uncovered many of the problems in determining which variables are
the causes and which are affected, or whether they affect each other. I published some
early work in this field with a coauthor: Robert D. Auerbach and Jack Rutner, "Time
and Frequency Domain Tests of Some U.S.-Canadian Relationships under the Auto-
regressive Filter," *Applied Economics* 8, no. 3 (September 1976): 165–178. Clive Granger
was the editor of the journal.

47. Except in Hawaii, where it took effect several years later. I assisted in the
preparation of this law, the Monetary Control Act of 1980.

48. These include money-market funds, which also offered checking services. They
could also buy U.S. Treasury securities and other debt instruments, such as bonds.

49. That meant all the banks had to keep a percentage—10 percent of checkable domestic deposits—in cash; the funds could be held on their premises, in automatic teller machines (ATMs), or at the Fed. In 1984, banks could earn over 8 percent interest on three-month Treasury bills instead of entrusting their money to the Fed, which until 2011 will pay no interest. The interest they earn could then be used to pay more on checking accounts to their favored (more profitable) customers.

50. Again, bank employees do not physically transfer money to the Cayman Islands, where the bank may have little more than a listed telephone in an office with many other banks. The money is merely listed in the Cayman Island account on the bank's records.

51. Credit card companies that calculate the net balance of daily debits and credits to a customer of the card issuer already eliminate some of the need to settle every transaction with bank checking accounts.

52. When a payment is required, say, for rent, a tenant can transfer checking-account money or many other assets, such as credit card credit or ninety-day Treasury bills, to a landlord in a matter of seconds. "Unit of account" simply means that the transaction is measured in units of dollars, even though no money as presently defined changes hands. A landlord may well accept many types of assets that can be traded at essentially zero cost for goods and services. Also, if a national system is developed as now exists for credit card systems, payments and revenues for individuals or businesses could be collected in real time and only the end-of-day balances would require the transfer of assets.

53. For example, credit card companies can accumulate balances during the day before they settle with the issuer. If they paid interest, the issuer might well be happy to leave the balances for a longer period.

54. This finding leads to some differences with Milton Friedman's assessment of the Greenspan Fed's money policies. Friedman argued that the lower average rate of inflation for the fifteen years following 1985 was due to the Fed's low average money growth. These Friedman averages do not explain the phenomenon pictured in Figure 11-2. Money growth was on a roller coaster, as shown in Figure 11-2. Its growth rate fell to under 2 percent for four years ending in 1995. It then took off, rising at a nearly 5 percent rate for two years, then over 7 percent for two years and over 8 percent in 2001. Meanwhile, the prices of goods and services, also shown in Figure 11-2, did not follow this roller-coaster ride. Even if Friedman were correct, relying on a fifteen-year average would not be a good guide for fine-tuning monetary policy, since the average could be significantly affected by the end points of the calculation. In "The Fed's Thermostat" (*Wall Street Journal*, August 16, 2003), Friedman explained that the poor performance assessment of the Fed "was amply justified for the first seven decades or so of the Fed's existence." He said this criticism was not valid for the period since 1985, when the Fed achieved low rates of inflation as a result of its control of the money supply. In a subsequent article ("He Has Set a Standard," *Wall Street Journal*, January 31, 2006), Friedman again repeats his praise for Greenspan's record. Friedman is cor-

rect in giving Volcker praise for taming the rapid inflation "beast" before Greenspan assumed the Fed chairmanship in 1987.

55. A case for inflation targets and a review of the literature are presented in William Gavin, "Inflation Targeting: Why It Works and How to Make It Work Better," Working Paper 2003-027B, Federal Reserve Bank of St. Louis, September 19, 2003; available at http://research.stlouisfed.org/wp/2003/2003-027.pdf.

CHAPTER 12

1. The editing should be done by governmental archivists in conjunction with Fed officials and staff under explicit rules. Any personnel decisions, proprietary information about other central banks, and items of national security should be redacted. Redacted material should not be removed from the source records.

2. Since twelve Fed Bank presidents and seven members of the Board of Governors would have to be nominated and confirmed, the process could become too burdensome to allow for the complete examination of each nominee. The presidents who serve on the FOMC in rotation should be allowed to serve more than their present, one-year term if other Fed Bank presidents have not yet been confirmed. Legislation authorizing these changes should specify that due consideration be given to knowledge, experience, and political diversity. Although these considerations would not be legally binding on the president, they would become an important factor in the selection of nominees. If the number of Board members were to fall below five, the president should make one-year interim appointments. The Board members would concentrate on monetary policy and appoint administrators for each of the Fed's facilities. All speeches to private-sector groups by Fed officials should be publicly announced in advance and open to the press; this has not been the case. Officials' comments that are intended to telegraph views on monetary policy and the future state of the economy should be limited to FOMC meetings. This means that most speeches should be stopped.

3. From the Web site of the Federal Reserve Bank of San Francisco: "The Twelfth Federal Reserve District includes the nine western states—Alaska, Arizona, California, Hawaii, Idaho, Nevada, Oregon, Utah, and Washington—and American Samoa, Guam, and the Northern Mariana Islands. Branches are located in Los Angeles, Portland, Salt Lake City, and Seattle. The largest District, it covers 35 percent of the nation's landmass, ranks first in the size of its economy, and is home to approximately 20 percent of the nation's population" (http://www.frbsf.org/publications/federalreserve/annual/2002/ack.html).

4. Hawaii's banking representatives expressed their views during the negotiations I was assigned to hold regarding the Monetary Control Act of 1980. They did not want a Fed facility because their bankers were more efficient at clearing paper checks with their own couriers than the Fed's slow, antiquated system. Their couriers carried paper checks from tourists back to distant mainland banks the following morning, whereas

the Fed was then taking up to two weeks to clear checks, long after the tourists had left, and some checks had bounced. Digitized check imaging, discussed in Chapter 7, may have changed the views of Hawaii's bankers.

5. State banks are regulated by state regulators as well as by some federal regulators. State regulators would not be discontinued, since they are necessary for a dual (state- and federal-chartered) banking system, a financial innovation that remains.

6. Since banks have been authorized to buy other businesses, such as brokerages, there will necessarily be some role for the SEC.

7. There have been attempts to legislate the one-regulator concept since at least 1964, when a consolidation bill was drafted by the late Grasty Crews (who was in the House legislative office and then on the staff of the Banking Committee).

8. Gonzalez, "Reduction in Regulatory Control of Federal Reserve Board Is Subject of Proposed Legislation," 2–3.

9. The Fed was one of five federal-government entities that reported to and paid a fee to support the FFIEC.

10. From the FFIEC Web site: "Federal Financial Institutions Examination Council (FFIEC): The Council is a formal interagency body empowered to prescribe uniform principles, standards, and report forms for the federal examination of financial institutions by the Board of Governors of the Federal Reserve System (FRB), the Federal Deposit Insurance Corporation (FDIC), the National Credit Union Administration (NCUA), the Office of the Comptroller of the Currency (OCC), and the Office of Thrift Supervision (OTS), and to make recommendations to promote uniformity in the supervision of financial institutions" (http://www.ffiec.gov/).

11. Federal Reserve, press release, March 18, 2003; available at http://federal reserve.gov/boarddocs/press/monetary/2003/20030318/.

12. Alan Beattie, "Fed Admits Its Ignorance in the Face of Global Uncertainty," *Financial Times* Web site, March 19, 2003, http://search.ft.com/ftArticle?queryText= alan+beattie+%22fed+admits&y=5&aje=true&x=14&id=030319000609.

13. Henry Reuss, "What the Secret Minutes of Federal Reserve Banks Meetings Disclose," speech on the floor of the House, May 24, 1977, *Congressional Record* 123: H 6236. This technicality may not hold.

14. Board of Governors of the Federal Reserve System, Office of Inspector General, *Semiannual Report to Congress*, April 1, 1994–September 30, 1994, 31.

15. *The Annual Report: Budget Review* (2002): "In conformance with statutory independence of the office, the OIG [Office of the Inspector General] presents its budget directly to the Chairman of the Board of Governors for consideration by the Board" (25).

16. Governor Kohn argued that the Fed should pay interest on the required reserves it held. There was bipartisan support for this position. I was opposed for a number of reasons, including the likelihood that the payment would not be substantially passed through to depositors in the form of higher interest payments on their accounts. I testified that $16.7 billion (the present value of the stream of payments, in my estimation) given by the government to banks could have positive welfare effects if

it were transferred to depositors as interest on their deposits. Some economists, by assuming that banking is a competitive industry, have theorized that this is what would happen; I said that this was the wrong model. The Financial Services Regulatory Act of 2006 authorized the payment of interest on these reserves.

17. Thomas F. Cargill, "The Bank of Japan: A Dependent but Price Stabilizing Central Bank."

18. Acton to Bishop Mandell Creighton, April 3, 1997; quoted in Louise Creighton, *Life and Letters of Mandell Creighton*, vol. 1 (1904). Lord Acton (John Emerich Edward Dalberg Acton, 1st Baron Acton), 1834–1902, was an English historian, a professor of modern history at Cambridge (1895–1902), and the founding editor of the twelve-volume *Cambridge Modern History* (1902–1912).

19. Senate Banking Committee, *General Accounting Office Report on the Federal Reserve System: Hearing before the Committee on Banking, Housing, and Urban Affairs . . . July 26, 1996*, 104th Cong., 2nd sess., July 26, 1996, 14–15; statement of Alan Greenspan; Greenspan's full statement is available at http://www.federalreserve.gov/Board docs/testimony/1996/19960726.htm.

APPENDIX

1. Footnote from the report: "April 26, 1994 speech to the Conference of First Vice Presidents of the Federal Reserve System, 'ITS COST ALLOCATION PRESENTATION,' p. 2."

2. Footnote from the report: "April 26, 1994 speech to the Conference of First Vice Presidents of the Federal Reserve System, 'ITS COST ALLOCATION PRESENTATION,' p. 1."

3. Footnote from the report: "The legal standing of the ITS was specifically noted in a 1984 Federal court case: 'There can be no doubt that the Federal Reserve Bank of Chicago is an "authority" of the government of the United States. As a member of the Federal Reserve System, it performs important governmental functions and exercises powers entrusted to it by the United States government. It is unquestionable that a court may review the action of either the Federal Reserve Board or its designated Banks in connection with the national check transportation system.' (Flight International Group, Inc., Plaintiff, V. Federal Reserve Bank of Chicago, Defendant, Civil Action C83-2696A, February 24, 1984, Order by Judge Marvin H. Shoob, United States District Court, Northern District of Georgia, pp. 7 and 9.)"

4. Footnote from the report: "Memorandum from Dave MacDonald to Banking Committee staff via the office of FRBB Executive Vice President and General Counsel William N. McDonough, 'Response to [Committee staff's] September 5th inquiry,' September 22, 1995, p. 1."

5. The U.S. Treasury requires that a certain percentage of Treasury checks be processed within four days unless the Treasury is notified of a delay. Thus, these checks do not have the same time sensitivity as other checks. Private-sector checks incur float because of double entry of the check balance in the checking accounts of both

the payor and the payee. If there is a delay in clearing these checks, the float increases. No such float problem arises with canceled U.S. Treasury checks because the Treasury operates according to authorized budget appropriations and does not increase its expenditures because of float.

6. By using airfreight forwarders or ground transportation, the cost to the Treasury and taxpayers could be reduced to between $0.25 and $1 a pound. The staff of the ITS verified this estimate.

GLOSSARY

American Continental Corporation (ACC). The real estate holding company that Charles Keating used to acquire Lincoln Savings.

Banking Committees. The banking committee in the House of Representatives is currently called the Financial Services Committee; its counterpart in the Senate is the Banking, Housing and Urban Affairs Committee. In this book, the two together are referred to as the Banking Committees. These two congressional committees are specifically charged with overseeing the Fed.

Bernanke, Ben S. (1953–). Fed chairman, 2006–present.

Board of Governors. A seven-member committee at the top of the Federal Reserve bureaucracy. Its members, who are nominated by the president and confirmed by the Senate, serve a fourteen-year term. They also are members of the Federal Open Market Committee.

Burns, Arthur F. (1904–1987). Fed chairman, 1970–1978.

Community Reinvestment Act (CRA). Enacted by Congress in 1977 to, according to the Web site of the Federal Financial Institutions Examination Council, "encourage depository institutions to help meet the credit needs of the communities in which they operate."

Equal Credit Opportunity Act (ECOA). This law ensures, according to the Web site of the Federal Trade Commission, "that all consumers are given an equal chance to obtain credit."

Equal Employment Opportunity Commission (EEOC). A federal commission that enforces laws against discrimination in employment based on race, color, religion, sex, national origin, age, or disabilities.

Equal Opportunity Office (EEO). The reference in the book is to the Fed's in-house civil rights office.

Fair Housing Act (FHA). Prohibits "discrimination by direct providers of housing, such as landlords and real estate companies as well as other entities, such as municipalities, banks or other lending institutions and homeowners insurance companies whose discriminatory practices make housing unavailable to persons because of: race or color, religion, sex, national origin, familial status, or disability" (Web site of the U.S. Department of Justice, Civil Rights Division, Housing and Civil Enforcement Section).

Federal Home Loan Bank Board (FHLBB). Former federal regulator of the savings and loan industry.

Federal Open Market Committee (FOMC). Policy-setting body of the Fed. It has twelve members: the seven members of the Board of Governors plus five of the twelve Fed Bank presidents; the New York Fed Bank president is always one of these. The FOMC targets short-term interest rates and controls the base of the U.S. money supply; it also makes loans to foreign countries.

Federal Reserve Bank (Fed Bank). A bank serving as a regional headquarters of the Federal Reserve. There are twelve Federal Reserve Banks, which have subsidiary Fed branch banks.

Federal Reserve System (the Fed). The central bank of the United States, comprising the Board of Governors, in Washington, D.C., and twelve regional Federal Reserve Banks and their branches. The twelve district Fed Banks are in Atlanta, Chicago, Boston, Cleveland, Dallas, Kansas City, Minneapolis, New York, Philadelphia, Richmond, San Francisco, and St. Louis.

Gonzalez, Henry B. (1916–2000). Democratic member of Congress from San Antonio, Texas. Elected to fill a vacancy caused by the resignation of Congressman Paul J. Kilday, he was reelected eighteen times, serving from 1961 to 1999. Gonzalez was House Banking Committee chairman from 1989 to 1994, and the ranking member until 1999.

Government Accountability Office (GAO). Until 2004, the General Accounting Office. The agency provides auditing, accounting, and legal services for Congress. It examines federal-government operations, including the Fed's and those the government contracts for with private-sector firms.

Greenspan, Alan (1926–). Fed chairman, 1987–2006.

Home Mortgage Disclosure Act (HMDA). Enacted by Congress in 1975, it is implemented by the Federal Reserve Board's Regulation C, which requires lending institutions to report public loan data.

Margin requirements. The maximum amount that can be borrowed to buy a financial asset. These requirements are stipulated by the Federal Reserve. The margin requirement for stock purchases has been set at 50 percent for many years, including during the Greenspan Fed period.

Martin, William McChesney, Jr. (1906–1998). Fed chairman, 1951–1970.

Member bank. A private-sector bank officially associated with the Fed.

Miller, G. William (1925–2006). Fed chairman, 1978–1979.

National bank. A private-sector bank that is chartered (given the right to operate) by the Comptroller of the Currency, a federal entity.

Patman, Wright (1893–1976). Democratic member of Congress from Texas; House Banking chairman, 1963–1975.

Proxmire, William (1915–2005). Democratic senator from Wisconsin. He was elected to the Senate in 1957 to fill the seat left vacant by the death of Joseph McCarthy. Proxmire was chairman of the Senate Banking Committee from 1975 to 1980, ranking member until 1986, and chairman again until his retirement, in 1988.

Reuss, Henry S. (1912–2002). Democratic member of Congress from Wisconsin; House Banking Committee chairman, 1975–1980.

State bank. A private-sector bank that is chartered (given the right to operate) by a state governmental entity.

Swap. As used in this book, the term refers to the Fed's international currency operations that are also called its "reciprocal currency operations."

Volcker, Paul (1927–). Fed chairman, 1979–1987.

BIBLIOGRAPHY

ARCHIVES

Arthur Burns Collection at the Gerald R. Ford Presidential Library and Museum, 1000 Beal Avenue, Ann Arbor, Michigan, on the University of Michigan's north campus.

Henry B. Gonzalez Papers, at the Center for American History, University of Texas at Austin.

BOOKS AND PERIODICALS

Abelson, Alan. "Irrational Adulation." *Barron's*, July 22, 2002.

Auerbach, Robert D. "A Budgetary Bias for United States Intervention in Foreign Exchange Markets." *Public Budgeting and Financial Management* 2, no. 3 (1990): 407–430.

———. "A Demand-Pull Theory of Deflation and Inflation." *Manchester School of Economics and Social Studies* 44, no. 2 (June 1976): 99–111.

———. "Far from Full Disclosure: When It Comes to Data and Access to Its Meetings, the Fed Can Be Two-Faced." *Barron's*, August 1, 1999, 31–32.

———. "Greenspan's Needle." *Barron's*, July 24, 2000, 17.

———. "G. William Miller." In Schweikart, *Encyclopedia of American Business History and Biography: Banking and Finance, 1913–1989*, 302–305.

———. "Henry S. Reuss." In Schweikart, *Encyclopedia of American Business History and Biography: Banking and Finance, 1913–1989*, 369–372.

———. "Institutional Preservation at the Federal Reserve." *Contemporary Policy Issues* 9 (July 1991): 46–58.

———. "Money and Stock Prices." *Monthly Review* [Federal Reserve Bank of Kansas City], September–October 1976, 3–11. Available at http://www.kc.frb.org/Publicat/econrev/EconRevArchive/1976/3q76-S-O.pdf.

————. *Money, Banking, and Financial Markets.* 3rd ed. New York: Macmillan, 1988.

————. "The Painful History of Transparency." *MarketWatch,* Dow Jones, May 8, 2006.

————. "Pensions, Planes and Priced Services." *FOMC Alert* 4, no. 1 (February 1–2, 2000): 8–10. Available at http://www.fmcenter.org/atf/cf/{DFBB2772-F5C5-4DFE-B310-D82A61944339}/Feb2000v4.pdf.

————. "That Shreddin' Fed." *Barron's,* December 10, 2001, 36.

Beckner, Stephen K. *Back from the Brink: The Greenspan Years.* New York: Wiley, 1996.

Bank for International Settlements. Committee on Payment and Settlement Systems. *Statistics on Payment Systems in the Group of Ten Countries: Figures for 1999* (Basel, Switzerland: BIS, 2001). Available at: http://www.bis.org/publ/cpss44.pdf.

Bartlett, Bruce. "Tax Cuts, the Right Way." *National Review Online,* July 26, 2004; http://www.nationalreview.com/nrof_bartlett/bartlett200407261019.asp.

Black, William K. *The Best Way to Rob a Bank Is to Own One: How Corporate Executives and Politicians Looted the S&L Industry.* Austin: Univ. of Texas Press, 2005.

Bureau of National Affairs. "Race/Retaliation; Black Woman Denied Job at Federal Reserve Awarded $150,000, Promotion for Race Bias." *Employment Discrimination Report* 3, no. 17 (November 2, 1994).

Cargill, Thomas F. "The Bank of Japan: A Dependent but Price Stabilizing Central Bank." *Public Budgeting and Financial Management* 5, no. 1 (1993): 131–139.

Davies, Stephen A. "Fed May Be Stifling Criticism by Hiring Outside Academics." *Bond Buyer,* November 4, 1994, 1.

Epstein, Gene, "No Place like Home; Looking for inflation, Chairman Greenspan? Have We Found Some For You!" *Barron's,* August 2, 1999, 27–30.

Financial Markets Center. "Uncivil Service: Pension Rebellion Stirs the Fed." *FOMC Alert* 4, no. 5 (August 22, 2000): 1–9. Available at http://www.fmcenter.org/atf/cf/%7BDFBB2772-F5C5-4DFE-B310-D82A61944339%7D/Aug00_FOMCAlert.pdf.

Friedman, Milton. "A Natural Experiment in Monetary Policy Covering Three Episodes of Growth and Decline in the Economy and the Stock Market." *Journal of Economic Perspectives* 19, no. 4, (Fall 2005): 145–150.

Friedman, Milton, and Rose Friedman. *Free to Choose.* New York: Harcourt Brace Jovanovich, 1980.

Friedman, Milton, and Anna Schwartz. *A Monetary History of the United States, 1867–1960.* Princeton, N.J.: Princeton Univ. Press, 1963.

Gavin, William. "Inflation Targeting: Why It Works and How to Make It Work Better." Working Paper 2003-027B. Federal Reserve Bank of St. Louis, September 19, 2003. Available at http://research.stlouisfed.org/wp/2003/2003-027.pdf.

Gowrisankaran, Gautam. "Why Do Americans Still Write Checks?" *FRBSF [Federal Reserve Bank of San Francisco] Economic Letter* 2002-27, September 20, 2002. Available at http://www.frbsf.org/publications/economics/letter/2002/el2002-27.html.

Greenspan, Alan. "The Challenge of Central Banking in a Democratic Society." Remarks at the annual dinner and Francis Boyer Lecture of the American Enterprise

Institute for Public Policy Research, December 5, 1996. Available at http://www .federalreserve.gov/BoardDocs/speeches/1996/19961205.htm.

———. "Recent Reports on Federal Reserve Operations." Testimony before the Senate Committee on Banking, Housing and Urban Affairs, July 26, 1996, 104 Cong., 2nd sess. Available at http://www.federalreserve.gov/Boarddocs/ Testimony/1996/19960726.htm.

Havrilesky, Thomas, and John Gildea. "The Biases of Federal Reserve Bank Presidents." *Economic Inquiry* 33, no. 2 (April 1995): 274–284.

Johnson, Rebecca Strand. "Arthur F. Burns." In Schweikart, *Encyclopedia of American Business History and Biography: Banking and Finance, 1913–1989,* 38–42.

Kahaner, Larry. *The Quotations of Chairman Greenspan: Words from the Man Who Can Shake the World.* Holbrook, Mass.: Adams Media, 2000.

Kroszner, Randall S. "Innovative Statistics for a Dynamic Economy." Remarks at the National Association for Business Economics Professional Development Seminar for Journalists, Washington, D.C., May 24, 2006. Available at http://www .federalreserve.gov/Boarddocs/speeches/2006/20060524/default.htm.

Lacker, Jeffrey M. "Payment System Disruptions and the Federal Reserve following September 11, 2001." *Journal of Monetary Economics* 51, no. 5 (July 2004): 935–965. Available at http://www.carnegie-rochester.rochester.edu/Nov03-pdfs/lacker.pdf.

Martin, Justin. *Greenspan: The Man behind Money.* Cambridge, Mass.: Perseus, 2000.

Maskell, Jack, and Richard S. Beth. "'No Confidence' Votes and Other Forms of Congressional Censure of Public Officials." Congressional Research Service, June 11, 2007, order code RL34037. Available at http://www.opencrs.com/rpts/RL34037_ 20070611.pdf.

McAndrews, James, and William Roberds. "The Economics of Check Float." *Economic Review* [Federal Reserve Bank of Atlanta] 85, no. 4 (2000). Available at http://www.frbatlanta.org/publica/eco-rev/rev_abs/00er/q4/roberds.pdf.

McTague, Jim. "Greenspan Has Himself to Blame for Fervid Interest in Transcripts." *American Banker,* December 1, 1993.

Meyer, Laurence H. *A Term at the Fed: An Insider's View.* New York: HarperCollins, 2006.

Mundell, Paul, and Paul Zak, eds. *Monetary Stability and Economic Growth: A Dialog between Leading Economists.* Northampton, Mass.: Edward Elgar, 2002.

National Commission on Financial Institution Reform, Recovery and Enforcement. *Origins and Causes of the S&L Debacle: A Blueprint for Reform; A Report to the President and Congress of the United States.* Washington, D.C., July 1993.

Osterberg, William P., and James B. Thomson. "The Exchange Stabilization Fund: How It Works." *Economic Commentary* [Federal Reserve Bank of Cleveland], December 1999. Available at http://www.clevelandfed.org/Research/commentary/ 1999/1201.pdf.

Pearce, Douglas K. "Alan Greenspan." In Schweikart, *Encyclopedia of American Business History and Biography: Banking and Finance, 1913–1989,* 175–182.

Rhoades, Stephen A. *See* U.S. Federal Reserve System, Board of Governors.

Roth, Andrew. "What the Fed Learned about Check-Handling after Sept. 11." *American Banker,* October 11, 2001.

Sargent, Thomas, Noah Williams, and Tao Zha. "Shocks and Government Beliefs: The Rise and Fall of American Inflation." Working Paper 2004-22. Federal Reserve Bank of Atlanta, September 2004. Available at http://www.frbatlanta.org/filelegacydocs/wp0422.pdf.

Schwartz, Anna J. "From Obscurity to Notoriety: A Biography of the Exchange Stabilization Fund." *Journal of Money, Credit, and Banking* 29 (May 1997): 135-153.

Schweikart, Larry, ed. *Encyclopedia of American Business History and Biography: Banking and Finance, 1913–1989.* Columbia, S.C.: Bruccoli Clark Layman, 1990.

Smale, Pauline. "Structure and Functions of the Federal Reserve System." Congressional Research Service, RS20826, June 15, 2005. Available at http://www.fas.org/sgp/crs/misc/RS20826.pdf).

Starobin, Paul. "The Fed Tapes: The Revelation That the Federal Reserve's Chief Policymaking Body Has Kept Secret Records of Its Meetings Has Raised Questions about the Fed's Integrity and Accountability to Congress." *National Journal,* December 18, 1993, 2984–2989.

Tuccille, Jerome. *Alan Shrugged: The Life and Times of Alan Greenspan, the World's Most Powerful Banker.* Hoboken, N.J.: Wiley, 2002.

U.S. Congress. *Congressional Record.* 95 Cong., 1st sess., 1977. Vol. 123.

———. *Congressional Record.* 103rd Cong., 2nd sess., 1994. Vol. 140.

U.S. Congress. General Accounting Office. *Federal Reserve Banks: Inaccurate Reporting of Currency at the Los Angeles Branch.* GAO/AIMD-96-146. September 30, 1996. Available at http://www.gao.gov/archive/1996/ai96146.pdf.

———. General Accounting Office. *Federal Reserve System: Current and Future Challenges Require Systemwide Attention.* GAO/GGD-96-128. June 1996. Available at http://www.gao.gov/archive/1996/gg96128.pdf.

U.S. Congress. House. Committee on Banking and Financial Services. *Conduct of Monetary Policy: Hearing before the Committee on Banking and Financial Services . . . July 25, 2000.* 106th Cong., 2nd sess., July 25, 2000.

———. Committee on Banking and Financial Services. Democratic Staff. *Waste and Abuse in the Federal Reserve's Payment System.* 104th Cong., 2nd sess., January 5, 1996.

———. Committee on Banking, Currency and Housing. *Federal Reserve Directors: A Study of Corporate and Banking Influence.* 94th Cong., 2nd sess., August 1976.

———. Committee on Banking, Finance and Urban Affairs. *Conduct of Monetary Policy: Hearings before the Committee on Banking, Finance and Urban Affairs.* 95th Cong., 1st sess., July 28–29, 1977.

———. Committee on Banking, Finance and Urban Affairs. *The Federal Reserve's 17-Year Secret.* 103rd Cong., 2nd sess., January 27, 1994.

———. Committee on Banking, Finance and Urban Affairs. *H.R. 28, the Federal Reserve Accountability Act of 1993: Hearing before the Committee on Banking, Finance and Urban Affairs.* 103rd Cong., 1st sess., October 1993.

―――. Committee on Banking, Finance and Urban Affairs. *Maintaining and Making Public Minutes of Federal Reserve Meetings: Hearings before the Subcommittee on Domestic Monetary Policy . . . October 27, 28, November 17, 1977.* 95th Cong., 1st sess., 1977.

―――. Committee on Banking, Finance and Urban Affairs. *Problems with Equal Employment Opportunity and Minority and Women Contracting at the Federal Banking Agencies: Hearing before the Committee on Banking, Finance and Urban Affairs.* 102nd Cong., 2nd sess., June 1992.

―――. Committee on Banking, Finance and Urban Affairs. *A Racial, Gender, and Background Profile of the Directors of the Federal Reserve Banks and Branches.* 101st Cong., 2nd sess., August 1990.

―――. Committee on Banking, Finance and Urban Affairs. *Status of Equal Employment Opportunity at the Federal Reserve: Diversity Still Lacking,* Parts 1 and 2. 103rd Cong., 1st sess., November 22, 1993.

U.S. Congress. Joint Economic Committee. *January 1962 Economic Report of the President: Hearings before the Joint Economic Committee.* 87th Cong., 2nd sess., January 30, 1962.

U.S. Congress. Senate. Committee on Banking, Housing, and Urban Affairs. *General Accounting Office Report on the Federal Reserve System: Hearing before the Committee on Banking, Housing, and Urban Affairs . . . July 26, 1996,* 104th Cong., 2nd sess., July 26, 1996.

―――. Senate. Select Committee on Ethics. *Preliminary Inquiry into Allegations regarding Senators Cranston, DeConcini, Glenn, McCain, and Riegle, and Lincoln Savings and Loan: Open Session Hearings before the Select Committee on Ethics.* 101st Cong., 2nd sess., November 15, 1990–January 16, 1991.

U.S. Federal Reserve System. Board of Governors. "Bank Mergers and Banking Structure in the United States, 1980–1998." Staff Study 174, prepared by Stephen A. Rhoades. August 2000, 31. Available at http://www.federalreserve.gov/pubs/staff studies/2000-present/ss174.pdf.

―――. Committee on the Federal Reserve in the Payments Mechanism. *The Federal Reserve in the Payments Mechanism.* January 1998. Available at http://www.federal reserve.gov/BOARDDOCS/PRESS/general/1998/19980105/19980105.pdf.

―――. Federal Open Market Committee. Conference-call transcripts. December 14, 1992. Available at http://www.federalreserve.gov/FOMC/transcripts/1992/decconf.pdf.

October 5, 1993. Available at http://www.federalreserve.gov/FOMC/transcripts/1993/931005ConfCall.pdf.

October 15, 1993. Available at http://www.federalreserve.gov/FOMC/transcripts/transcripts_1993.htm.

February 28, 1994. Available at http://www.federalreserve.gov/FOMC/transcripts/1994/940228ConfCall.pdf.

April 18, 1994. Available at http://www.federalreserve.gov/FOMC/transcripts/1994/940418ConfCall.pdf.

———. Federal Open Market Committee. Meeting minutes. July 2–3, 1996. Available at http://www.federalreserve.gov/FOMC/minutes/19960702.htm.

———. Federal Open Market Committee. Meeting transcripts.

November 1, 1988. Available at http://www.federalreserve.gov/FOMC/transcripts/1988/881101Meeting.pdf.

December 18–19, 1989. Available at http://www.federalreserve.gov/FOMC/transcripts/1989/891219Meeting.pdf.

March 27, 1990. Available at http://www.federalreserve.gov/FOMC/transcripts/1990/900327Meeting.pdf.

July 2–3, 1991. Available at http://www.federalreserve.gov/FOMC/transcripts/1991/910703Meeting.pdf.

November 17, 1992. Available at http://www.federalreserve.gov/FOMC/tran scripts/1992/novmeet.pdf.

March 22, 1994. Available at http://www.federalreserve.gov/FOMC/transcripts/1994/940322Meeting.pdf.

May 17, 1994. Available at http://www.federalreserve.gov/FOMC/transcripts/1994/940517Meeting.pdf.

November 15, 1994. Available at http://www.federalreserve.gov/FOMC/transcripts/1994/941115Meeting.pdf.

January 31–February 1, 1995. Available at http://www.federalreserve.gov/FOMC/transcripts/1995/950201Meeting.pdf.

February 4–5, 1997. Available at http://www.federalreserve.gov/FOMC/transcripts/1997/19970205Meeting.pdf.

May 19, 1998. Available at http://www.federalreserve.gov/FOMC/transcripts/1998/980519meeting.pdf.

September 29, 1998. Available at http://www.federalreserve.gov/FOMC/transcripts/1998/980929meeting.pdf.

———. Office of Inspector General. *Semiannual Report to Congress, April 1, 1994–September 30, 1994.*

Weber, Max. *From Max Weber: Essays in Sociology.* Translated, edited, and with an introduction by H. H. Gerth and C. Wright Mills. New York: Oxford Univ. Press, 1958.

Wheelock, David C., and Paul W. Wilson. "Trends in the Efficiency of Federal Reserve Check Processing Operations." *Review* [Federal Reserve Bank of St. Louis] 86, no. 5 (September–October 2004): 7–20. Available at http://research.stlouisfed.org/publications/review/04/09/Wheelock.pdf.

Woodward, Bob. *Maestro: Greenspan's Fed and the American Boom.* New York: Simon and Schuster, 2000.

INDEX

House Banking Committee for overseeing, 1-2, 6; salaries of officials at, 16-17,
30, 126-129, 183; secrecy at, 16-17, 87-105;
shredding of official records by, 8, 46, 47,
103-105, 182; and transparency, 46-47,
105, 212n39; Web site of, 103, 141, 145-
146, 225n42. *See also* Board of Governors;
check-clearing operation; Federal Open
Market Committee (FOMC); inflation;
interest rates; money supply; stock market; Treasury Department, U.S.; *and
specific chairmen of Federal Reserve System*
Federal Reserve System Accountability Act
(1993), 223n18
Fed stock, 190-191
Fedwire, 108, 227n5
Feldstein, Martin, 152
Ferguson, Roger W., 52
FFIEC. *See* Federal Financial Institutions
Examination Council (FFIEC)
FHLBB. *See* Federal Home Loan Bank Board
(FHLBB)
financial derivatives, 146-147
Financial Services Committee. *See* House
Banking Committee
Financial Services Modernization Act (1999),
118, 162-163, 186, 241n41
Financial Services Regulatory Act (1996),
249n16
Financial Times, 4, 177-178
Fitzwater, Martin, 152, 237n13
Foley, Thomas, 3
FOMC. *See* Federal Open Market Committee
(FOMC)
Ford, Gerald R., 13, 34, 35-36, 45, 209n13
foreign central banks, 75, 78-79
foreign currency traders, 80-81
foreign loans, 8, 55, 65-73, 217-218n42,
218n51, 218nn54-55, 226n57
Forrestal, Robert P., 235n22
Francis, Darryl R., 138, 233n5
Frank, Barney, 162, 212n39, 239-240n36
Freedom of Information Act, 92-93, 223n21
Friedman, Milton: comparison of Fed chairmen by, 139; on economists employed
by Fed, 142-143; education of, 12, 139;
on Great Depression, 221-222n4; on
inflation, 16, 246-247n54; on MODS
("Memoranda of Discussion"), 88, 90;
on monetary growth and stock market,
169, 242-243n17; University of Chicago
seminar by, 140; writings by, 88, 98

Fuller, Mary Falvey, 210n22

Galbraith, John Kenneth, 93
GAO. *See* Government Accountability Office
(GAO)
Garment, Leonard, 32
Garn, Edwin Jacob "Jake," 40, 109
Garn–St. Germain Depository Institutions
Act (1982), 211n26
Garzarelli, Elaine, 77
gasoline prices, 35, 205n19
General Accounting Office. *See* Government
Accountability Office (GAO)
Gergen, David, 151-152
Germany, 112, 192, 238n25
Gervais, Sister Generose, 126
gifts for Fed officials, 61-63
Glass, Carter, 184, 240n38
Glass-Steagall Act, 162, 240n38, 241n40
Glenn, John, 40
gold policy, 69-71, 217n40
Gonzalez, Henry B.: and airplane operations
of Fed, 106, 108, 112-113, 116-117; attacks
against, 6-7, 11; award for, 11; and bank-
examination practices, 63, 64; on bias in
lending, 129-130; as chairman of House
Banking Committee generally, 1-4, 6;
Congressional career of, 2; and Drogoul's
testimony on money to Saddam Hussein,
65; and economists for Fed, 141-142, 147,
235n21; education of, 201n2; and embezzlement at Fed, 56; ethical conduct of,
3, 7, 11, 61-62; and falsifying accounting
records by Fed, 58-60; and FOMC records,
92-102, 224n39, 224-225nn41-42; and
foreign loans, 71-72; and gifts for Fed
officials, 61-62; illness of, 3; and leaks of
inside information from Fed, 77-80; and
lobbying by Fed, 159-160; and responsibilities of House Banking Committee for
overseeing Fed, 1-2, 6; and savings and
loan crisis, 3-4, 11, 39, 63; staff meetings
with, 201n2; Texas Senate filibuster by, 3;
and transparency of Fed, 105, 212n39; and
videotaping of FOMC meetings, 92, 154;
and Volcker, 202n6; and *Waste and Abuse
in the Federal Reserve's Payment System*,
113, 195-199; and Watergate scandal,
21-22, 25, 28. *See also* House Banking
Committee
Government Accountability Office (GAO):
audit of Los Angeles Fed Branch Bank

National Bureau of Economic Research,
203n1, 244n31
National Commission on Terrorist Attacks
Upon the United States, 10–11
National Records Act, 104, 105
Neal, Stephen L., 89–90, 93, 238n27
New York Fed Bank: bailout of Long-Term
Capital Management (LTCM) by, 177–
178; bank-examination practices of, 61–
62; board of directors of, 165; Coombs at,
217n41; economists at, 142; and Federal
Open Market Committee (FOMC), 136;
and foreign-currency operations, 70–71,
72; manager of open-market desk at, 140;
research publications of, 146; salary of
president of, 30; Volcker as president of,
13, 30, 89
New York Times, 53, 81, 139, 152, 207n42
New York University, 32, 33, 36–38, 208n5
Ney, Robert, 117
9/11 attacks, 10–11, 103, 111
9/11 Commission, 10–11
Nixon, Richard: and Burns as Fed chairman,
13, 15–16, 236n3; Ford's pardoning of,
36; and gold policy, 71; and Greenspan,
32, 34, 210n19; resignation of, 28; and
Volcker, 30; and wage and price controls,
15–16, 234n8; and Watergate scandal, 8,
20–28, 36, 207n42
nondisclosure agreements for economists,
143–146

O'Brien, Lawrence, 207n42
OCC. *See* Office of the Comptroller of Cur-
rency (OCC)
Office of Government Ethics, 215n24
Office of Management of Budgeting, 117
Office of the Comptroller of Currency (OCC),
216n30
oil prices, 16, 35, 205n19
Okun, Arthur, 145
Olson, Mark W., 52
Organization for Economic Cooperation and
Development, 70
Ottawa University, 77

paper checks, 108–112, 173, 227–228n8,
229n20. *See also* check-clearing operation
Parry, Robert T., 52, 226n53
Patman, Wright, 13, 15–17, 25, 88, 89, 124–125,
221n3

pension fund, 117–118, 230n33
Pepper, Claude, 210n22
Philadelphia Fed Bank: and FOMC records,
90, 101, 224n39; and impact of interest
rates on stock market, 168; lobbying by,
237–238n21; media coverage of, 114–115;
Prichard at, 197; and Watergate scandal,
21, 22, 24–25, 28; woman official at, 126
phishing, 120
Phoenix Fed facility, 185
Planin, Eric, 206n33
Poole, William, 233n5
Powers, Richard A., 25
preservation hypothesis, 9
pre-Wash meetings, 136–137
price controls. *See* wage and price controls
Prichard, Blake, 197
pricing system, 106, 107, 113, 118, 195–199,
230nn30–32
Proxmire, William, 14, 21, 25–29, 34
Public Company Accounting Oversight
Board, 62–63

Raghavan, Anita, 77
Rand, Ayn, 9, 33–35
Reagan, Ronald: appointments by, to Board
of Governors, 77, 152, 153; and Burns, 13;
and Greenspan, 31, 43, 210n21; monetary
policy of, 151–152, 236n6; and tax reductions, 38, 151, 210n19; and Volcker, 151–
153, 236–237n13
recessions: double-dip recession of 1980–
1982, 30–31, 152, 166, 208n51, 236n3; and
Ford presidency, 209n13; Greenspan's
prediction of, in 1989, 43, 45, 211–212n34;
of 1973–1975, 35, 209n10; of 1990–1991,
156, 166, 212n36; and rapid contractions
in money growth, 181; of 2000–2001, 47,
166, 174–176, 244n31
redlining, 129–130
Regan, Donald, 151, 210n21
Reid, Harry, 49–50, 118
Reno, Janet, 108, 113
Reuss, Henry: and Auerbach, 5, 8, 19, 218n48,
227n4; and Burns, 13, 15, 28–29; and
FOMC records, 18–20, 88; and foreign
loans, 72; and GAO study of Fed directors,
17–18; as intellectual, 221n3; and interest
rates, 28–29; and lobbying by Fed, 5–6,
156–159, 189, 237–238n21; and Monetary
Control Act (1980), 106, 227n4; on murder at Richmond Fed, 20; and racial and

secretary of, 29; prices for U.S. Treasury
bonds, 82
Trowbridge, Alexander B., 210n22
Truman, Harry, 5, 235n3
Truman, Mr., 67–69
Ture, Norman, 151

U.C.C. (Uniform Commercial Code), 109
unemployment, 30–31, 35, 152, 167, 175, 181,
208n51, 209n11, 241n2. *See also* employ-
ment rates
Uniform Commercial Code (U.C.C.), 109
University of California, 13–14, 59
University of Chicago, 14, 126, 140,
209–210n15
University of Missouri, 211n30
University of Pennsylvania, 126
University of Texas. *See* LBJ School of Public
Affairs
Urbina, Ricardo, 130–131
USA Today, 6, 53, 86, 146

videotaping of FOMC meetings, 92, 154,
223n18
Vietnam War, 16
Volcker, Paul: and Board of Governors, 53,
152, 153, 183; and FOMC records, 98; and
Gonzalez, 202n6; and inflation, 30–31,
45, 150, 166, 192, 207n48, 236n3, 244n38,
246–247n54; and money supply, 207n48;
as New York Fed Bank president, 13,
30, 89; Reagan on, 151–153, 236–237n13;
resignation of, 152–153, 183, 236–237n13,
237n16; salary of, 30; tenure of, as Fed
chairman, 5
von Hoffman, Nicholas, 84, 85, 221n35

Wachovia, 161
wage and price controls, 15, 16, 34, 234n8
Waggonner, Joe, Jr., 210n22
Wall, Danny, 40
Wallace, George C., 122
Wall Street Journal, 53, 75, 77, 83, 86, 97, 119,
161, 175, 186
Washington Post, 8, 20, 22, 24–25, 53, 75–76,
79–81, 83–85, 98, 114, 151, 153, 221n35
*Waste and Abuse in the Federal Reserve's Pay-
ment System*, 113, 195–199
Watergate scandal, 8, 20–28, 36, 207n42
Waters, Maxine, 134, 168
Weber, Max, 9
Web site of Federal Reserve, 103, 141, 145–
146, 225n42
Weill, Sanford, 165
Weiner, Tim, 207n42
Weintraub, Robert E., 13–14, 236n3
Wessel, David, 77, 83, 97
whistle-blower protection, 117
Wilke, John, 86, 119
Wilson, Woodrow, 234n6
Winn, Don, 231n7
wire advice of returned checks, 228n10
wire-transfer system (CHIPS), 108
Woodruff, Judy, 212n42
Woodward, Bob, 24, 31, 33, 40, 42, 46, 47
WorldCom, 163–164, 243n19
World War II, 204n10

Y2K problems, 111, 229n16, 242n16

Zickler, Joyce, 226n57